A long overdue addition to the catalog of sexuality writing and resources. Chen thoughtfully positions asexuality not as its own unique category or identity but as one more point on the vast, diverse spectrum of human sexual identities. A must-read for everyone: ace, allo, or anywhere in between.

—LUX ALPTRAUM, author of *Faking It: The Lies Women Tell About Sex—And the Truths They Reveal*

Angela Chen's tenacious search for the precise language to describe her experiences is deeply moving and relatable. This book will inspire you to interrogate every assumption you've made about yourself, your sexuality, and your relationships. *Ace* is a revelation. We can't stop thinking about it.

—AMINATOU SOW and ANN FRIEDMAN, authors of *Big Friendship: How We Keep Each Other Close*

Accessible and eloquently written, *Ace* sensitively and accurately spotlights an interconnected series of outsider experiences. Few asexual-spectrum narratives so authentically and diversely capture the truths, the quirks, the tragedies, and the triumphs of our lives without alienating non-ace readers or appealing only to one subset of the ace population. *Ace* creates an inclusive tapestry of validating and eye-opening narratives that will give some readers an experience they may have never had before: seeing our 'anomalous' perspectives and emotions given the sensitive examination and validation we've always been denied. This book is a welcome addition to a very niche field and puts so many nuanced experiences into relatable, empathetic language.

—JULIE SONDRA DECKER, author of *The Invisible Orientation: An Introduction to Asexuality*

Though Angela Chen is a science journalist, *Ace* is nothing less than a cultural feat. It's a powerful book that interweaves reporting and research about asexuality in ways that will remain with readers long after they've turned the last page. Asexuality has long been misunderstood, but after reading this masterpiece I know asexuality will be at the forefront of all of our minds as we think more deeply about who gets sidelined in broader conversations about gender identity and sexual orientation, and what that reveals about how we benefit from oppressing those different from us. Angela has achieved something that seems so simple but is actually difficult: allowing people to talk about and for themselves within a book that's so heavily driven by hard-hitting reporting. *Ace* announces a new dawn, one in which asexual people are voicing their experiences without fear or shame. They're here, simply living and demystifying misconceptions in the process.

—EVETTE DIONNE, editor in chief of Bitch Media and author of *Lifting as We Climb: Black Women's Battle for the Ballot Box*

Through painstaking research and her considerable skill as a storyteller, Angela Chen brings needed attention and nuance to an often overlooked spectrum of asexual experiences, encouraging readers to consider what exists and what is possible in terms of human connection, consent, understanding, and acceptance. A book that makes room for questions even as it illuminates, *Ace* should be viewed as a landmark work on culture and sexuality.

—NICOLE CHUNG, author of *All You Can Ever Know: A Memoir*

ACE

ACE

What ASEXUALITY
REVEALS *About*
DESIRE, SOCIETY,
and the
MEANING *of* SEX

....

ANGELA CHEN

BEACON PRESS
BOSTON

BEACON PRESS
Boston, Massachusetts
www.beacon.org

Beacon Press books
are published under the auspices of
the Unitarian Universalist Association of Congregations.

24 23   8

This book is printed on acid-free paper that meets the uncoated paper
ANSI/NISO specifications for permanence as revised in 1992.

Text design and composition by Kim Arney

Library of Congress Cataloging-in-Publication Data
Names: Chen, Angela, author.
Title: Ace : what asexuality reveals about desire, society,
and the meaning of sex / Angela Chen.
Description: Boston : Beacon Press, [2020] | Includes bibliographical
references and index.
Identifiers: LCCN 2020002390 (print) | LCCN 2020002391 (ebook) |
ISBN 9780807014738 (paperback) | ISBN 9780807014110 (ebook)
Subjects: LCSH: Sex. | Asexuality (Sexual orientation) | Desire. |
Sexual attraction. | Sex (Psychology)
Classification: LCC HQ21 .C456 2020 (print) | LCC HQ21 (ebook) |
DDC 306.7—dc23
LC record available at https://lccn.loc.gov/2020002390
LC ebook record available at https://lccn.loc.gov/2020002391

For everyone
who has wanted to
want more

If you're *not* having sex, what's there to talk about?

—STAR JONES, *The View*

CONTENTS

AUTHOR'S NOTE

THERE IS NO ONE ASEXUAL (OR ACE) STORY and no book can capture all of ace experience. This book is meant to be a big-picture exploration of ace issues, and what they can teach all of us about sexuality and desire in a very particular context. It is deliberately limited to the people that psychologists call WEIRD: Western, educated, industrialized, rich (or at least middle class), and democratic. Most are also American and liberal—a word I use throughout this book to mean culturally liberal and, typically, sex positive. The book is deliberately contemporary. The stories are grounded in the present, drawing from my own life as well as extensive interviews with other aces. I offered anonymity to each person I spoke with, so in many cases I use a person's first name only or a different name entirely.

The word *we* shows up frequently in this book and its meaning changes too. Sometimes I use *we* to mean the community of aces, since I identify as ace, and sometimes I use it to mean the bigger *we*, which is the society of liberal, primarily upper-middle-class America. I hope many more books will be written about the experiences of those outside this world. There is so much more to say.

PART I

SELF

PROLOGUE

I LET JANE PICK THE RESTAURANT, since I was in Silver Spring for the day anyway and she had driven down from Baltimore to see me. Those who knew us both liked to joke that we were the same person—bookish, interested in neuroscience, and she had even cut her hair short after I did—but it was our differences that interested me now.

"I have a question for you," I said, as soon as we settled into our booth at the Burmese place she had chosen. "What does sexual attraction feel like?"

Jane shifted in her seat. We were both twenty four. She was a virgin who had never had a boyfriend, while I was in the middle of my second serious relationship. My boyfriends enjoyed sex, as did I, and I considered myself lucky to have such an uncomplicated sexual history. Yet there I was, asking my friend what sexual attraction felt like from the inside. I wanted a blueprint, something I might lay side by side with my own experience to see where they matched up and where they diverged.

"I don't mean what it feels like when you think someone is good-looking," I continued; I knew how that felt. "Or what it feels like to want a relationship with someone, or to love them." I knew that feeling too, had known it so deeply that it had shamed me. I didn't have a problem becoming physically aroused during sex and I was not naive enough to believe that physical desire was the only reason to have sex. People had sex to feel closer to their partners or better about themselves, to counteract boredom and to distract from their problems.

What I didn't know was what it felt like to want sex without a specific person in mind. To think about sex at all when I was alone. To feel any physical urge for sex distinct from wanting the emotional intimacy it

3

created. I had more sexual experience than Jane, but she was the one who spoke openly of lust and libido. Meanwhile, the language of sexual drive did not quite make sense to me.

Jane took a bite of tea leaf salad, then tapped her fork against her plate. "I want to be close to someone, physically, even if they're just a stranger," she said. "I get jittery. I start fiddling with things. I feel warmer."

She stumbled as she continued, then apologized because her answer was not particularly precise. "I don't know," she said. "It's just a feeling."

But it was answer enough. Jane's cautious description revealed that what I had passed off as sexual attraction even to myself was something else entirely: aesthetic appreciation, a desire for emotional and physical closeness, a certain possessiveness. All were related to sexual attraction, components that could build upon and amplify it, but they were not the same as sexual attraction itself.

"Is this just an intellectual exercise?" Jane asked.

"No."

CHAPTER 1

ARRIVING AT ASEXUALITY

AT FOURTEEN, I came across the word *asexuality* the same way most people do: online. I read the words prominently displayed on asexuality .org, the website of the Asexual Visibility and Education Network (AVEN):[1] "An asexual person is a person who does not experience sexual attraction." Asexuality, I learned, is a sexual orientation, just like homosexuality and pansexuality and heterosexuality are sexual orientations. A person who is homosexual is sexually attracted to the same gender; a person who is asexual is sexually attracted to no one.

All of this made sense. Growing up in Silicon Valley had helped me develop a healthy appreciation for alternative lifestyles, and I was pleased that my latest Wikipedia rabbit hole had taught me something new about the world and about other people. I had no trouble believing that asexuality was normal, healthy, and valid, and that these asexual people, or aces, were entitled to long and happy lives without the rest of us pointing and laughing. But learning the term did not change how I viewed myself. I misinterpreted "a person who does not experience sexual attraction" to mean "a person who hates sex"—and so I, personally, could not be asexual. I hadn't had sex yet, but the idea held great promise. That's the strange thing about this orientation and all the misconceptions it carries. It is possible to be ace and not realize it, to see the word and still shrug and move on. Definitions are not enough; one must plumb deeper.

Since I assumed I wasn't asexual, asexuality seemed irrelevant to my life. In this, too, I was wrong. Sexuality is everywhere, and in every place that sexuality touches society, asexuality does too. The issues that aces struggle with are the same issues that people of every orientation are likely to confront at some point in their lives.

Let's take, for example, the question of how much sexual desire a person is supposed to have. How much is too little? When is too little unhealthy? How might one's answers, or the answers that are assumed, change depending on gender identity, race, or disability? What does the amount of desire we experience mean about our politics, our personalities, and our prospects for relationships? What *should* it mean?

These are broad questions of human experience. The answers look different from the ace perspective—and this book tries to match one with the other. To do so, I interviewed nearly a hundred aces, both over the phone and in person. I asked questions about attraction and identity and love. The answers they provided were rarely simple, as my own experiences have not been simple, as no one's ever are. The ace way of thinking has many new terms and nuances. Like anything that is honest, it can be messy.

There's the man who grew up in a religious environment and followed all the rules, only to realize after marriage that sex was not the wonder he had been promised. The woman who ordered blood tests in high school because she was convinced that her lack of desire for sex was a symptom of serious illness. Disabled aces can have trouble fitting into either community, wondering where their disability ends and their asexuality begins, and whether finding that border should matter. Aces of color and gender nonconforming aces question whether their asexuality is a reaction against stereotypes. Everyone wonders how to separate friendship and romance when sex is not part of the equation. Aces who don't want romantic relationships wonder if there's room for them in a world hyper-focused on a particular type of partnership. And aces who do want romantic relationships point out how consent practices don't make room for their needs.

Even in the absence of simple answers, these stories provide a shift in perspective that can shed light on how we all, ace and non-ace alike, relate to our sexualities. Most people are constricted by sexual norms; aces even more so, at times to the point of exclusion. This affords aces the ability to observe the rules of society from an outsider's vantage and with an outsider's insights. Aces draw attention to sexual assumptions and sexual scripts—around definition, feeling, action—that are often hidden and interrogate the ways that these norms make our lives smaller. Aces have developed a new lens that prioritizes what is just over what is supposedly natural.

· · · · · · · · · ·

At fourteen, I knew only that my experience of sexuality didn't match the experience of aces profiled in magazine articles. I thought I was a straight woman, like almost all my friends and a good portion of the population.

In contrast, many of the aces I read about in articles or interviewed for this project spoke of sensing difference from a young age. Their stories sounded like that of Lucid Brown, a visual artist who recently graduated from Emerson College in Boston. "My mother tried to give me 'the talk' three separate times when I was a kid, and I ditched halfway through all three times," they say. (Lucid, like many people I interviewed, is nonbinary and uses they/them pronouns.)

In middle school, Lucid tells me, everyone hid behind a tree and watched two classmates kiss. The others seemed to feel a thrill of titillation, but Lucid felt only bewilderment, not understanding the appeal of kissing or why anyone would care. Puberty, of course, can be baffling no matter one's orientation. For aces, the confusion comes not only from being unable to navigate sexuality, but also from feeling excluded from sexuality entirely and watching others participate. Gossip revolves around crushes and kisses. Sex—who's having it, who might have it, who wants to have it—becomes a key topic of conversation even if no one is doing anything. The new, collective obsession can seem incomprehensible, like everyone else's brains have been hijacked.

No matter how often Lucid heard whispers about the excitement of sex, they wanted no part of it. The idea of sex, and everything related to sex, remained repulsive. (Different aces have different tolerances. Throughout this book, I use the word *sex* to mean partnered sexual activity, from making out onward.)

Many sex-repulsed aces say that their reaction to the idea of sex is disgust, "as if you told a straight person you were into bestiality." For Lucid, the reaction was even stronger. Being exposed to sexual images and comments provoked a physical response that felt like eels squirming and writhing. The eels lived in different parts of Lucid's body: one in the gut, one along the spine. Accompanying them would be an instant fight-or-flight response, complete with nausea, heart pounding, and freezing in place.

Lucid's reactions weren't predictable or intuitive, not as simple as explaining that talking about sex caused a little repulsion while watching sex scenes on TV caused more. An in-depth discussion of a sex act might be worse than an image of a naked body, but it was hard to say why. Such physical reactions were obvious to others, and all this made Lucid a target for a particular flavor of bullying: kids yelling sex jokes at them and "essentially using my sex repulsion against me."

So, Lucid thought, it was obvious that they weren't straight. Many aces assume they are gay before wondering whether *gay* is the correct descriptor. Others come up with the word *asexual* independently, looking at the other sexual orientations and deducing that this is the only option left. Lucid identified as "nonsexual" until the day they came across a Dear Abby column syndicated in the *Maui News*.[2] New England ACE asked when it would be necessary to disclose their orientation to dates. Abby responded that there was no obligation to tell others right away, adding that the letter-writer wasn't the only asexual person out there and including a reference to AVEN. Lucid, age thirteen, stole that copy of the newspaper off the dining room table.

The word alone was an answer that made perfect, immediate sense. Lucid was clearly asexual but hadn't known that there existed a label for this experience. Few do, because it is so widely assumed that everyone is allosexual (or allo), the term for people who do experience sexual attraction. In other words, allosexuals are people who aren't ace.

"Finding the word *asexuality* was such an explanation of things that had already happened to me," Lucid says. "It's the first time I heard, 'You can just not have sex,' and that was incredibly freeing, because as a kid you hear the talk about this big scary thing that's going to happen and how you're going to want it, and that's just terrifying, absolutely terrifying."

They pause. "It was like the first step, the key that opened the box that had a lot of confusing other boxes. Asexuality was just the clearest one and it helped me get more into the complexities of my identity." The word granted access to important knowledge that had been unavailable before.

• • • • • • • • •

I spent middle school gossiping about crushes on boys. In high school, I fell into a complicated and ambivalent relationship with a female classmate that first made me wonder if I was bisexual and then, when I didn't like touching or being touched, made me decide I was probably straight after all. Even through college, there was little reason to suspect I might be ace, only that I might be neurotic, shy, and inclined to like men.

The notion that I might be asexual seemed laughable. I found Adrien Brody attractive and Channing Tatum less so and had a vulgar sense of humor, full of sex jokes and sly insinuations that made my more proper friends blush. I spoke of longing and listened intently to stories of sexual adventures, and never did it occur to me that my friends and I might be using the language of desire differently. For them, a word like "hot" could indicate a physical pull of the type Jane had described. For me, "hot" conveyed an admiration of excellent bone structure. Their sexual encounters were often motivated by libido; I didn't even know that I lacked a libido.

I was a little curious about sex with men because everything—books, television, friends—told me it felt fantastic. But I was *very* curious about what it would be like to be desired, to be loved by someone that I desired too, desired wholeheartedly in a way that hadn't been the case with my high school ex. That was the real root of my longing.

Then, Henry. Henry and I met when we were twenty-one. After our first conversation, I wrote "BE STILL MY FUCKING HEART" in my journal, just like that, in all caps. That conversation took place over the internet, he in Texas and I in California. We fell in love anyway, over emails and chats and hours of talking.

I wouldn't meet Henry in person for nearly a year. A few months after that would be the last time I saw him, but the aftershocks of our relationship would stretch into the future far beyond the amount of time we had actually spent together. A through line can be traced from that first conversation to the question I asked Jane at the Burmese restaurant for this book. Henry will always be one of the ways that I mark "before" and "after" in my life—not just for learning about asexuality, though our relationship provided the impetus for me to do so, but also for understanding romantic love and the obsessive pain of loss.

First love always feels like a miracle. That I fell in love with someone far away, someone I had met believing nothing could happen other than friendship; that we needed to coordinate our lives to be together; that what we felt inside really did change outer reality—all of that made this moment in time, this person, feel even more extraordinary. Our investments marked the relationship as special, and the seriousness of our plan became evidence of the seriousness of our feelings, testaments that our tie went beyond vanity and was more than infatuation. In this, I remain sure, we were not wrong. Nothing then or since has shaken my belief that no matter how excruciatingly immature we might have been, at their core the feelings were both rare and very real.

Texas and California are far apart, but it was senior year of college and everyone's lives were about to split open anyway. The deal was that we would both move to New York City after graduation. I would take a journalism job and he would go to graduate school. But when Henry was not accepted into any universities in the area, he chose to attend a school in the South and pushed for a five-year, long-distance open relationship.

I was not equipped to handle this arrangement—I, so untrusting and wary of vulnerability that I had written this to myself in my journal: *Another thing you need to remember, and something that, for some reason, has never really occurred to you before: You can ask things of others too. You can ask them to compromise. It is not always you who have to.*

I should have said no, but I was afraid of losing him. So I made a mistake and said yes.

· · · · · · · · · ·

Before Henry headed to the South for graduate school, he arranged to be in New York for the summer, ostensibly to take language classes but in reality to be with me. Without having met in person, we agreed to find a place together. The months we would spend together already seemed painfully short compared to what we had expected. There was nothing else we wanted so much; commuting would be a waste of time.

That summer was painful and there are many reasons we did not work out. Sex was not one of those reasons—not exactly. Our strange courtship might have created problems in many other areas, but we found each other beautiful and I enjoyed having sex with Henry. It felt intimate, like I privy to an experience that others were not. It gave me the feeling I had always wanted: not sexual pleasure, but the thrill of specialness.

Sex itself did not cause problems, but my fear of a specific aspect of sexuality did. Though we were functionally monogamous during those months, the prospect of five years of an open relationship terrified me, and the fact that Henry wanted to have sex with others was hard to take. Convinced that Henry would fall in love with someone else after sleeping with them, any mention of sexual attraction—his or anyone else's—prompted tortured projections of abandonment.

Soon, dread of an uncertain future overshadowed the safety I had in the present. I wanted to be strong and wanted to run away in equal measure, and that produced the toxic cocktail that ruined the time we did have together. Over and over, I could feel my emotions spinning out of control as I acted in ways I knew were wrong but felt powerless to stop. My panic manifested in constantly trying to break up, so afraid was I of being left. During the nonstop fights, I waved my hand and gave as reasons any number of issues that never directly included the words *fear* or *insecurity*. I could neither say that I was afraid nor admit how much I cared.

One day, on the way home from work, I passed a flower shop and on a whim bought red carnations for Henry. When I arrived home and he asked me where I'd gotten the flowers, I became overwhelmed by the prospect of admitting to a kind, spontaneous gesture. I said that I had taken the flowers from someone at work and thought they'd look nice on the dining room table.

· · · · · · · · · ·

Henry eventually had enough and broke up with me, rightly, in the fall. He was gone, but my mind continued to wrap itself around the endless conversations we'd had about why an open relationship was necessary: Henry saying that men would always want to stray because it was natural, that clinging to monogamy was old-fashioned and that I could defeat that desire if I really tried, just a little bit harder.

Henry's statements created a new, gut-deep fear of anything related to flirting or sex or romance. When my roommate started watching old seasons of *Scandal*, a glance at the protagonists kissing in some dark hallway sent me to my room with the door shut. If anyone tried to hug me on a date, I drew back immediately. I had never liked being touched by strangers, but, clammy and cynical, I now actively feared it. I missed Henry terribly and now believed that every relationship would end either in betrayal or with the other person feeling trapped.

One evening, nearly two years after I had last seen Henry, I found myself telling my friend Thomas about how badly everything had ended. By this point, I was well-practiced at reciting the events. I was obsessed with them, convinced that people couldn't understand me without knowing about Henry and convinced that I couldn't understand myself unless I could answer the question of why we failed—which to me was the same as the question of why I behaved the way I did when I knew better. So many people had heard this story, but Thomas couldn't understand why I had been worried that Henry might be attracted to someone else and leave me.

"I get being jealous," Thomas said, "but not your worry that he couldn't control himself at all. Being sexually attracted to other people happens to all of us."

"I know, and that's what terrifies me," I said. "It'll happen to everyone and then someone will always be fighting this desire and wanting to cheat, even if they don't cheat. That seems miserable."

"I mean, yes," he said. "Sort of. But also, not really. I'm sure you've been sexually attracted to someone that you're not dating, but it's often just *attraction*. Physical. That happens all the time and you manage it. For most people, it's not some horrible thing you can't deal with, though I guess it can be. Almost all the time it's no big deal. We all learn to deal, you know?"

I didn't know. Nothing he said sounded familiar. I had never experienced "just attraction," a physical impulse—only emotional desire that manifested physically. I wanted sex with someone only when I was already prepared to change my life for them, so I did not believe Henry when he claimed that wanting sex with others did not automatically threaten me. When he talked about how everyone was sexually attracted to everyone else all the time, I could not understand attraction as anything but how I experienced it: emotional yearning—love, really—overpowering and overwhelming, a disaster for our relationship if targeted toward anyone but me. It sounds illogical now, and like incredible naivete, but for me, desire for love and desire for sex had always been one and the same, an unbreakable link. I had been curious about sex but had never wanted to have sex with any person before Henry.

Talking to Thomas prompted me to question why statements he took for granted were revelations to me. I wondered what else I did not know that I did not know about sexual desire. A few months later, I had lunch with Jane and asked her what sexual attraction felt like. It was my first time asking the question, but by then, I already suspected that her answer would not line up with my view of the world.

· · · · · · · · ·

Ten years after I first came across the term *asexuality*, I returned to the topic, wanting to figure out what I had misunderstood. I had long known that sexual attraction and sexual behavior are not the same and that one does not necessarily limit the other. I knew that, generally speaking, sexual behavior is under our control while sexual attraction is not. It was always clear that a gay man or a straight woman could each have sex with women without that affecting who either is attracted to. I had understood that asexuality is the lack of sexual attraction while celibacy is the lack of sexual behavior.

Reading more, I understood for the first time that it is possible to lack the experience of sexual attraction without being repulsed by sex, just like it is possible to neither physically crave nor be disgusted by a food like crackers but still enjoy eating them as part of a cherished social ritual. Being repulsed by sex can be a fairly obvious indication of the lack of sexual attraction, but a lack of sexual attraction can also be hidden by social performativity or wanting (and having) sex for emotional reasons—and because the different types of desire are bound together so tightly, it can be difficult to untangle the various strands. "People who have never felt sexual attraction do not know what sexual attraction feels like, and knowing whether or not they have ever felt it can be difficult," writes ace researcher Andrew C. Hinderliter in a 2009 letter to the editor of the journal *Archives of Sexual Behavior*.[3] Yes, exactly.

Sexuality as allos experience it was completely foreign to me, and realizing this in my midtwenties recast much of my life. The switch that turned on for others at puberty had never flipped for me. During this time, most people started masturbating, had wet dreams or sexual fantasies, and became hyperattuned to touch and physicality—the smell of hair or the sight of an exposed shoulder. For some, these developments happen a little later. For others, like me, none of it happened at all. I had grown taller and become moody but did not one day look around and start noticing bodies, let alone start wanting anything from them. My crushes as a teenager, though intense, were little different from the ones I had earlier in life, based on aesthetic attraction and thinking a person clever. Even in fantasy, they never progressed beyond the point when someone I liked said I was worth dating.

Asexuality explained why I had been so perplexed when a high school classmate got pregnant. It was so *easy* to never have sex, I thought. It was the default state and it took real effort to do anything else. What could have compelled her to take such risks? Now I understood why it hadn't been so easy. Our experiences had been fundamentally different but not in a way obvious enough to make me question them.

Now I could see the ways my asexuality had protected me. Being ace spared me from sexual distraction, from slut-shaming internal or external, from bad hookups or any hookups at all, from casual relationships that ended in ghosting and confusion. I saw, too, the ways my asexuality—or rather my misunderstanding of it—had hurt Henry and me. Asexuality was never the reason we failed. For that, I have life circumstances, immaturity, and the feedback loop of our worries to blame. Still, being ace and not knowing it inflated the fears that ended us. I had been terrified in large part because I lacked, and did not realize I lacked, personal experience of sexuality—what it means and what it's like to manage it. Limited by my knowledge, constrained by my experience, I saw monsters where there were only shadows.

· · · · · · · · ·

Lucid's story is easy for people to accept; mine, less so. Lucid's sex repulsion—the eels, the nausea—seems very different from the experience of allos, so people think that's what asexuality should be like. My experience, on the other hand, might sound typical for a less sexual person in a sexual society, not like anything out of the ordinary or anything that requires a separate identity label. Many allos may find my story familiar and prefer not to identify as asexual. So why do *I* identify as ace when I could identify as an allo woman who is not sexually motivated?

First, it is because many parts of my experience—like the fact that I never think about sex involuntarily and could be celibate for life with little trouble—line up with the experiences of other aces. Learning about asexuality provoked a shock of recognition and I wanted to honor that. I have always been a stickler for using the word that fits, even when I didn't like either the experience or the word.

Yet the word *asexual* by itself would be pointless if it only described an experience and did not connect me to people who helped make that experience legible. *Asexuality* has always been a political label with a practical purpose, and the more important reason I identify as ace is because it has been useful for me. After my relationship with Henry ended, I had trouble understanding myself or others until I learned about asexuality. I had strong, complicated feelings around romance and sex but lacked the language to express them. Other aces understood. Their presence and writings helped me make sense of myself and my life. Though the process of accepting asexuality involved a lot of internal resistance, it clarified my experience in meaningful ways. It showed me a new way of viewing the world.

The world is not a binary of aces and allos. It is a spectrum, with people like Lucid further from the allo end and people like me closer to it. I am not interested in thinking about aces as a discrete group completely separate from "normal" people or of ace membership as a goal achievable only with a tidy checklist. I refuse to hold ace identity to higher standards of legitimacy than any other orientation. No one thinks that all allosexuals are the same or that they experience sexual attraction at every moment. Their sexual status is not questioned each time they turn down sex. Aces are not a monolith either—and if a more fluid, inclusive definition means that the lines of ace and allo blur and more people can be considered ace, that would only strengthen what we have to say.

This is a book that centers ace experience. Aces today are not concerned with how to have sex, but we are not anti-sex either. We don't ask people to stop having sex or feel guilty for enjoying it. We do ask that all of us question our sexual beliefs and promise that doing so means that the world would be a better and freer place for everyone. I hope that ace readers see themselves here and feel understood. I hope that non-ace readers also recognize parts of themselves and gain concepts and tools to help them puzzle out their own confusions around how to be in the world. We are all still figuring it out.

CHAPTER 2

EXPLANATION *VIA NEGATIVA*

PEOPLE WHO COULD be described as asexual have existed for a long time. They were certainly around in the 1940s, when sex researcher Alfred Kinsey was developing his model of sexual orientation. Kinsey believed that sexual orientation was more than a binary of homosexual and heterosexual. He created a scale (a line, really) that runs from zero to six: zero for someone who is exclusively heterosexual, six for someone who is exclusively homosexual, three for bisexual.[1] Today, the Kinsey scale is famous and has become the main way of thinking about sexuality and sexual orientation in the West.

It does not make room for asexuality, even though Kinsey knew about asexual people. During the thousands of interviews that he conducted, Kinsey had come across people who didn't fit onto his line—who, in his language, had "no socio-sexual contacts or reactions."[2] Faced with data that didn't fit this theory, he didn't revise his line to make it more multidimensional. Instead, Kinsey marked these people into a separate category called X and carried on. Heterosexual, homosexual, and bisexual dominated, while Group X was mostly forgotten.

This matters, because language is a form of power. It creates categories that help us interpret the world, and that which is not easily available in language is often ignored in thought itself. A shared vocabulary makes ideas more accessible while a lack of language can render an experience illegible. It can isolate.

The internet would be instrumental in reversing that erasure. Sixty years after Kinsey's interviews, those who once would have been marked X found each other on message boards and forums and blogs. They started talking about their lives, what they wanted that others didn't and what others wanted that they didn't, marking territory for experiences that didn't always match Kinsey's numbers. Asexuality is not an "internet orientation," and the internet did not lead to the invention of asexual people. People had identified as asexual for decades before and in the 1970s bonded over asexuality in self-published work and zines.[3] The people already existed; the internet helped facilitate these discussions at a scale and volume that had not been possible before.

Those who were posting on these message boards and forums during the early 2000s had enormous influence in shaping the contemporary understanding of asexuality. These early activists, some of whom spoke to me for this book, are now considered elders despite most being only in their thirties. They don't own asexuality. No one does, and no group or person has the legitimacy to speak for all aces. Yet these activists did build, through intention and trial and error and sometimes pure accident, the foundations of the ace movement. Young people talking to each other developed the basic framework that is still used by those discovering the orientation for the first time, by allo researchers who want to study the identity, by journalists like me, and more. From their discussions came the very definition of *asexual* and the dominance of the term as opposed to other options like *nonsexual*. Much of this knowledge was created through informal means, which is why I explicitly cite and quote from bloggers. Tenured scholars are not the only people who produce knowledge or who deserve credit for their expertise.

In the span of human history, the internet is very young and so, too, is the contemporary ace movement and the corresponding exploration of asexual experience. The ace movement, then, is in some ways a real-time experiment in the promise of the internet to bring together people to create a social movement and a new culture, one that pushes against the societal obsession with sex and makes room for everyone—ace, allo, or questioning—who wants the freedom to find pleasure in a different way.

• • • • • • • • •

The first well-known website that gestured at asexuality was Haven for the Human Amoeba, a Yahoo! group that began in 2000.[4] In 2001, a Wesleyan University freshman named David Jay started the Asexuality

Visibility and Education Network (AVEN), hosting it on his student web space. The next summer, he bought the asexuality.org domain for $25 in cash from a guy in a beat-up car and set up the forums.

To the wider world, *asexual* was a word from high school biology, used to describe organisms that clone themselves without sex. Members of these early online communities—which also included the Official Asexual Society and several LiveJournal groups[5]—debated what the word might mean when applied to people and which behaviors might qualify or disqualify someone from claiming the label. Some people, called *anti-sexuals*, believed that aces were superior to people who weren't ace. Others thought that the label of *asexual* should only be reserved for those who didn't masturbate.[6]

David Jay wanted AVEN to offer a different perspective. Long interested in social justice, he had no interest in debating whether a lesbian was still a lesbian if she slept with a man; of course she was. Aces weren't inherently better than allos, and aces who didn't masturbate weren't better than those who did. It was all variation, not superiority, not inferiority. It would be better, he thought, to conceptualize asexuality as a sexual orientation and identity label that could build bridges with the greater LGBTQ+ community. A definition that emphasized sexual attraction rather than behavior could distinguish asexuality from celibacy and also make it a natural fit with the logic of other sexual orientations. If *heterosexual* describes someone who is sexually attracted to the opposite gender, a person who is asexual must be sexually attracted to no one. (David initially described an asexual person as someone who is not sexually attracted to either gender. After experts told him to avoid assuming a gender binary, he changed the definition to emphasize "not experiencing sexual attraction.") The inclusive ethos and simple explanation helped make AVEN the de facto asexual group.[7]

Unfortunately, the decision to define asexuality using the same linguistic and theoretical logic as other sexual orientations turned out to be a trap. To explain asexuality and what it means to not experience sexual attraction, aces must define and describe the exact phenomena we don't experience. It requires us to use the language of "lack," claiming we are legitimate in spite of being deficient, while struggling to explain exactly what it is we don't get.

To the best I can tell, sexual attraction is the desire to have sex with a specific person for physical reasons. Sexual attraction can be instantaneous and involuntary: a heightened awareness, a physical alertness combined with mental wanting. My allo friends say they feel sexually attracted to people they have just met, to people whose company they don't enjoy, to people they don't like or even find good-looking.

Fair enough. Aces don't experience this. Aces can still find people beautiful, have a libido, masturbate, and seek out porn. Aces can enjoy sex and like kink and be in relationships of all kinds.

To many allos, this is unexpected. Their surprise reveals a failure not in naming, but in the fact that few people think about sexuality and sexual attraction closely enough. It turns out that the key to capturing ace and allo experience alike is explaining sexual attraction *via negativa*, or explaining what it is not and what a lack of sexual attraction does not prevent us from doing. Sexual attraction is so often conflated with sexual drive and other types of attraction. These things are distinct, but—and this will become a running theme in this book—when any two things often go together, people wrongly assume that they must always go together. The various components of sexuality and attraction are tangled together for allos too, but—and here's another running theme—allos haven't had to grapple with their confusion as much because it hasn't caused problems for them in the same way. Aces have been forced to take a closer look.

• • • • • • • •

After Sarah, an ace editor in her thirties, came out to a friend, he tentatively suggested that she try masturbating. "He didn't know that I'd been masturbating since I was very young," she says, "but attraction does not factor into it at all for me." Sarah masturbates when she gets—her voice becomes high-pitched and facetious—"a tingling in my nethers," but the fact that seeing a person or an act can cause physical changes in one's own body or desire in one's mind does not compute. "I cannot comprehend how attraction works," she continues. "You look at a body and it turns you on? I don't get it."

Repeat after me: sexual attraction is not sex drive. These two phenomena are often treated as interchangeable, but understanding that they are separate helps explain ace experience.

Simply put, sex drive (or libido) is the desire for sexual release, a set of feelings in the body, often combined with intrusive thoughts. It can come out of nowhere and for no obvious reason and not be about anyone. It's an internal experience of sexual frustration that does not depend on sexual orientation. A woman can be gay and have a high sex drive—that is, she frequently wants sexual release. A man can be straight and have a low sex drive. A person can be ace and have no desire for sexual release at all. Or a person can be ace and have a so-called undirected sex drive, that tingling in the nethers. An undirected sex drive isn't a quirk of ace experience; it's another way of saying "being horny," which can afflict anyone because horniness does not need to include sexual attraction. Imagine a gay man with a high sex drive surrounded by women. It is possible for him to feel horny and want to get laid even if he's not interested in anyone around him.

Sexual *attraction*, then, is horniness toward or caused by a specific person. It is the desire to be sexual with that partner—libido with a target. To use a food metaphor: a person can feel physiological hunger, which would be like sex drive, without craving a specific dish, which would be more like sexual attraction. And just as people have different sex drives, they also experience different levels of sexual attraction. Some aces have a libido and some don't, but we all share the lack of sexual attraction, and most of us have low desire for partnered sex. (As a side note, it's important to clarify that neither sexual attraction nor sex drive are the same as physical arousal. People can have random erections or be aroused during medical exams with no libido or attraction involved. Research from the University of British Columbia psychologist Lori Brotto suggests that self-identified ace women and allo women experience roughly the same amount of genital arousal when showed sexual imagery.[8] And most ace men, at least anecdotally, report that they have no trouble getting erections.)

Sarah feels the desire for sexual release, that libido for no reason, but it's not triggered by other people. Nor is the idea of inviting other people to help out appealing whatsoever. The bodily sensations simply don't turn into desire for others. Similarly, Vesper, an ace blogger, noticed a difference in sex drive but not sexual attraction after they started taking testosterone (often called T). "It was very easy for me to ignore genitalia because I'm not interested in sex and, aside from the monthly hell [of menstruation], I didn't have to acknowledge its existence," they say. "But when you start T, it's much more in your face that this is a *thing* and libido exists." Having a libido is a new experience for Vesper and a disorienting one. "But I would be asexual regardless of whether I'd have a high libido because it still would not be directed at a specific person," they continue. "There is no specific person causing that libido." (For the sake of linguistic simplicity, in the rest of the book I will use terms like *sex drive* and *sexual desire* as shorthand for "sexual desire for partnered sex.")

Because Sarah is not sexually interested in other people, no amount of libido or masturbation can change that, as she puts it, "my brain is ace." The prefix *a-* means *without*, and so she is considered to have no sexuality. It's right there in the name. But consider what David Jay calls "the masturbation paradox."[9] Aces who have a sex drive and masturbate participate in what should be "the purest form of sexual desire out there." Masturbation is sexual arousal and sexual release without the complicated social and emotional dynamics of partnered sex, he writes. It's more purely sexual than a hookup. It's more purely sexual than holding hands and kissing or a night flirting at the bar. It's more sexual than almost anything.

So why do we say that people who do the most sexual thing there is lack a sexuality completely? In other words, why is the word *sexuality* used so narrowly and usually as a synonym for sexual orientation? When someone asks about a person's sexuality, we understand the question and answer appropriately with *gay* or *straight* or *bisexual*.

If sexuality is nothing but sexual attraction toward a certain gender, then it's true: Sarah has no sexuality. But this simplistic understanding doesn't make room for her sexual fantasies. "Thinking about a penis inside me doesn't interest me. Thinking about a person I'm doing this to doesn't interest me," Sarah says. "If I envision people, they don't have faces or names or bodies; it's more of a concept. But having someone in control of me in some way, acting like I 'have to do these things,' or like I am like an inanimate object, works for me. That's sort of my fantasy." To better reflect Sarah's experience, the way we use the language of sexuality may require rethinking.

Most people intuitively acknowledge that sexuality, often vaguely described as "how people express themselves sexually," is more than sexual orientation and more than liking partnered sex. A Twitter search for "my sexuality is," for example, brings up answers like "beautiful women in suits" or "Harry Styles," not "bisexuality." It's a meme and a joke, but it's also self-expression, signaling a belief that sexuality can be very specific. Yet there is little serious, systematic discussion, at least among the general public, about what these other components of sexuality might be.

To my mind, sexual orientation is one part of sexuality, but so much else—kinks and fetishes, aesthetics and fantasies—can fill those borders. So much room can be available in which to explore the boundaries of sexuality beyond the heaviness of orientation. This idea is certainly not new in alternative sexual communities, but it has yet to fully move into the mainstream and be absorbed into the way we consider the nuances of our sexual lives.

· · · · · · · · · ·

Now, if you are not ace and would like to experience the world like many ace people do, this is possible. For that, I have the British television show *Naked Attraction* to thank. Though eagerly described to me as a "naked dating show," it is not, as one might suspect, about two people going on a date while naked. It is better.

It is a game show. One lucky person looking for love stands on the stage, faced with six neon-colored tubes arranged in a half-circle. Inside each of these tubes is a naked person of the gender the main contestant prefers. Round one: The neon screens lift from the ground up to show everything from the waist down. Nothing is blurred out or obscured. It's all penises and vaginas.

The contestant walks around the circle, peering into each tube and commenting on various bodily crimes (gray pubes, "not standing confidently enough") while the camera zooms in on the genitals. The owners, likely desperate to exploit any possible advantage, sometimes sway their hips back and forth to appear more enticing or at least appear to have a personality. Sometimes, all the genitals are displayed side by side in a colorful graphic that resembles an "every body is beautiful" diagram for children about to face puberty. Finally, one person is eliminated.

Round two: The screen lifts up further and reveals the body up to the neck, the better to judge chest hair or breasts. More discussion, another person eliminated. The other rounds include face and voice (which is mostly about accent and class), and then the contestant gets naked too, picks the winner, and the two go on a date without ever having had a full conversation.

All this might sound obscene, but when I watched a few episodes with female friends one afternoon, we agreed that *Naked Attraction* is one of the least erotic examples of television imaginable. It is practically endearing. The premise is tongue-in-cheek, and the bodies are simply *there*, not oiled up, not provocatively posed, not trying to sell J'Adore by Dior, just looking perfectly normal despite being inside these neon chambers. It had the atmosphere not of a meat market but of a Russian sauna full of no-nonsense people who are determined to get clean.

Though I was the only ace person in the group, none of us felt any flutters of excitement. The bodies are not attractive. They're not unattractive, either, but it's not easy to decide whom to eliminate by looking at genitals alone, divorced from all other context. Don't their hobbies matter more than testicle size? He might have too much chest hair, but surely he could wax it. Or maybe, if you knew him better, a little extra hair wouldn't matter so much.

Please watch this show and marvel at how utterly unsexy it is. Observe the genitals, stripped of personality and desexualized, just some folds of skin stippled with hair. Nothing is titillating. The contestants themselves appear unmoved; they're more likely to laugh than to lick their lips. Nothing means anything, and yet you're supposed to make a decision about who is more or less appropriate as a partner. Nothing means anything, though it could—but it simply doesn't yet.

Take it one step further and pretend: Nothing means anything, but other people are getting something out of it that you're not. They are seeing the same floppy bodies that you are, but the bodies mean something different. The bodies are provoking some kind of reaction that you are not having. The show makes them think about what they might want to do with *their* body to the other bodies on display. It doesn't make sense. Take that feeling of bafflement and magnify it. Apply it to everyone all times. Welcome to the ace world.

· · · · · · · · · ·

The ace world today has become broad enough to include many types of people. There are many types of aces, for one, who describe ourselves as sex-repulsed, sex-indifferent, or sex-favorable depending on how averse we are to sexual material and sexual activity. The ace world also includes people who identify as gray-asexual, or gray-A, a more catchall phrase that encompasses experiences like only occasionally experiencing sexual attraction or not experiencing it very strongly.

For some, these terms have great value because more precise language leads to more precise discussions. Not everyone agrees. Many people roll their eyes at the ever-more-specific terms that crop up and believe that the more words there are, the less legitimate each particular one is. For skeptics, these terms smack of Tumblr and fake identities and people under the age of eighteen who are special snowflakes.

Few terms are more the victim of this attitude than *demisexuality*. Demisexuals, who only experience sexual attraction after an emotional bond has developed, are considered a subset of gray-A's, and they are often mocked. Even those who respect asexuality as a sexual orientation disparage demisexual as a self-righteous term used by "normal" people who want to signal that they're deep, unlike the horndogs who will bone anything that has a pulse. "When I tell people that I'm demisexual and explain to people what it means, some people think it's another label that people use to feel special, or that I despise people who sleep around, when that's not the case," says Zhexi Shan, a student at Columbia University. The widespread disdain led him to abandon the word completely and switch to simply saying, "It takes me a while to have attraction to other guys," a description that tends to alienate people less.

Like anyone, aces can be assholes, so somebody out there is probably using the concept of demisexuality to slut-shame. Demisexuality itself, however, is not about despising people who are promiscuous or even preferring to have sex after there's an emotional connection. It has nothing to do with preference at all. "Someone who isn't demisexual can generally walk into a bar and find someone they find sexually attractive," explains Lola Phoenix, a thirty-three-year-old writer in London who identifies as demi. "They might not go *home* with them, of course—there are a lot of different factors that play into that decision—but I can't walk into a bar and just find someone attractive, regardless of whether I'd be willing to sleep with them or not." Lola can have sex with a stranger whenever they want, but that's not the same as being able to be sexually attracted to a stranger.

Branding problem aside, the real risk is not that people don't like these terms, but that emphasizing separate identities can perpetuate misconceptions about sexual behavior. The label of demisexuality, for example, can create the impression that there exist "categories of 'normal' sexual people and then these 'weird sexual people' who only want to have sex with people they're emotionally attached to," Lisa Wade, a professor of sociology at Occidental College and author of *American Hookup: The New Culture of Sex on Campus*, tells me. In her research, Wade has found that the majority of students want to be in a relationship but believe that everyone else wants only casual sex. She worries that adopting demisexuality as a distinct identity can reinforce falsehoods that are not supported by the data. "It's a little dangerous," she continues. "It's buying into the hookup culture idea that everyone should feel one way, that everyone wants casual sex and if you don't, it's distinct enough that it's part of your identity." Though Wade makes an important point, I believe that the benefits of the term outweigh the costs. Over-sexualization existed long before the word *demisexual* became popular, while I suspect that avoiding the term will do little to prevent people from thinking that everyone else's sex life is better.

Plus, these words don't need to create separation and difference. They can be useful descriptors used by anyone, not mutually exclusive identity labels used to divide people. (*Impatient*, for example, is a useful descriptor and not necessarily an identity category.) Allos are sexually repulsed by plenty of people. Many spend the majority of their time sexually indifferent as well. The proportion is usually different—sex-repulsed aces are usually sex-repulsed 100 percent of the time—but adopting this language at a more granular level, to describe feelings day by day and track experience, can be helpful. "Asexuality has taught me a language—a vocabulary for sex-neutral, sex-repulsed, sex-positive, and then I can place myself on that scale for the day and try to initiate sex and try to create a better sense of connection," says Alicia, an ace scholar with an allo partner.

In fact, *demisexuality* and *gray-asexuality* not only *can* describe allos; they actually refer to many who could technically be considered allo. Asexuality is about who you're sexually attracted to: no one.

Demisexuality describes the conditions under which someone develops sexual attraction (after an emotional bond is formed), and gray-asexuality can be about how often someone develops sexual attraction (rarely). It is possible to be pansexual and demisexual, or gray-A heterosexual, or any number of other combinations.

The contradictions are supposed to be there, says CJ Chasin, a long-time ace activist and PhD candidate in psychology at the University of Windsor in Canada. Just as the world isn't a straight line from homosexual to heterosexual, the ace world isn't a straight line with ace people on one side, non-aces on the other, and demis somewhere in the middle. It's an umbrella that covers different, diverse, and sometimes inconsistent experiences, including ones that don't perfectly hew to the "lack of sexual attraction" definition. *Ace* is so broad that academics are still arguing over how best to define asexuality for the purposes of research, since a study that includes self-identified aces will likely return different results than a study that only includes celibate aces.[10]

Porous borders are intentional. Aces offer up all these terms to whoever might benefit, and one line of thinking is that anyone can identify as ace if they like. The purpose is not to encourage people to behave rigidly as a condition of being accepted, but to embrace complexity and let people identify how they wish and allow their sexualities to change and overlap. The ace world is not an obligation. Nobody needs to identify, nobody is trapped, nobody needs to stay forever and pledge allegiance. The words are gifts. If you know which terms to search, you know how to find others who might have something to teach. They are, like Lucid said, keys. Intellectual entryways to the ace world and other worlds. Offerings of language for as long as they bring value.

• • • • • • • • •

Here is something else that aces want to tell everyone: sexual attraction is not the only kind of attraction. Nobody in *Naked Attraction* provoked lust or seemed much more sexually appealing than the next person, but that doesn't mean I had the same reaction to every single contestant. It's not hard to imagine how, with a lot more time to get to know a contestant, preferably with all parties clothed in accordance with social rules, more romantic interest could develop—and there were some people that

I thought had more potential than others. Sexuality is more than sexual orientation, and attraction is more than sexual attraction, yet humans can act as though sexual interest is the only reason we find ourselves compelled by others.

Not experiencing sexual attraction doesn't prevent aces from experiencing aesthetic attraction, which means finding someone beautiful without that beauty being a sexual motivator. Aesthetic attraction is the reason I preferred the taller, lankier contestants on *Naked Attraction* despite being just as sexually apathetic to them as to the shorter, stockier folks. It's the reason a straight woman might say that she prefers the model Bella Hadid to her sister Gigi without wanting to end up in bed with either. She might admire Bella's hair and skin in the absence of any desire to touch or kiss, just as I have gone on dates with men I think are handsome and have not wanted any physical contact with them. The amount of aesthetic attraction people experience can vary too. As one person put it: "Almost everyone looks the exact same to me in terms of attractiveness, except Matt Bomer. He's pretty."

Aesthetic attraction can guide romantic attraction, or the feeling of being romantically interested in or having a crush on someone. Romantic orientation, then, denotes the gender that people usually develop crushes on. (Chapter 7 covers the question of how people distinguish romantic and platonic interest in the absence of sexual attraction.) These use the same linguistic constructions as sexual orientations, swapping out the "sexual" part: heteroromantic, panromantic, homoromantic, and so on. People who don't experience romantic attraction toward anyone are called *aromantic*, or aro. The concepts of aromanticism and asexuality developed alongside each other, so aros have long been part of the ace community, though some people are aromantic and not asexual.

Aces didn't discover these experiences. We merely paid attention and tried to better describe them. Breaking the link between aesthetic and romantic and sexual attraction makes it possible to understand each type on its own terms instead of mistaking one for the other. New ways to talk about attraction mean new ways to think about attraction, to more clearly evaluate a bond.

Learning about the complicated ways that attraction works—and the ways that different types don't always line up—helped me understand my high school relationship with my classmate Jennifer. I first thought I might be bisexual because I enjoyed our close relationship and didn't mind the idea of dating her. Then I thought I wasn't bisexual because I didn't like doing anything physical with Jennifer, even as I remained curious about sex with men. A decade later, I've realized that the situation was more complicated than bisexual or not bisexual. I identify as biromantic and don't experience sexual attraction to any gender, yet I am ultimately more averse to sex with women than with men. All these caveats sound complicated, and they are, but they are also more accurate than painting myself with a broad brush. Allos, too, might decide that they are heterosexual and biromantic, or bisexual and heteroromantic.

In addition to these three main types of attraction, aces also discuss touch attraction or sensual attraction, emotional and intellectual attraction, and more. The separation of attraction into smaller and smaller components challenges us to think more about the building blocks of desire. The specificity of language can force us to look more closely at what we want and what leaves us cold.

·········

After all of those technical details, perhaps the best description of asexuality is the one I heard from Shari B. Ellis, a filmmaker in her forties who is also the codirector of Ace Los Angeles. When she's being flippant, Shari likes to say that Duran Duran made her asexual.

Shari started to think she was asexual in high school, long before the online community existed and before she knew that there were others like her. About eight years ago, while cleaning her house, Shari found an old journal where she had written about attending a Duran Duran concert. The entry describes a pivotal moment when singer Simon Le Bon starts taking off his shirt and rolling around on the ground.

"The way I described it in that entry was revealing," she says. "I was excited about it, but I certainly wasn't talking about it in the same way that other people, particularly women, were talking about it. It wasn't in that 'I wanna do him' kind of way. There was this level of distance in the way I was talking about it that made me realize, oh, I'd known all along that I was asexual, and I just let people talk me out of realizing it for myself."

Soon, other examples from her past became apparent. As a teenager, Shari had enjoyed writing fan fiction, including smut. "I just remember letting a friend read my stuff and she commented that there was a level of distance and lack of passion in the way I was writing these scenes, and I was like, 'I didn't know any other way of writing,'" she says. In college, she tried to talk to a friend about being a virgin and struggled to explain that it had nothing to do with morals or saving herself for marriage. "My friend said, 'I feel like other people put out a certain energy when they want to attract someone,'" Shari remembers, "and I still don't have any idea what this energy is."

I still don't have any idea what this energy is. This may be the unifying ace call, one I have heard again and again from aces, whether they are sex-favorable or sex-repulsed, irrespective of their romantic orientation and aesthetic types. Regardless of whether we have sex, we don't relate to sexuality the way that, seemingly, allos do. We do not center sexuality in our lives.

And, so, aces spend an inordinate amount of time wondering about this energy that other people are detecting, and experiencing, and expressing, that we are not. People think about sex even if they don't want to? What makes one person sexually attractive on that visceral level and not another? Allos can even be sexually attracted to people they find ugly? *What?* Like anthropologists after a day of fieldwork, we commiserate about the mysteries of the local culture, even though it is actually the culture that we were born into—just one that, for a long time, had no room for us and our way of being. There is room now.

An entire ace culture has developed all over the world. Ace colors: black and gray and white and purple. An ace flag: those colors, in that order, in horizontal stripes. An aromantic flag too: stripes of dark green, light green, white, gray, and black. Symbols—a black ring on the middle finger of the right hand—and in-jokes: images of cake (because, as the joke goes, cake is better than sex), and the ace of spades, the term "asexy." Many of those small, early-2000s groups are gone, but they've been succeeded by more zines, a thriving network of bloggers, and a popular group blog called *The Asexual Agenda*. AVEN is still around and David Jay's dream of building bridges with the LGBTQ+ community came true. For the most part, aces are considered part of the LGBTQ+ community, though some people disagree and think that cis heteroromantic aces should not be considered queer. (To be clear, all aces are queer because none of us are heterosexual.)

The ace world has moved offline too, to meetups and conferences, which is a boon because it's very rare for aces to run into each other in the wild. Every time I am surrounded by aces, I am both surprised and moved by how free I feel, how the discussions come with an extra sense of lightness and ease. Though I would never say that I am restricted in my daily interactions with allos, there is a palpable difference among aces, a stripping away of defensiveness because I know that I will not need to explain asexuality or represent asexuality or educate others on all the ways that someone can be asexual. I can be myself and also ace, not myself defined by asexuality. We talk about books and music and film and families, like anyone else, and also about the confusions and conflicts of ace experience.

. . . .

That aces can point out contradictions around sexuality and language does not mean we need to solve them or that we are capable of doing so. The lack of tidiness frustrates me, but reality is rarely simple. Sexuality can be more than sexual orientation and aces can still lack a sexuality. People who experience sexual attraction can still be part of the ace community. Kink can be sexual for some and only about emotional dynamics for others.

A careful balancing act is necessary. Aces understand by isolating, *via negativa*, by splitting attraction into categories and then calling it a model, but that gives everything a gloss of scientific legitimacy that almost no explanation can fully claim. It is equally important to acknowledge that, all too often, these different attractions blend together and cannot be cleanly extracted.

In the fall of 2016, I began taking the antidepressant Wellbutrin, which has the well-known side effect of increasing sex drive. I felt no different at first, yet when I began a relationship a few months later, I found myself more eager to have sex with this partner than any partner before and questioning my asexuality for the first time. Was it because of Wellbutrin? Was it because he and I were compatible in ways that previous partners and I were not? Was it because I was simply older and better equipped to deal with the stresses of a relationship without shutting down?

It may be impossible to know. Life is not a science experiment. Nobody can run multiple simulations of their experiences, tweaking one factor here and another there to see how the outcomes differ. Sexuality of any kind never exists in a vacuum. It is not broken down easily but is affected by biology and culture, by our emotional state and mental health, by race and class and gender and the passing of time. Shari the filmmaker and Vesper the ace blogger are Black and I am a Chinese immigrant, and our experiences of asexuality are shaped by race. Sebastian Maguire, who is the legislative director for New York City councilmember Daniel Dromm, identified as allo and gay before realizing he was ace and homoromantic. His process of coming to asexuality, and how he experiences asexuality, has been different from ours.

Over and over, I return to an aphorism coined by the Polish philosopher Alfred Korzybski: the map is not the territory. The saying contains both tension and promise. A map is a simplified representation of what is actually there and the landscape is always richer than the markings captured on the page. Yet maps and simplification can still be helpful—after all, all models are wrong, but some are useful. All representations are limited, but better ones can still broaden the gaze. It is time for new and more detailed maps. Asexuality offers these more precise maps, but we must remember that a map is still a map and that the phrase "Welcome to the ace world" is a misnomer. There is no one ace world. It should be "Welcome to the ace worlds," one of many entry points for understanding.

CHAPTER 3

COMPULSORY SEXUALITY AND (MALE) ASEXUAL EXISTENCE

WHEN HUNTER WAS VERY YOUNG, his parents would take him to the local superstore and let him hang out at the video game display while they bought groceries. One day, seeing that an older kid was already there playing the demos, Hunter asked if he could take a turn for five minutes.

"Yeah, right," the kid said. "You'll hog it."

"No!" Hunter insisted. "I'm not lying because *I'm a Christian*."

Religion was the beating heart of his childhood, and Hunter had not yet realized that Christians could lie too. His family prayed before every meal and attended church each Sunday, but the greatest source of moral pressure, always, came from Hunter himself. As a child, he had a strong moral sense fortified by the teachings of the Bible. As he grew older, this turned into a form of scrupulosity that he would one day look back on with bemusement.

No one talked about sex. During all those childhood Sundays, only a single sermon directly addressed sex, and that was a warning against temptation. Yet while nobody was talking about sex, everybody learned that sex was good, a gift from God and a pleasurable reward so long as enjoyed only within marriage.

Sex bound men and women together in a way that nothing else could—"like a superior connection," Hunter says, a quality so notable that it could almost be seen. People became different around each other, more tightly integrated, like an unofficial marriage. Hunter longed for that connection and knew that God would provide if he remained chaste. To uphold his end of the bargain, Hunter began training himself to resist temptation and in college picked up a book called *Every Man's Battle* that promised a system for staying pure.

The gist of *Every Man's Battle* is that avoidance is the answer to the problem of lust. Readers are instructed to "bounce your eyes," Hunter explains, which means immediately looking away from anyone who might trigger an impure thought. Visual repression starves the sexual appetite, supposedly. "I totally bought into that," Hunter says, "just telling myself not to look at people because you can't lust. In hindsight, it maybe brought me some harm in other ways because there was nothing sexual to begin with, so I was constantly looking away from strangers who happened to be attractive."

Avoidance was easy for Hunter, ridiculously so. Lust was not as much of a struggle for him as it was for others. He did not consider that lust might not be a struggle at all, that he had invented a struggle because he was told that he must have something to struggle against. Today, now that he has told old friends that he is asexual, they laugh and say it's not fair that he had no sexual urges to suppress. "Hunter," they say, "you had cheat codes the whole time."

•••••••••

The assumption that everyone struggles against sexual temptation—the "every" of *Every Man's Battle* and *Every Woman's Battle* and the rest of this best-selling Christian series—shows that religion, too, emphasizes the ubiquity of sexual desire. Despite its emphasis on purity culture and the importance of abstinence, religion is not entirely free from compulsory sexuality or the belief that lust is universal and to be otherwise is to be abnormal.

If the phrase *compulsory sexuality* sounds familiar, that's because it borrows from the poet Adrienne Rich's concept of compulsory heterosexuality. In her 1980 essay "Compulsory Heterosexuality and Lesbian Existence," Rich argued that heterosexuality is not merely a sexual orientation that happens to be the orientation of most people. Heterosexuality is a political institution that is taught and conditioned and reinforced.[1]

Compulsory heterosexuality is not the belief that most people are heterosexual. It is a set of assumptions and behaviors—that only heterosexual love is innate, that women need men as social and economic protectors—that support the idea of heterosexuality as the default and only option. It makes people believe that heterosexuality is so widespread only because it is "natural," even though, as Rich writes, "the failure to examine heterosexuality as an institution is like failing to admit that the economic system called capitalism or the caste system of racism is maintained by a variety of forces, including both physical violence and false consciousness."[2]

Building off this idea, compulsory sexuality, an idea central to ace discourse, is not the belief that most people want sex and have sex and that sex can be pleasurable. Compulsory sexuality is a set of assumptions and behaviors that support the idea that every normal person is sexual, that not wanting (socially approved) sex is unnatural and wrong, and that people who don't care about sexuality are missing out on an utterly necessary experience.

Make no mistake: Sex is political, and its meaning is always changing. The world is big and complicated and the amount of compulsory sexuality, and the way it is expressed, changes according to context. Sex is associated with impurity and sin, and celibacy is required for some members of the clergy. Generally, heterosexual married sex is celebrated far more than unmarried sex, more so than gay sex or kinky sex. The world has not encouraged sex for those who are poor or for people of color. As Illinois State University gender studies scholar Ela Przybylo points out in an interview, sex negativity exists alongside compulsory sexuality; people celebrate queerness even while homophobia is rampant.

For Hunter, taught that same-sex desire was not consistent with religious teachings, compulsory sexuality was packaged neatly into compulsory heterosexuality. Hunter is romantically attracted to women, so he already fulfilled the hetero part—and it is the *hetero* part of *compulsory heterosexuality* that receives the most attention—yet he still found the elevation of sex and the expectation of sexuality hard to fulfill.

Compulsory sexuality separate from compulsory heterosexuality exists too. In queer subcultures where heterosexuality is not enforced as strongly, compulsory sexuality can be expressed as the expectation that gay men be hypersexual or the worry by lesbian women about supposed "lesbian bed death." In many cases, lack of sexual attraction is a problem regardless of whom that attraction might have been directed toward. Zii Miller, a trans man in Florida who grew up in Europe, did not have to contend with either compulsory heterosexuality or purity culture. However, when he told his mother about being ace, she blamed America, believing that her son would be different if the family had stayed in France. There, Zii would have been exposed to so-called healthy, open sexuality, instead of America's Puritan values and discomfort around bodies. American values, she thought, had caused him to be repressed. The United States had made her child weird.

· · · · · · · · · ·

One of the more obvious examples of compulsory sexuality is the fear of a sexless population. It is a great irony that despite hand-wringing over loose morals, Americans are having less sex than before. According to the Centers for Disease Control and Prevention, 41 percent of high school students in 2015 reported having had sex, down from 54 percent in 1991.[3] As for American adults, in the 2010s, they had sex about nine fewer times per year than a quarter-century earlier.[4]

Such findings have prompted cover stories about "sex recessions"[5] (a recession, naturally, is not a good thing), articles about how the sex recession could lead to an economic recession[6] and hand-wringing comments over how young people are doing it wrong and are boring now. Economic worries could be to blame,[7] or anxiety over unclear dating norms, or the popularity of Netflix and social media.[8] Americans, according to some researchers, have traded the pleasures of genital stimulation for the pleasure of likes on social media and binge-watching *The Great British Baking Show*. In one *Washington Post* article about the decline of sex, an eighteen-year-old is described as sitting in front of "several screens simultaneously: a work project, a YouTube clip, a video game." For him, abandoning this setup for a date or a one-night stand "seems like a waste."[9]

Often implicit in this framing are these questions: Isn't it *sad* that people are having less sex and that a one-night stand now seems like a waste? Isn't it *pitiful* to be playing video games instead of feeling sexual pleasure?

Shouldn't we be worried that people don't care about sex anymore? For truly passionate people, sex—the pursuit, the experience—is always better than a movie, a book, a game. The loser of today has three computer screens and no sex drive.

Such articles imply not only that sex is normal and wonderful but also that sex is the main source of adventure, reflecting what journalist Rachel Hills calls "the sex myth" in her book of the same name. The sex myth, which is an extension of compulsory sexuality, has two parts. One is obvious: sex is everywhere and we are saturated in it, from song lyrics to television shows to close-ups of women's lipsticked mouths eating burgers, meat juice trickling down their throats. The second part is the belief that "sex [is] more special, more significant, a source of greater thrills and more perfect pleasure than any other activity humans engage in."[10] No sex means no pleasure, or no ability to enjoy pleasure.

The result is that anyone who isn't sexual enough or sexual in the right way becomes lesser. The label of *asexual* should be value neutral. It should indicate little more than sexual orientation. Instead, *asexual* implies a slew of other, negative associations: passionless, uptight, boring, robotic, cold, prude, frigid, lacking, broken. These, especially *broken*, are the words aces use again and again to describe how we are perceived and made to feel.

The existence of these associations can be traced back, in part, to the commodification of sex. Sex sells, and sex makes other things easier to sell. Hugh Hefner's *Playboy*, often credited for this shift, did not merely provide photos of naked women. *Playboy* provided a vision of the good life, of what real men did with their time and money, and that included using their purchasing power to buy the attention of gorgeous models and access to orgies.[11] When sex is a commodity, having and flaunting sex becomes a form of conspicuous consumption, used to signal that we are not passionless, uptight, boring, and robotic but instead have the financial and social capital to be hip and fun and high status and multiorgasmic.

Aces do not comply and so are dismissed and told that our experience is depression or delusion or childish innocence, and that we cannot play with the big kids. We are not quite right, or not quite worthwhile—made in the shape of a human but with faulty wiring and something lost, something fundamental to the good life.

· · · · · · · · · ·

The religious narrative that dominated Hunter's life warned to wait until marriage, but always running alongside that message was the simple, secular one: sex is cool. Sex *makes* you cool. Compulsory sexuality told Hunter that he was naturally lustful. The cultural legacy of *Playboy* and coming-of-age movies like *American Pie* further taught Hunter that sex would take away his worries about being masculine enough. "Watching [*American Pie*], it was like, 'Oh yeah, that kid was a loser and he became the hero of the movie and the catalyst for that was having sex.' That's what I wanted," he says. "I wanted sex on an *intellectual* level. I wanted everything that sex was supposed to bring me." Hetero and white and male, the very model of privilege, Hunter nevertheless felt enormous pressure to be different from how he was. The way that compulsory sexuality intersected with gender expectations and religious teachings would be the source of much of his pain. His faith was strong, but the dictates of faith couldn't obliterate the message that real men are sexually aggressive.

Surveys of the ace community show that far more women identify as asexual than men—about 63 percent versus 11 percent, according to the most recent numbers[12]—likely in part because asexuality is a greater challenge to male sexual stereotypes. Men are taught that they are not *men*, and therefore not deserving of respect or status, unless they can sleep with as many women as possible. (Women talk about sex, too, but are socialized to discuss relationships and emotions while men's conversations are more laser-focused on the sexual.)

In *Inside Greek U.: Fraternities, Sororities, and the Pursuit of Pleasure, Power, and Prestige*, Indiana University scholar Alan D. DeSantis observes an exaggerated example of this dynamic, the ur-model of male sexuality. DeSantis describes fraternity brothers who "engage in the old fraternal tradition of 'kissing and telling,' or more aptly put, 'fucking and bragging,'" chronicling their conquests while laughing and giving each other high fives. The gossiping ritual "continues for another ten minutes until everyone's dirty laundry has been aired" and we learn that, as DeSantis writes, "as far as these fraternity brothers are concerned, the ideal masculinity is hypersexual, promiscuous, and heterosexual."[13]

Plenty of men aren't in fraternities, but this scene lines up with a 2017 Pew Research survey that tracked attitudes toward masculinity and femininity. According to the survey, nearly 60 percent of millennial men said that they feel pressure to join in when others are talking about women sexually.[14] "But what happens when all your friends start talking about sex and you're still a virgin?" asks sociologist Colby Fleming in an interview with *MEL Magazine*. "A male virgin can effectively be locked out or outright shamed."[15] Performing sexuality provides access to formative friendships and respect; it can be more social than personal. The lack of the right kind of sexual behavior is a barrier to connection, so men's talk and behavior can be less about wanting sex than it is about wanting friends.

The lesson that real men have a lot of sex is responsible for the experiences of two seemingly opposite groups. One group, of course, is ace men. The other is the incels, or involuntary celibates: misogynistic, usually heterosexual men who are angry at women for not having sex with them.

Ace men, who are often voluntarily celibate, have trouble relating to discussions of sex because of a genuine lack of interest. Przybylo, the gender studies professor, interviewed several ace men for an academic article on asexuality and masculinity.[16] All, unsurprisingly, experienced tension between gender expectations and what they actually wanted. They "played along" with male friends by pretending to have crushes on women or had unwanted heterosexual sex with partners. "Some people just can't wrap their heads around" a man not wanting sex, said one interviewee, Billy. "Some people will react like, 'How can you not love it?' I wish I knew. Apparently it's the best feeling in the world, but I wish I could appreciate it," he told Przybylo, adding that he wondered whether he would feel less alienated if he were gay but not asexual.[17]

Gay men, too, feel intense pressure to be sexual. "I think we assume that a single gay man is having sex," a man named Craig told *GQ*, "There's a focus on appearance, categorization, youth, and the like that colors dating and sex in our community."[18] For him, being twenty-two and gay and not having a lot of sex is embarrassing. Men who are ace and homoromantic tell me that compulsory sexuality in the gay community makes them feel doubly ostracized.

Beliefs about the voracious nature of male sexuality are so strong that they can lead ace men to doubt their gender identity. One ace man I interviewed said that he initially wondered whether he was trans because he knew that women were supposed to be the ones uninterested in sex. Antony, who talked to Przybylo, said that the more a person identified with the gender label of male, the more he would feel the pressure to go out and meet women to have sex.[19]

For ace men who are trans, the intersection of gender and sexuality can be confusing too. "I've connected being transgender and asexual," says Zii, the trans man from Florida. "I've sometimes thought that I'm transgender *because* I'm asexual, since I hit puberty and developed secondary sex characteristics and never felt comfortable using them. I wanted to get rid of them." During his first visit to the endocrinologist, Zii said that he didn't want to be anything—he'd rather be "neutral"— but he especially didn't want to be female, not when being female meant having to shave and wear particular clothes and be hit on by guys.

From his current vantage point, Zii can see important differences in how he was treated when presenting as female versus now. His lack of interest in sex was viewed as natural then, because girls are supposed to be hesitant. "And as a man," he tells me, "they say, 'You gotta get out there and stop thinking like that.'"

• • • • • • • •

Incels, on the other hand, are desperately interested in sex. Incels have also absorbed the lesson that real men have sex with women, but they lack the sexual expertise needed to participate in the rites of masculinity. For this I have sympathy. Exclusion and social rejection are painful, and in fact, the first incel website was started by a woman who wanted to create a supportive community for the lonely.[20]

Incels, however, are not merely lonely. They are also entitled, and here my sympathy ends. Instead of questioning the narrative of masculinity that prioritizes sexual conquest, incels lean into it, misusing evolutionary psychology to make themselves more miserable and falling into reductionist theories about genetic fitness and how the purpose of men is to impregnate as many women as possible.

Some affiliated groups, like Men Going Their Own Way, avoid engaging with women at all.[21] In other cases, the hatred has terrible consequences. The subreddit r/incel had about forty thousand subscribers before being banned for inciting violence.[22] It had become affiliated with people like Elliot Rodger, who murdered six people at a California university in 2014 because women wouldn't have sex with him.[23] Four years later, twenty-five-year-old Alek Minassian went on a rampage with a van in Toronto, killing ten. Before his murder spree, Minassian had made posts on his Facebook that praised Elliot Rodger and claimed that "the incel rebellion has already begun."[24] All this rage and violence from not having sex.

But it is not really about sex. As Tim Squirrell, a researcher who studies online extremist groups, tells me: "If it were just about the sexual thrill, why wouldn't incels resort to increasingly elaborate forms of wanking?" If sexual frustration were the only problem, incels could try to pay for sex. Yet, many incels refuse to "debase" themselves by going to sex workers. They divide women into the blonde, large-breasted Stacys, and the Beckys, plain women who commit gender crime by refusing to accentuate their femininity, Squirrell explains. Incels scoff at Beckys, hoping to score exclusively with Stacys because Stacys alone are the sexual currency that will lead to admiration. It's about the status.

I am no incel apologist. Many people feel unattractive and undateable without believing that others owe them sex or resorting to murder. Still, it's undeniable that the rage of the incels is connected to cultural expectations around men and sex, and that the same is true of the alienation of ace men. These groups, so different in desire, are both constricted by the same sexual norms. Making sexual experience less of a prerequisite for male social inclusion—and less of a requirement for acceptance and status generally—would help both groups.

For now, though, male sexual stereotypes remain so strong that voluntarily celibate aces are sometimes conflated with incels. Ace men tell me that people of all genders assume that they are secret incels who hide behind a made-up identity. Such is the trap: Even when a man doesn't want sex, he can be lumped in with the men who will kill in their desire to have it. Men cannot be simply uninterested; there must always be something else at work.

. . . .

The promises of faith trumped the temptation of being cool, so Hunter and his girlfriend followed every precaution. No rooms with closed doors, no fooling around, and no sex until they married when Hunter was twenty-five.

Sex was nothing like Hunter had expected. "I'd always heard people saying that 'Oh, one thing leads to another,' but that was not it," he says. Sex felt "forced and unnatural"—not forced as in nonconsensual, more like he had to force himself to initiate. Not unnatural as in uncomfortable, but rather that it was unintuitive and he had to focus intently on the movements from moment to moment. Like learning to ride a bike, only your limbs never quite synchronize properly. Years of bouncing his eyes had not prepared Hunter for an act that was okay but nothing spectacular, nor had he expected his own indifference. Afterward, no special, superior connection materialized.

Inexperience was the obvious culprit, but that explanation became less and less legitimate as the years went by. Age became the next scapegoat as Hunter wondered whether waiting until twenty-five had caused him to miss some kind of physiological trigger for enjoying sex. *Every Man's Battle* could be to blame, or maybe his religious upbringing more generally was at fault. Maybe the fact that no one talked about sex had made him repressed, "almost like self-conversion therapy, but away from heteronormative sex."

None of this explained why Hunter had Christian friends who married later and loved sex, saying it was their favorite part of marriage. He couldn't relate when coworkers joked about being "thirsty" and wanting to hook up, but he didn't mind hearing these stories either, so repression seemed unlikely. He hadn't been abused. He didn't have erectile dysfunction. A visit to the doctor to ask if everything was okay "down there" revealed that his testosterone levels were on the higher end of average.

The doctor's visit had been Hunter's last resort. It provided no answer to a question that would not go away. His marriage was official in the eyes of the law and his wife never complained—she was busy and didn't have a high sex drive anyway—but once again, the moral pressure came from Hunter himself. "Because the sex never clicked, there was always this feeling that I was still infantile," he says. He was not truly married, not truly an adult and not truly a man.

If sex is a gift from God and wonderful if you do everything right, what does it mean when you do everything right and the sex disappoints time and time again? Where does that leave you? "That's what brought me to the darkest places," Hunter says. "I never experienced this great thing and I didn't know why, for years on end with no explanation."

· · · · · · · · ·

Nine years into his marriage, Hunter saw an article about asexuality on Facebook. It made asexuality sound like a medical problem and the doctor's visit had busted that theory, so he closed the tab and moved on. A few months later, working the night shift at a factory, the term *gray-A* in an Instagram bio caught Hunter's eye and he casually googled the term to learn more. By the end of the night, the interest was no longer casual. If asexuality wasn't about sickness, it might explain what theories about repression and out-of-whack hormones and religion had not. It might provide some measure of self-acceptance

Hunter's story is one answer to those who mock asexuality and ask why aces need to make a big fuss about not wanting sex. Years of Hunter's life had been spent wondering what was wrong until he learned about asexuality from an Instagram bio, yet it's not uncommon for ace activism to be considered a nuisance and a joke.

In 2012, for instance, Fox ran a segment about asexuality that starts with the host asking guest Brooke Goldstein, founder of the Lawfare Project, whether she buys that asexuality is a legitimate sexual orientation. "Oh, I buy it," Goldstein replies. "Asexuality has been around for a very long time. It's called being a woman every three and a half weeks. It's a wonderful excuse to get out of obligations."[25]

The host laughs at this quip. No one remarks on the fact that if anyone needs to make up an identity to get out of having sex, *that* is the bigger problem. It is a failure of society if anyone needs to say "I have a partner" to turn someone down, and it is a failure of society if anyone needs to invoke a sexual orientation to avoid unwanted sex because saying no doesn't do the job.

Goldstein even continues on to say that aces "are normal in an uber-sexualized society, so we've had to invent this asexuality."[26] Yet this point is not addressed any further. Goldstein does not discuss the possible downsides of such an uber-sexualized society and the expectations present around how much sex is necessary and when it is okay to opt out and what happens if anyone tries to hold off for too long. Instead, the host says that because aces lack a sexuality, they'll be "treated as lepers," while a different guest, Fox contributor Bill Schulz, is incredulous at the idea that aces face any discrimination and asks if we can "stop recognizing things." "If [aces are] that small a portion of the population, do I have to recognize you?" he asks. "Like, oh, recognize me because I wear sock-monkey hats! Okay, there's a couple people that wear sock-monkey hats, I don't need to recognize you. Yes, you exist. Move on."[27]

Completely by accident, this dismissive segment, which ends with the host saying that he doesn't trust aces, has painted what I believe would be a utopia for aces: not needing to be recognized. Nobody needs to recognize the sock-monkey-hat people because there's not much pressure against wearing sock-monkey hats. Doctors won't tell them they're sick. Immigration lawyers won't ask them to prove that sometimes they don't wear sock-monkey hats in order to verify a marriage. Television shows don't frequently mock people who wear sock-monkey hats. Society does not center sock-monkey hats in any way.

Society does center sexuality. In the West today, sexuality is considered an essential part of identity. Sexuality is not merely what you do, it is part of who you are, part of the truth of you. As philosopher Michel Foucault argues in his *History of Sexuality*, this social emphasis on sexuality is the result of historical and political forces.[28] I do not think that it must always be this way.

In many ways, the ace movement grew out of opposition to this idea that sexuality must be a cornerstone of both identity and existence. Though asexuality has become a sexual identity in itself, it can also be understood as a way of living that simply refuses to care about personal sexuality. As Julie Sondra Decker, author of *The Invisible Orientation: An Introduction to Asexuality*, tells me, "We're whole people who just lack that 'driving force' and it's understandable in the same way that it's understandable that someone doesn't have 'crafts' as their driving force." (Or in the way that people don't have "not wearing sock-monkey hats" as their driving force.) "I'm not a 'non-crafter'; I'm only asexual because there's a word for it and because people have an objection to me not wanting to have sex. If they didn't, my life would not have involved very much of talking about it," she says.

Sexuality-as-identity is not necessarily the enemy. Compulsory sexuality is. Compulsory sexuality is at the root of the objection against a life like Julie's and it is the force aces define ourselves against. If there were no compulsory sexuality, aces would not need a community for support. It would not be so meaningful for aces to find each other and realize that we're okay. Any visibility we have is, in some ways, a reminder that compulsory sexuality exists and that it affects more than us, that it can punish anyone seems to deviate from the expected. If aces make a big deal out of being ace and demand to be recognized, if we have created groups of our own, it is because we want a place away from sexual pressure. If we fight for visibility and change, it is because we want that pressure to be lifted for others too.

· · · · · · · · ·

For Hunter, the ace community provided permission to be as he was, after nearly a decade of searching for a fix. To explain everything to his wife, Hunter wrote a six-page letter, going through three drafts and five prefaces just to lay the groundwork. It was important that she understand what had been going through his mind all those years and why, from her perspective, he had always been preoccupied with sex, always the one talking about sex and initiating it. He needed her to know that he had put sex on a pedestal and thought himself wrong for not loving it, but that this would no longer be the case. "It was an apology for ways that I'd behaved too," Hunter adds, "because there were times when I made myself more distant because I didn't want to deal with that frustration as much."

Life together didn't need to change, he wrote. Actions could be the same. He wouldn't initiate anymore, but she could always tell him when she wanted sex and he would be happy to please her. "The actual act of sex, I don't really mind," Hunter says. "Whatever was bad before was the uncertainty of why I was broken and that weird tension." What had been bad was knowing that he had sex out of insecurity. It was the dream of sex as the promised act versus what it turned out to be.

Agency is present in a new way and accepting asexuality has brought Hunter clarity of other kinds. He had become a queer ally before identifying as ace, but learning about asexuality helped him understand that others emphasized sexual orientation because sexual attraction was an active force in their lives. He has become more critical of male gender roles too. Rejecting one form of social programming makes it easier to start questioning everything else.

"It's like, Oh, okay, those expectations I had of what a man is or does or likes or wants are expectations that were given to me culturally, and they're not necessarily the default," Hunter says. "I've experienced this my whole life but never noticed it, and [asexuality] turned everything on its head, and now I'm way more skeptical of all those narratives. I no longer feel infantile, that subconscious mindset of having never attained adulthood. I finally felt more free to be an adult at thirty-four—which is a little late, but whatever."

PART II
·············
VARIATIONS ON
A THEME

CHAPTER 4

JUST LET ME LIBERATE YOU

TWO WEEKS AFTER I TURNED TWENTY-TWO, I asked my friends to take me to a bar and help me pick someone up. A request like this was unprecedented. I did not drink, I did not go to bars, and I avoided so much as holding a person's hand. Furthermore, I had blabbed about Henry and our plans to meet over the summer. It was now April, and with that meeting only a couple of months away, it seemed stupid not to wait.

But I hadn't told my friends about my insecurities. I hadn't told them that I felt so old-fashioned and backward for only wanting sex if it came with love. They knew that Henry and I planned to have an open relationship, but I had not been honest about the extent of my fears around this situation. Neither the entire history of human relations nor the testimonies of male and female friends alike assuaged my rumination. Nothing could stop my suspicion that Henry was lying when he said that sex without love was common and that he could have sex with others without becoming emotionally entangled. Filled with doubt and also guilt for doubting, I decided to prove to myself that sex without attachment was possible and, hopefully, make myself more amenable to free love. I needed to live up to the goals I had set for myself: to be modern instead of old-fashioned, a good feminist who lived out my beliefs, and to not be repressed.

"Repressed" is the opposite of "liberated." An insult. In culturally liberal circles, the sexually conservative woman is often considered to be sexually repressed—and the sexually repressed woman is a symbol of a time before freedom. She is uptight and in denial, white-knuckling her way through life. She is the perfectly coiffed fifties housewife, lacking the ease of liberated counterparts who are in touch with their bodies and secure with their place in the world. The sexually repressed woman is an object of pity and a reminder of the importance of progress. She is embarrassing.

I believed all of the assumptions embedded in this archetype of the woman who doesn't embrace sex: that she is prudish and prim, that she hasn't done the proper work of liberating herself from shame, and that she is politically conservative too.

None of this aligned with my goals. The words used to describe women who didn't have sex (celibate, abstinent, pure, chaste) seemed either clinical or moralistic in a way I disdained. The words used to describe women who did (free, empowered, bold) I liked and wanted to apply to me. I absorbed the language of archetypes and aesthetic tropes—the repressed woman, the liberated woman—instead of thinking more critically about whether these stories were true and, if so, what they might imply about how we connect sex and politics and power. I reuse these archetypes and aesthetic tropes now because they represent the way these messages were handed down. Few people would explicitly say that sexually conservative women are wallflowers, but popular culture made that insinuation clear, and so I had a vague, unquestioned feeling that the women who pursue sex are more fun and feminist than the women who don't. Perhaps my attitude can best be summarized by anti-rape activist Alexandra Brodsky, who told journalist Rebecca Traister that she hears from women who believe that "not having a super-exciting, super-positive sex life is in some ways a political failure."[1] I could easily have been one of them.

. . . .

My ideas about the humiliation of repression and the meaning of liberated sexuality did not come from nowhere. For so long, women have been encouraged to deny our sexual needs and instead serve the needs of men. Our worth is tied to sex. We are sexualized until we are too old, yet shamed and policed for being sexual ourselves, prevented from exploring what we desire or are allowed to desire—and this is doubly true if the women in question aren't straight.

The politics of sex became central to American feminist discussion in the 1970s and 1980s. During this period, activists Catharine Mac-

Kinnon and Andrea Dworkin led the movement that would be known as sex-negative feminism. MacKinnon and Dworkin might not have thought of themselves as sex negative, but their work certainly did not focus on the liberatory possibilities of orgasm. With titles like *Sexual Harassment of Working Women* and *Woman Hating,* their books focused less on the pleasure of sex and more on the ways that sexuality could be used to harm.

The very basic argument was that unequal power dynamics are the backdrop to heterosexual sex, always, so true consent is almost impossible to achieve. Their structural analysis concluded that sex under patriarchy was inevitably compromised and unfree. Activist groups that sprang from this tradition were against pornography, sadomasochism, and sex work, all of which they deemed exploitative ways for men to degrade and hurt women.

In 1982, when the annual Barnard Conference on Sexuality decided that its theme would be "pleasure and danger," members of the group Women Against Pornography protested, wearing shirts that read "For a Feminist Sexuality" on one side and "Against S/M" on the other.[2] The next year, MacKinnon and Dworkin tried to a pass a law to ban pornography in Minneapolis. After that effort failed, a similar ordinance was introduced in Indianapolis, endorsed by conservatives and the avowedly anti-feminist lawyer Phyllis Schlafly.

MacKinnon and Dworkin were a well-matched team, writes New York University professor Lisa Duggan in a retrospective of the period published in *Sex Wars: Sexual Dissent and Political Cultures.* MacKinnon, with a degree from Yale Law School, was the polished, patrician, rational one, Duggan recounts, and Dworkin the fiery speaker who told supporters to "swallow the vomit you feel at the thought of dealing with the city council and get this law in place." Her words were memorable and she was not afraid of appearing extreme. "See that the silence of women is over," Dworkin said, "and that we're not down on our backs with our legs spread anymore."[3]

The Indianapolis anti-porn ordinance was signed into law. Similar ordinances were suggested—and narrowly defeated—in places like Los Angeles, New York, and Cambridge, Massachusetts. Challenges to these ordinances made it all the way to the Supreme Court, which ultimately supported the idea that these porn bans are unconstitutional.[4]

Feminists have never all agreed with each other and feminist attitudes toward sex have never been static. For feminists like Ellen Willis and Susie Bright, the MacKinnon-Dworkin approach encouraged a sexual conservatism that did not serve women. In a landmark 1981 essay titled "Lust Horizons: Is the Women's Movement Pro-Sex?" Willis struck back at the attitudes that, as she put it, "tap into the underside of traditional femininity—the bitter, self-righteous fury that propels the indictment of men as lustful beasts ravaging their chaste victims." Bitterness was not the same as an actual solution, and the doom-and-gloom hyper-focus of sex negativity pushed women to "accept a spurious moral superiority as a substitute for sexual pleasure, and curbs on men's sexual freedom as a substitute for real power." Plus, she continued, "in this culture, where women are still supposed to be less sexual than men, sexual inhibition is as integral to the 'normal' woman's identity as sexual aggression is to a man's. It is 'excessive' genital desires that often make women feel 'unfeminine' and unworthy."[5] MacKinnon and Dworkin may have helped women become more aware of how complicated sex could be, but they hardly helped anyone have better sex.

Sex-positive feminists like Willis and Bright did not believe that porn was always demeaning. They did not approve of the conservative allegiance to ban it or of giving politicians (who were so often men) so much power in controlling women's sexuality. It was important to undo the social conditioning of shame. Pleasure was possible, even under patriarchy. Women had agency and were not such fragile creatures, easily broken.

. . . .

Having sex is cool; not having sex is less so. Sex is not only a commodity for men to buy. Women can now participate, too, conspicuously consuming sex to show off and also to be able to say that this consumption is empowering because we are using our power to have the same rights as men. Female horniness is to be cultivated. This is not an explicit memo but a feeling in the air that makes "prude" a gendered pejorative and motivates aces to rush to claim that we are not judgmental about sex at all.

Samantha Jones, played by Kim Cattrall in the blockbuster show *Sex and the City*, is one iconic representation of this modern, sex-positive woman. She's a high-powered publicist, ambitious and confident, with some of the funniest and best lines in the show. An unapologetic sexual libertine, Samantha talks a big game about her many affairs and calls herself a "try-sexual," as in, she'll try anything once. "I will not be judged by you or society," she says, in a memorable scene that has been GIF'ed all over the internet. "I will wear whatever and blow whomever I want as long as I can breathe and kneel."

Twenty years after *Sex and the City* premiered, HBO debuted the teen drama *Euphoria*. Fictional teens of today, as represented by the show, treat sex cavalierly, with hotel room trysts and hookups at other people's houses. In one early episode, the character Kat Hernandez confesses to being a virgin and is told, "Bitch, this isn't the '80s. You need to catch a dick!" Kat does, losing her virginity and gaining confidence by becoming a cam girl.

In real life, too, women talking about sex can build up a certain cultural cachet. *Cosmopolitan* continues to provide readers with sex tips, articles in other publications combat the stereotype of the sexually demure woman by claiming that "women are horny as heck,"[6] and the women's magazine *The Cut* has a week of content dedicated to being horny.[7] Last December, the *New York Times* declared 2019 "the year women got 'horny.'"[8] Cool-girl singer Tove Lo sings about being wet through all her clothes and Charli XCX insists she's "no angel" who likes to fuck in the hotel but it doesn't mean anything. In her song "Das Me," rapper Brooke Candy says that "slut" is now a compliment, "a sexy-ass female who running shit and confident." Top stars like Ariana Grande, Cardi B, and Nicki Minaj boast about sex and sexual prowess in both their music and their public personas.

Nicki Minaj's "Feeling Myself" has a line where Nicki brags about a lover telling her, "Damn, bae, you so little, but you be really takin' that pipe." That line was the cause of overwhelming disorientation for a friend of mine while she was listening in the car one day. How strange, she thought, that being able to have rough sex was a rap-worthy compliment, that it would be described as taking (making the woman seem like a recipient instead of a participant) a pipe (a brutal metaphor), that Nicki would brag about being able to get fucked and that she, listening, would instinctively understand why Nicki was bragging and also like the song. It all felt mixed together and messed up.

. . . .

If having sex were merely cool, this would have bothered me little. However, sex had also become *feminist* and this I cared about. Through a subtle series of twists, like in a game of telephone, sex for liberal women has become more than a way to enjoy ourselves or even prove that we're desirable. Conspicuous consumption of sex has become a way to perform feminist politics.

First, the important message that most women are conditioned to be sexually inhibited was delivered with a lack of nuance. "It seems that the message is 'we have liberated our sexuality, therefore we must now celebrate it and have as much sex as we want,'" says Jo, an ace policy worker in Australia. "Except 'as much sex as we want' is always lots of sex and not no sex, because then we are oppressed, or possibly repressed, and we're either not being our true authentic selves, or we haven't discovered this crucial side of ourselves that is our sexuality in relation to other people, or we haven't grown up properly or awakened yet."

Jo is far from the only one who feels this way. In college, the ace blogger Framboise (who writes as Radical Prude) was heavily influenced by sex-positive feminism and "talked endlessly with my feminist friends about desires and throwing off repression."[9] Throwing off repression is necessary, according to sex-positive feminism, because men control and shame women into not having sex. Shame can be so ingrained that it feels natural, so active work is required to overcome hesitation. Encouraging women to try whatever necessary to enjoy sex is praxis. None of this is wrong, but taken too far, Ellen Willis's claim that conditioned sexual inhibition is "integral to a 'normal' woman's identity" becomes the belief that sexual inhibition is the only reason women don't want sex.

It is then the strong, brave women who think critically about shame, who break free from patriarchy and reclaim their pleasure. Enjoying sex is proof that someone has done the work of self-liberation while staying at home alone can feel like disappointing the activists who worked so hard to offer women other and more exciting options. When Framboise spoke of her ambivalence toward sex, other feminists reacted by suggesting that she try masturbation and kinkier sex to help her process, explore, and defeat this repression. Notably, a certain *other* option is rarely presented. "[I was] never once told, 'Eh, maybe you just don't want sex. That's okay,'" Framboise writes. There was "little to no prominent affirmation of non-desire in sex positivity and a lot of suggestions on how to 'fix' yourself."[10] It was taken for granted that every woman would love sex, if only she could figure out how.

And if having sex liberates, then kinkier and more transgressive sex will be even more liberatory, both personally and politically. This belief is an inversion of a concept called the charmed circle, coined by anthropologist Gayle Rubin in her 1984 paper "Thinking Sex: Notes for a Radical Theory of the Politics of Sexuality."[11] The charmed circle illustrates the existence of a hierarchy of sex acts. Inside the charmed circle is everything that is socially acceptable, which traditionally means monogamous, married, vanilla, heterosexual sex in private. Outside these borders would be, for example, promiscuous sex, group sex, and so on. The charmed circle represented the conservative, rigid status quo.

Instead of realizing that the problem is the very existence of the charmed circle, liberals simply reversed it. Now, much of what was on the outside has become charmed and elevated. As University of Missouri gender studies professor Elisa Glick writes, the quest for a feminist sexuality free of male violence "is replaced by the quest for a politically incorrect sexuality that transgresses movement standards."[12] In other words, the more "transgressive" the act, the more inherently liberated it is from old norms and old politics and the better it is, and the more liberated you are when you do it. New rules are put in place.

Finally, as this vision of sexual liberation dominated the feminist platform, not having sex—or only wanting vanilla sex or only having sex within the confines of monogamous, heterosexual relationships—becomes a sign that someone is allied with backward, conservative political beliefs. Sexuality, which is already a maturity narrative where sex leads to adulthood, then becomes a *political* maturity narrative as well, an evolution in thought and practice. An imaginary line runs from "immature," both sexually and politically, to "fully realized."

On one end is our old friend, the sexually repressed woman. She is heterosexual, probably a Republican, maybe a WASP. She is blonde and stays at home with her kids and clutches her pearls when she's not clutching a cross. On the other end is a woman who is down for anything: threesomes,

polyamory, kink, sex clubs. She has multiple orgasms and multiple partners and wants to abolish ICE.

All this creates pressure for feminists to deprogram ourselves by
moving along the line from frigid and conservative to lusty and liberal.
"In queer radical circles and in much of the left, the worlds in which I
operate, there's a widely held idea that one's political radicalism can be
attached to one's sexual practices," writes activist Yasmin Nair.[13] "And
too often, we hear of people coming out into radical queer communities, often at very young ages, being told that they can't possibly be
radical enough unless they've entered into polyamorous and orgiastic
relationships. I've heard from too many people that they felt pressured,
especially as young and vulnerable new activists, to be particular kinds of
sexual beings and made to feel less political simply because a particular
sex scene wasn't really their scene."

At first glance, the connection between political radicalism and sexuality seems to make sense. The politically conservative are often also
sexually conservative, at least in their public personas. People who are
gay or trans are less likely to support conservative politicians that op-
pose their rights, and the power of association is strong. Once again,
just because two things are often paired does not mean they must be
paired. Yet a new kind of sexual normativity has developed. Preferences
are judged if they do not align with this correct—politically *incorrect* to
conservatives—vision of female sexuality. Transgressive sex becomes a
political act against patriarchy; its opposite, submission to patriarchy.
Asexuality does not exist but is only the byproduct of male oppression.
None of this is what the sex-positive feminists wanted. It's doubtful
they would have approved of this change or other changes, like the way
that sex has been commodified and feminism has become a buzzword
to sell products and television shows and personal brands. That hasn't
prevented good ideas from being co-opted and turned into material for
manipulation.

· · · · · · · · ·

The writer Lauren Jankowski knows this well. Lauren is a fantasy author,
an adoptee, and a feminist. Today, she runs a website called Asexual Artists and is fierce in her resolve that one does not need to want sex to have

a happy life, though at one point that belief had brought her to places of stark self-doubt.

After graduating from high school, Lauren took classes at the local community college. But what she really wanted was to be a novelist, so her father arranged for their next-door neighbor Chris to be her writing coach. Chris was a journalist, he and his wife were good friends with Lauren's family, she had babysat for their son, and it appeared to be a good fit all around. The two met for a few hours every Sunday in his dining room, an area that was kept perpetually dark because the family had stopped cleaning the windows after birds kept flying into them. The other walls were covered with shelves packed with books, and one of the shelves held a fish tank. Lauren would look at the colorful fish swimming around, trapped in there, and think that she knew how they felt.

Lauren came out to Chris early on because it was the easiest way to explain why she wanted to write ace characters. For her, identifying as asexual was already a victory. In high school Lauren had been convinced that her disinterest in sex was caused by cancer or a brain tumor, going so far as to order blood tests to diagnose her mysterious condition. It was important that no one else go through that same anxiety and uncertainty.

The first thing Chris said was that asexuality wasn't real. It was an idea made up by misogynistic men to keep women from being sexually liberated. Chris knew this because he was a worldly professional, a writer who could name-drop artists and liked to talk about Freud. She was his shy, anxious neighbor, a teenager who looked up to him and had attention deficit disorder to boot. Her opinion would not matter here.

Chris told Lauren to keep a dream journal and went through the entries with her, taking on the job of interpreting her dreams, which he claimed were all about her sublimated desire for sex. He edited her first novel, a fantasy murder-mystery about queer women, so that the main character was no longer asexual. Another character, who was both ace and aromantic, he turned into a villain, because evil was the only reason a woman wouldn't want a relationship. "It felt like something that I loved had been tainted," Lauren says, "and I didn't understand why I felt that way and it didn't really click until much later. But I'd remember going through those lines and thinking, 'That doesn't sound like me, but he's happy so it must be good, and I must be good.'"

Soon, nearly every meeting included a mention of the downsides of asexuality. Either the ADD medication was to blame and Lauren wasn't actually asexual, or she was and it was a great tragedy. Chris's lectures had a showy logic to them, demonstrating step by step how asexuality would lead—inexorably—to the ruin of all Lauren's ambitions. Being asexual means you can't have passion, he'd say. If you don't have passion, you can't write. Therefore, if you don't have sex, you can't be a writer. Identifying as ace means you're brainwashed by the patriarchy and you need to work harder to fight that. Otherwise, you can't be a feminist, and you certainly can't be an artist.

It must be said that Chris is almost too convenient. He is the literal voice of compulsory sexuality, the perfect avatar spewing warped beliefs. In one way, he is nothing new: men have long used shame to control women. The genius of Chris's manipulation was not that he used his power as an older male authority figure. It was that he updated the tactic, directly connecting Lauren's asexuality to her feminist politics and sense of identity, to her dream of being a writer and what she could hope to understand of life. He twisted the language of female sexual liberation to serve his own ends—which were revealed when he confessed to Lauren that he was in love with her. When Lauren didn't reciprocate, he called her a lazy, talentless failure and stopped working with her. Chris took the idea that women should be free to pursue sex and turned it into the idea that women aren't free unless they have sex—with him. Old male entitlement armed with a few new ideas, now hijacked in service of his libido. He is like Robin Thicke in "Blurred Lines": *Just let me liberate you.* He, and the feminists that Framboise knew in college, and myself when I was twenty-two, are all wrong.

· · · · · · · · · ·

One more time: sex is political. The questions of who deserves pleasure and what is considered transgressive and the very definition of sex are political. The meaning of sex and feminism and liberation is different for poor women and women of color, disabled women, and women of faith. Wealthy women with many partners are more likely to be considered liberated, for example, while working-class women with many partners are more likely to be considered trashy. Queer women have to deal with homophobia, the stigma of hypersexuality, and fetishization. Trans women are shamed and their gender identities are denied. All this can make it difficult for women to express their sexualities at all.

That doesn't mean every sexually indifferent woman is repressed. Patriarchal control is often responsible for women not enjoying sex. It is not always responsible. The truth of the gender inequality in sexual freedom, and the importance of teaching women to honor their sexual desires, has distorted into the belief that female sexual liberation only looks like one thing—and that's the opposite of what women's lives looked like before. Overcorrection doesn't solve the problem. It only redistributes the shame and the stigma.

To believe Chris and the rhetoric that female sexual apathy is always caused by repression is to forget that there have always been many ways to want sex and have sex. It is to be a victim of what Rubin, the anthropologist, called "one of the most tenacious ideas about sex," that "there is one best way to do it, and that everyone should do it that way."[14] This belief is wrong when only heterosexual, monogamous sex is accepted. It will still be wrong in a world where only heterosexual, monogamous sex is not accepted.

People may realize that they enjoy certain acts, but there is a difference between addressing desires that are already there (or exploring to see what you might like) and going searching for what *must* be there. It is true that many women are inhibited and perhaps do not yet know it. It is not true that inside everyone unwilling to try a threesome is a freak desperate to let her flag fly. Perhaps there is no flag.

The assumption of a ubiquitous, voracious libido ignores the reality of sexual variation. The idea that there always exists some secret sexual self to liberate only makes sense if you believe that we are all the same deep down—that everyone wants the same things, only some of us don't know yet that we get off on being flogged. Because sexual variation exists, there is no universal vision of liberated sexuality. The personal is political, but what's best for each person may be different. Liberated sexuality—that is, sexuality free from social shaming—can look like promiscuity or it can look like celibacy. And because liberated sexuality exists in many forms, there is no reason that being sexually conservative must mean being sexually repressed and no reason that being sexually conservative must prevent one's political radicalism.

It is also troubling if the focus on personal liberation takes attention away from the true power of political organizing. Having transgressive sex can be individually powerful, but it rarely changes the greater structure of politics, law, and culture that continues to shame alternative lifestyles and sex (and enforce other forms of regressive norms) for everyone else. An emphasis on personal, transgressive sexuality can result in a situation where "queerness, for example, is revalued, [but] the political and economic conditions that are responsible for its devaluation remain unchallenged,"[15] writes Glick, the University of Missouri scholar.

Political gatekeeping based on sexuality also alienates feminists for whom sex is not the priority. One such feminist is Rafia Zakaria, a Muslim lawyer and activist who first learned about sex-positive feminism in a graduate seminar. "In the competitiveness that graduate seminars breed, my classmates rambled on about threesomes, triumphant and unceremonious dumpings of emotionally attached lovers (who has time for that?) and in general lots and lots of sex," she wrote in an essay for the *New Republic*.[16] "Our smug professor, nose-pierced and wild-haired and duly sporting the scarves and baubles of the well-traveled, encouraged it all. The question of how and when sexual liberation had become not simply the centerpiece but the entire sum of liberation in general never came up."

Zakaria did not fit in among her graduate school classmates, aware that she would be labeled as a prude, "a Muslim woman to save, to school in the possibilities of sexual liberation."[17] Hardly in need of saving or schooling, she instead rejected the idea that the free love ethos would be the most fulfilling for every woman and the idea that sexual liberation needed to be the keystone of female liberation, as if the two were one and the same. As a Muslim feminist, an identity that some foolishly see as incompatible, she found it hard to explain that she was opposed not to sexual pleasure, but to the way that it has been constructed and the stories about sex that have been taught, the hollow example of more sex as more liberation that sometimes overshadows other issues. It is not a coincidence that the types of sex-positive spaces Zakaria describes are often the domain of upper-class white women who are demographically similar to many of the feminists who ignited the discussion and who are often the loudest voices in the room. White upper-class women, less affected by racism and classism, are also less likely to see the need for a broader vision of feminism that emphasizes these concerns and, therefore, are more likely to center this narrow vision of sexual liberation as female liberation.

Sex was not the center of Zakaria's feminism. Sex is not the center of my feminism either, and I do not have time for those who would say that this calls my feminism into question. I am no longer concerned with having a super-exciting sex life. Even if I put in the work to make my sex life the envy of all, that would mostly help me alone. Pursuing pleasure can be wonderful, but not having a super-exciting sex life does not make one a political failure, not when there is so much other work to be done, on issues of violence and economics and education and more. The woman who hates sex and may be repressed but who supports comprehensive sex education and pressures legislators to pass equal pay laws is a political success. The one who brags about using men but ignores the need for any greater action, less so.

Or, as Nair writes, "The revolution"—the one that helps all of us—"will not come on the tidal wave of your next multiple orgasm had with your seven partners on the floor of your communal living space. It will only happen if you have an actual plan for destroying systems of oppression and exploitation."[18] Sexual diversity of all kinds is important, and one's personal sexuality does not create the limits of their political activism, in either direction.

. . . .

Twenty-two years old, arrogant and reckless and also scared, I did not challenge the compulsory sexuality of mainstream feminism. I also clung to a related mutation of feminist values: that women should not only be able to do what men supposedly do but that they were *superior* if they could do what men do—which in the realm of sex meant hookups and sex only for physical pleasure. This (misguided) version of sexual liberation felt necessary, yet I berated myself for being so conservative and unable to change. I read *The Ethical Slut* and blog posts promising to teach me how to "hack myself into being polyamorous," and filled out worksheets to "map my jealousy" and try to contain it or, better yet, obliterate it. I believed that my desire for monogamy and disinterest in casual sex were not preferences worthy of honoring, but political and moral failings that must be overcome. I thought I was weak and stupid.

So my friends and I went to a tiny bar in Pacific Beach, a neighborhood in San Diego. It had neon lights, a single television showing sports, and maybe four men total. I couldn't bring myself to approach a single person and ended up insisting that we leave *right now* but at least get carne asada fries on the drive back to make up for a wasted evening.

The next morning, I logged onto OkCupid and messaged someone who periodically visited my profile page and seemed nice enough. I no longer remember his username. I no longer remember his actual name either, or anything about him other than that he was twenty-eight and had brown hair and was happy to go along when I explained what I wanted.

An hour later, the two of us were sitting outdoors at a strip mall near where I lived. He ate sushi from one of those clear plastic grocery containers. I ate nothing. He told me that he liked technology and occasionally thought of applying for a fellowship at *Wired*. I told him I had considered applying for the same fellowship. We drove in separate cars back to his place.

The detail that will always stand out has nothing to do with the man or having sex. Burned into my memory is the surprise I felt when I entered his house and it was filled with children. At least four of them, probably relatives, were piled on an enormous couch and watching a movie featuring an animated princess with long blonde hair. (A week later, I looked it up. It was *Tangled*.) Nobody so much as glanced at me, a small blessing for which I remain grateful.

The sex was painful and perfunctory and over quickly. I dressed and left, triumphant. Emotionally, I hadn't felt anything—which, after all, had been the point. So my fears about Henry's claims had been wrong! Sex without feeling was possible. So my fears about myself had been wrong too. I was not repressed, not clingy. I was all of those words I had hoped to embody: strong, individualistic, bold, and, dare I say it, empowered by my own apathy.

Falling into any female stereotype, like wanting emotional commitment before sex, felt like defeat, so the sole hookup of my life had been in pursuit of political growth, not for anything remotely close to pleasure. By going out and having sex "like a man," I had destroyed the possibility of myself as the caricature of a sentimental damsel waiting for true love. For that assurance, having a one-night stand—a one-afternoon stand, really—seemed a small price to pay. For once, I was progressive enough.

When I told Henry, he said congratulations and that he was happy for me. Later that summer though, one night in the dark, he told me that part of him had felt weird about the whole thing. He had intuited, correctly, that in some ways my action was a punishment and a sign of distrust. And he felt weird because maybe some small part of him had wanted to be my first.

• • • • • • • • • •

What I had called feminism was spite and fear disguised as performance. It was partly about verifying for myself what everyone else said was possible about sex separate from love. (Though, since I had not actually felt attracted to this man, it never reassured my fears about what being sexually attracted to others meant.) It was also about control and distance and ego and politics and insecurity.

I didn't want Henry to be the first person I slept with. I was not sure I could handle it because I was afraid of falling too much in love with him. Denying him this was a way to assert power, to take away something that I could give and something that people seemed to think I should save. It was the one thing I had been told might hurt him and make him feel a little bit of the discomfort that I did.

My actions were the result of a funny reversal of the importance of sexual purity. I had thought myself feminist in rejecting outdated notions of waiting for love, but being motivated by disproving outdated notions shows that those expectations continue to exert influence. As anyone who has done reverse psychology on a child knows, acting against the status quo only because it is the status quo makes you easy to manipulate. As with the charmed circle, a reversal nevertheless holds power. The righteous woman once guarded her virginity jealously to prove that she's pure. Now it can be more appealing to throw it away at first glance to prove she doesn't believe in purity. She once hewed to gender stereotypes to prove she belonged; now she is valorized for having sex the way men stereotypically do, though maybe more men should have sex the way women supposedly do.

It would be disingenuous to blame feminism for my decision when my own personality flaws are a big factor. It would also be naive to think that certain strains of sex-positive feminism had nothing to do with my choice. I don't regret losing my virginity in the way that I did; it did not harm me and I rarely think about it. The real price I have paid is not any trauma from this encounter, but that I feel such awkwardness around the topic of asexuality, a constant management of my own defensiveness because I know what many people believe about asexuality and, by extension, about me. The stakes of this new kind of sex normativity were never that young women might lose their virginity to strangers—I don't care about that—but that women are presented with more rules for how to be instead of fewer. I am affected not by my one-night stand, but by the assumptions that led me to the one-night stand in the first place.

If asexuality, mine or anyone else's, comes up in discussion, it must always be qualified. It feels like I can't say "I'm ace" and let that stand on its own; I must always fight the impulse to tack on frenetic caveat after frenetic caveat.

ONE: Asexual isn't the same as celibacy!

TWO: I'm asexual, but I'm also kinky!

THREE: Many aces are in relationships!

FOUR: I have a raunchy sense of humor, and I'm not judgmental!

I dislike both these caveats and the fact that I am tempted to use them. "I'm X but Y" always throws someone under the bus. "I'm a girl, but one of those cool girls" emphasizes the default view that girls are not cool. "I'm ace, but I'm kinky and not celibate" is an insult to those who are vanilla or celibate. "I'm ace, but not ace in the boring way that you're thinking" is still a dart, a subtle reinforcement of all the lessons taught about what it means to be frigid. Celibacy can be eroticized because the supposed restraint implies a rich appetite underneath. After all, Eve was the woman who took a bite out of the apple. It can be interesting to be a lusty broad with a hearty appetite that she is denying. It is not interesting to have no appetite at all. That's just nothingness.

· · · · · · · · · ·

None of this is to downplay the good work that sex-positive feminists have done. The lesson that women deserve sexual equality has always been worth championing. Thanks to these activists, sex education has become more comprehensive and LGBTQ+ and alternative families have become more acceptable.[19] The sex-positive movement gave us lesbian-run erotica magazines like *On Our Backs* (its name a spoof of the anti-pornography magazine *Off Our Backs*) and the legendary woman-owned sex shop Good Vibrations. Sex can obviously be a source of positivity, and women have agency even in situations with tricky power dynamics.

Hard-won gains don't mean that the work of fighting sexual inequality is finished. Beyond and even within these liberal corners of the world, old ideas hold; horny women are still feared and women receive plenty of pushback for speaking out. The article exploring the "sex recession" highlighted that, despite all the cheering over new sexual freedom, young people remain anxious and unsure about how best to proceed.[20] My most feminist, sexual friends tell me of instinctively slut-shaming themselves, though they also know they have done nothing worthy of shame.

"Feeling Myself" and *Euphoria* and every example I listed earlier have value. I agree with *Sex and the City*'s Samantha that everyone should wear whatever and blow whomever they want (if they want). Explicit lyrics and content about desire are not a problem, but that this type of content can dominate or be relentlessly pushed in young, liberal, queer spaces is. Dominance of any one idea can be harmful. It can skew the lesson.

So the other side needs attention as well. It isn't necessary to follow in the exact steps of MacKinnon and Dworkin—I do not share their views on porn or BDSM or sex work—but their more critical attitude toward sex is worth revisiting. In fact, the shift may have already begun.

In 2015, the *New York Times Magazine* ran an article titled "The Return of the Sex Wars," which discussed feminist arguments over how to deal with campus sexual assault.[21] Two years later, the #MeToo movement spurred more analysis over the dangers of sex and sexual aggression, with some claiming that the movement has gone too far and others, not far enough. Andrea Dworkin, once the figure women cited to say they were feminist, "but not like her," is the latest figure to be appreciated anew. A collection of her essays was rereleased in 2019.

The important thing now, as Arizona State University gender studies scholar Breanne Fahs writes, is to integrate these perspectives, which represent what philosopher Isaiah Berlin called the two kinds of freedom: positive and negative liberty, or "freedom to" and "freedom from."[22] Sex-positive feminists have focused on the freedom to: freedom to have sex, freedom to enjoy ourselves, freedom to do the things that men do without the unjust inhibition caused by a double standard. They were right. Sex-negative feminists were concerned with freedom from: freedom from being treated as sexual objects, freedom from feeling obligated to have sex to show that we are cool, freedom from the idea that sex is by default good. Transgressive personal sexuality shouldn't be the price of entry to radical spaces and sexual liberation shouldn't be the sum of women's liberation. They were right too, but they received less attention.

All these perspectives deserve consideration. I, for one, am not pro-sex. I am not sex-positive or sex-negative. I am pro-pleasure, which does not need to include sex at all, and I am pro-sexual choice—real choice. It is not enough to say that everyone should only do what they want. That's a bromide that anyone can parrot and it ignores the ways that society pressures us to want certain things. Back it up. Show us examples of powerful, enviable women who are openly indifferent to sex, secure in that decision, and not constantly challenged by others. Don't reinforce the new charmed circle with comments about how polyamory is more evolved than monogamy, or look down on vanilla sex. Stop assuming that sexual behavior must be linked to political belief or that horniness is an interesting personality trait. That's closer to what I mean by real choice.

I am what sexuality scholar Lisa Downing calls "sex-critical,"[23] aware of both women's personal agency and the continuing inequalities of society. It is possible to encourage others to experiment while trusting them if they say sex doesn't do anything for them. Someone shouldn't be feted either because their sex acts are very kinky or because their number of partners is very low. It is cause for celebration whenever anyone is, to the best of their ability, making their own choices free from pressure—and also working to change the social and political structures that will let everyone else have that same sexual freedom, and freedom of other kinds, too.

All this is what I wish I had known at twenty-two, when I was jumpy with anxiety and unsure about myself, desperate to fit into the charmed circle and terrified of vulnerability. *I got exactly what I wanted*, I wrote in my journal right after my one-night stand. *I was in control the entire time, and I still have Henry, whom I love dearly*. I got what I wanted then, but, of course, the decision looks different now, years later. I wish now that I had wanted something else, something other than to always be in control, something other than to push Henry away, something other than to use sex to prove myself.

CHAPTER 5

WHITEWASHED

IN 2014, MORE THAN A DECADE after the first forum members began discussing questions of ace definition and identity, a group of volunteers with statistical training began running the annual Ace Community Survey.[1] The survey is far from perfect, since the only people who take it are those who already know enough about asexuality to find the survey in the first place. It's more of a snapshot of the online ace community than it is representative of asexual people in general, but it remains a valuable resource for anyone trying to understand who identifies as ace.

A few trends stand out. Far more cis women than cis men identify as ace, and many members are trans or gender nonconforming. Plenty of aces are neurodivergent. The vast majority are young. Numbers from the 2016 survey, the most recent year for which summary information is available, show that the average age of a respondent is twenty-three and the average age of coming out is to an allo person twenty, with one-third of the respondents first finding out about asexuality on Tumblr.[2]

And a lot of aces are white. The whiteness of the ace community—over 83 percent of respondents in 2016 global survey identified as white only[3]—is glaring, though not necessarily surprising. White people typically have more economic, political, and cultural power than people of color. They are usually given more credit when championing a cause and are more likely to become the figureheads.

So far, the asexual movement has followed this pattern. The most visible early activists, like David Jay, were white. Today, Tumblr and message boards and other online spaces still feel white in a way that people acknowledge without quite being able to define. "The asexual culture online is very white in a weird way," says Kendra, a Black ace writer who has contributed to Everyday Feminism and *Ebony*. "I think as I got more into the community I did start looking for more people of color just because there were so many white things." The ace community symbols—like the cake emoji to welcome newcomers and the colors black and gray and purple—don't appeal to her. "The pun jokes aren't that funny to me and who voted on cake? Who chose those colors?" she jokes. "Can we not get some sweet potato pie?"

Many early figureheads were white, so a white culture with white artifacts developed. White people feel most comfortable in this community and join it, therefore making it even more white. Yet asexuality isn't only associated with whiteness because of its most famous faces. Asexuality is also associated with whiteness because of the complicated ways that sexuality itself intersects with race.

· · · · · · · · · ·

Until high school, Selena, a Bay Area workplace consultant, thought of herself as a straight boy with a high sex drive. She craved intimacy and romance and hated the stereotype of East Asian men as emasculated and sexless. "Before I identified as trans it was important for me to fight that stereotype by 'wanting to have sex,' maybe more than I really wanted to," she says.

The specifics of sex drive, however, remained low on Selena's list of priorities. The more general question related to sexual orientation and self-expression and how one might limit the other. Selena wanted to wear women's-cut T-shirts, dresses, and skirts and believed that doing so required her to follow certain rules. "I thought, 'I want to wear this clothing, and to wear this clothing I need to be gay,'" she says. "Some of the conditions for being gay include only dating men, and I thought that I could accept that kind of exchange."

After coming out as trans junior year of high school, "the trans thing superseded the gay thing," and Selena decided that wanting to wear dresses did not need to restrict whom she could date. But as her identity shifted, her experience of attraction did too, because attraction is influenced by social and psychological factors. Many old friends, who were East Asian like her, had distanced themselves after her transition, which changed her dating pool and who was around and who she found appealing in any way. As Selena's hair grew longer and she began wearing makeup, it was no longer necessary to counter the stereotype of the sexless Asian man. That stereotype didn't apply anymore, but as one restriction lifted, another replaced it. Selena now wanted to have less sex to spite the fetishists who were suddenly interested in her new presentation as an Asian woman.

Sexual stereotypes tied to race affected the desire she had for others and the desire that Selena had for others and the desire that others had for her. Her experience of sexual attraction is inextricable from other facets of her identity, she says. Selena cannot talk about being ace without also talking about being trans and being Asian.

The Combahee River Collective, a Black feminist lesbian group that existed in the 1970s, would have understood what Selena was expressing. Their famous Combahee River Collective Statement coined the term "identity politics" and discussed the ways that multiple identities overlap. The Combahee members observed, as many would after them, that "major systems of oppression are interlocking." Racial oppression is difficult to separate from class oppression and from gender-based or sexual oppression because they are experienced simultaneously and "the synthesis of these oppressions creates the conditions of our lives," resulting in, for example, "racial–sexual oppression which is neither solely racial nor solely sexual."[4] Asian men and Asian women share a race but not a gender, and sexuality is mediated by both, so the experience of identity and sex for, say, me and for one of my male cousins can be very different. Scholar Kimberlé Crenshaw addressed this phenomenon when she coined the term *intersectionality* in a 1989 law article that pointed out a major weakness in anti-discrimination law: it only acknowledges a single axis of oppression.[5]

· · · · · · · · · ·

As we have seen, compulsory sexuality exists for straight white men. But for people who come from more vulnerable communities and are weighed down by extra layers of social conditioning, figuring out whether one's asexuality is human variation or externally imposed is fraught with cultural and historical baggage.

Control of sexuality is a classic tool of domination, used by men against women, by white people against people of color, by the abled against the disabled—or, to cut a long list short, by the powerful against the less powerful. It can be expressed in many ways, like rape as a form of political conquest or slave owners marrying off their slaves and splitting families apart. It can look like enforcing purity rules only for women, perpetuating racist sexual stereotypes, or assuming that some groups have no sexual desires at all.

Life is a continuous process of unlearning for minorities and anyone with less power. These groups—women, people of color, and, in the next chapter, disabled people—can find it very difficult to claim asexuality because it looks so much like the product of sexism, racism, ableism, and other forms of violence. The legacy of this violence is that those who belong to a group that has been controlled must do extra work to figure out the extent to which we are *still* being controlled.

Call it variations on a theme. The theme is oppression; the variations are the exact ways that oppression manifests and how it affects asexual identity. The question of who gets to be ace versus who is considered deluded or naive matters beyond the borders of each specific community. The details of why some groups find it harder than others to accept asexuality, or be accepted as ace, reveal the outlines of how sex and power and history have combined.

When it comes to race, so many different, complicated threads keep the ace community white. Asexuality has been idealized and it has been denied. Both are problematic. Asexuality is tied to whiteness because white people (and especially white women[6]) are often assumed to be sexually "pure," whereas Black and Latinx people are often considered hypersexual—and these racialized sexual stereotypes are a form of control themselves. At the same time, asexuality can *also* look suspiciously similar to racial tropes like the mammy or the China doll, which again keeps people of color away.

Picture whiteness as a neutral backdrop, a white wall. It is easier to paint a white wall light blue than it is to paint a dark green wall light blue. The dominant media is filled with images of many types of white people; white people, for the most part, have the freedom to be anything they like. People of color need to scrub away the dark green—racial stereotypes and expectations—before determining whether we are *really* ace. We carry an extra layer of awareness that comes from knowing how, specifically, our sexuality is supposed to be and what our wanting should look like. The project of self-knowledge is complicated by both racial stereotypes and our desire not to be controlled by these stereotypes.

· · · · · · · · · ·

Racial stereotypes are complex and exist in multiple directions at once. Asian women are fetishized, as Selena found, and sometimes considered hypersexual. In other contexts, Asian women are desexualized portrayed as the geisha girl or China doll: soft-spoken, servile, and submissive. In the US today, East Asians are considered the well-behaved model minority, enough so that members of the white supremacist far right seem to like dating Asian women.[7]

The stereotype of the well-behaved Asian woman, with little desire and little thought of her own, was the one most pervasive in the early life of Sebastian, a Chinese Canadian model who is genderqueer and socialized as female. Identifying as asexual felt pointless. "Why would I bother to assert something that was already assumed?" Sebastian asks. Acknowledging asexuality made Sebastian feel as though they were confirming racist stereotypes and therefore doing a disservice to all Asian people. Over time, however, Sebastian decided that avoiding a label because of what others believed was still a form of deference. Sebastian no longer hesitates to use a label because it might *not* surprise others.

Like Sebastian, I am Chinese. Unlike Sebastian, I had no qualms about using the term *ace*. From the moment I decided I was ace, I knew that I would use the word, but I was not happy about being asexual, even less so about being asexual on top of being female and Asian.

Once, I disdained the thought that race negatively affected me in any way. After leaving China as a kid, I ended up in California's Silicon Valley, an area with a large Asian population. To this day, no one has called me chink or pulled back the corners of their eyes to imitate me or made fun of my food. Place of birth, family culture, my ability to speak Mandarin, and my face all permanently marked me as Asian, but I could see no opportunity denied me.

The counterpoint is that I never knew what it was like to live without my race being a part of my awareness and my awareness of how others perceived me. I had often felt the pressure of being an ambassador, a metaphor instead of a person. In elementary school, I noticed people looking at me when we talked about the Chinese laborers who built the California railroads, never mind that I had arrived in the state only five years earlier. My Japanese friend hated how people would turn to her when Pearl Harbor came up during history class. We didn't know what it would have felt like otherwise, to be white and represented everywhere, and to never have anyone turn to you during a lesson about what white people have done.

It was not slurs that affected me but the lack of vision, tired tropes that I learned against my will: that Asians are not creative or interesting, that we are all engineers, that we are timid. All the same, these expectations did align with how I believed my family wanted me to be: rule-following, docile, someone who would grow up to be an engineer like my engineer parents. I took piano lessons and violin lessons, became frustrated when I was not particularly good at math, and was told to keep my head down.

Expectations aren't only imposed from the outside, but they take on a different meaning in a minority context. Were we all in China, my parents might have given me the same advice, but there I would not have internalized this specific image of what it meant to be Asian in America, which is a product of the white gaze. It's less likely I would have strained against the stereotype of being a submissive Asian woman. In the US, I did not encounter many others like me, famous or otherwise, who modeled a different way to be. I became aware of the presence of these stereotypes only when I started questioning my attitudes and saw these statements lurking in the shadows of so much of what I believed and how I behaved.

It was frustrating enough that Asians were boring engineers and women were weak and not as good as men, especially if they didn't publicly break the bounds of patriarchy by loving sex. Now, I had *asexual*, a label that sounded clinical and reminded me of one-celled organisms. I was already introverted and uninterested in drinking; being asexual seemed to reinforce this cascade of stereotypes, further marking me as not worthy of notice. Here was yet another place I was found to be wilting and wanting.

· · · · · · · · · ·

Part of the problem is that aces in general have very few depictions in popular culture, and the options for aces of color are even more limited. All of us who consume popular media absorb messages about what certain groups are like, even when the messages are biased and wrong, even when we know that they are biased and wrong. We learn, and we grow biased too. Limited representation is a near-ubiquitous problem, but because asexuality already has so little visibility, the consequences are heightened.

Forget film entirely, and best-selling books don't do much better. In television the first portrayal of an asexual human is likely Sebastian the Asexual Icon, a character portrayed by comedian Craig Kilborn in a 2003 segment on CBS's *The Late Late Show*. Shot in black and white, these short clips of Sebastian illustrate a dangerous aspect of asexuality, which is that it's just logical enough that people assume they know what it is without doing any further research. As critic Sara Ghaleb writes in her retrospective of ace representation on TV, "The character made it obvious the writers had no idea asexuality was a real orientation, turning the very idea of being nonsexual into a punch line."[9]

Spectacled, nasally, and clad in a scarf, Sebastian is a mockery of effeminate stereotypes. In high school, he was excused from gym class with a doctor's note claiming that "this boy's groin is a parched wasteland." Whenever Sebastian has the urge to "touch it," he maces himself. His dream is that instead of genitals, he has a third pinky, the better to hold one more cup of tea. The word "wood" makes him uncomfortable, he "lost the keys to my libido," and his therapist shot himself.[9]

To the great fortune of aces everywhere, Sebastian remains mostly unknown. Only a few explicitly ace characters have influenced popular culture in a meaningful way, few enough that I can mention most of them in the next two paragraphs. Varys from *Game of Thrones* was one. Varys is a castrated eunuch in a fantasyland, which real ace people are not, but at least he is not a joke. Varys is shrewd and good-hearted and conveniently touts the benefits of asexuality, saying that after seeing what desire has done to people and to politics, he is "very glad to have no part in it."[10]

Another explicitly ace character, Raphael Santiago, graced the campy teen drama *Shadowhunters*. Raphael is a young-looking vampire in his seventies—which, again, is what real aces are not—but at least he's witty and hot.

Most important of all was Todd Chavez from *BoJack Horseman*, an animated show set in a world of anthropomorphic animals. (Todd is human.) In season four, Todd suspects he might be asexual and attends an ace meetup. The dialogue was heavy-handed—"asexual just means you're not interested in sex, some asexuals are also aromantic but others have relationships like anyone else!"[11]—but that's unavoidable given that the episode essentially doubles as an educational special. Watching the writers get it right was surprisingly moving. The specificity of ace imagery (the meetup featured a sign in ace colors) and attention to detail were a sign of respect. Todd is sometimes confused and a bit of a screwball, but he is well-meaning and beloved. His asexuality was not obscure. It was portrayed without mockery. And, in a testament to why representation is important, the mere existence of Todd has raised the number of aces there are in the world.

Put another way: "If there was more ace representation, then I probably would have realized I was ace a lot sooner," Coy, a twenty-seven-year-old ace blogger, told me a few years ago, before Todd came out on *BoJack*. Coy's comments are part of the reason I hesitate when asked how many ace people exist. The most common statistic, taken from a 2004 study,[12] is 1 percent of the population. Yet because there are so many misconceptions about what it means to not experience sexual attraction and so few positive examples of aces in popular culture, I suspect the number may be much higher. You can't be what you can't see but thankfully, Todd has done a lot of that visibility work for the general public. Julie Kliegman, a journalist for *Sports Illustrated*, told me she realized that she was ace while reporting a story about how the asexual community reacted to Todd. Another friend told me that her childhood friend had begun wondering whether he's ace. I was surprised that he knew the term; it turns out he had learned it from *BoJack*. Representation not only reflects, but actually changes reality.

Cherished as he is, Todd is not a perfect solution. For one, *BoJack* has ended, and so have *Game of Thrones* and *Shadowhunters*. There are now zero asexual characters on prime-time television,[13] according to the

GLAAD Media Institute, which tracks queer characters in television and started including asexual characters a few years ago.

More to the point, no one character can or should become the face of any orientation. While Todd, Varys, and Raphael have educated audiences and helped some viewers recognize their aceness, the vast majority of aces are still left without any portrayal that reflects them. Sebastian and Varys are white, Raphael is Latino, and it remains a mystery whether Todd Chavez is white or not. (He is voiced by the white actor Aaron Paul, and *BoJack* creator Raphael Bob-Waksberg has said he is "embarrassed to admit" he never considered that Todd might be Latino.[14]) This group is joined by a handful of mainstream television characters who are sometimes read as ace: the serial killer Dexter Morgan from *Dexter*, who had a girlfriend but initially has little sexual interest in her, plus Sherlock Holmes and Dr. Who, who often don't have romantic plotlines. All (at least until the most recent Dr. Who) are men. Most share the quality of being reserved and incredibly rational and can be portrayed as less than fully human, whether that means being a murderer or, in Dr. Who's case, literally not human. Nobody is Black or trans or Asian. There's little vision for what an ace person like me, Sebastian, Kendra, and others can be or hope to be.

· · · · · · · · ·

While Sebastian (the ace model, not the TV character) and I worry about sliding too neatly into stereotypes, others struggle because their asexuality seems too dissimilar to what is expected. Latinx aces say they chafe against the "spicy Latina" or "exotic Latin lover" formula that makes their ace identity seem less believable. Cassie, a twenty-nine-year-old therapist in Chicago, is blunt about what their body signals to others. "I'm perceived as a Black cis woman, with large tits and a large ass," they say. "There's absolutely no way in hell, societally speaking, that I could possibly *not* be a sexbot."

Not when white Americans have long considered Black women to be sexually promiscuous jezebels, the opposite of the pure and proper white lady and a target of racist anxieties over miscegenation. The term *jezebel* may seem outdated today, but Black women are still over-sexualized, with young Black girls perceived as knowing more about sex than their white counterparts.[15] And as Boston University

English professor Ianna Hawkins Owen has shown, the opposite stereotype also exists—that of the sexless and sexually undesirable mammy, the racist Southern trope of the Black nursemaid to white children who is safe to employ because she won't sexually tempt the white master.[16] "Being a Black asexual woman often feels like living in the shadow of the mammy, a caricature whose asexuality is conceived of only because she is expected to mother everyone around her," writes essayist Sherronda J. Brown. "Mammy is allowed to be free of the racialized hypersexualization only because it permits her more time, energy, and space to perform her endless duties. She is not allowed to have desire or desirability, not allowed to seek out sexual pleasures and intimacies, because her entire focus should be on her domestic and emotional labor."[17]

For Cassie, it is the assumption of "easy" sexuality that others more readily apply to her. The sexbot remark is facetious, but in high school, when a friend suggested that Cassie might be ace, Cassie thought the friend was being kind of a bitch. In rural Illinois, Cassie and their brother were often the only Black students in the school district. Already hyper-visible and already used to standing up for themself, Cassie refused to be associated with anything weird. Asexuality? No, that had to be rejected immediately.

It wasn't until Cassie joined a BDSM group in college that they began to reconsider that old comment. When the group leader, who identified as asexual, asked Cassie about their experiences with sex, Cassie explained that they found all genders aesthetically attractive but, "It would be cool not having sex with anyone, because it just seems gross." *Oh.*

Sex is not a given in Cassie's relationships. When this realization dawns on others, people are disappointed that what they've learned about the hypersexualization of Black bodies isn't true and that Cassie is not a source of "free sex" or going to be their "sexy Black mama." Cassie's refusal is more than a disappointment on its own terms. It is accompanied by a bewilderment, conditioned by the images of mass media, that might not be there if Cassie were not Black.

· · · · · · · · ·

It's hard if you confirm a stereotype and it's hard if you violate a stereotype and it's hard if you think you're violating the stereotype only because you hate it so much. May, a Black college student studying to be a teacher, found herself in the third situation. She didn't think that she experienced sexual attraction but hesitated to call herself as asexual because she was unsure of the correctness of her motivation.

May has seen the worst of both worlds. People claiming that Black asexual men don't exist because "all Black men want sex." People claiming that asexuality is a tool of white supremacy, that Black aces are confused, that a Black woman must want—must *need*—a man in her life and is selfish if she doesn't want to have kids and uphold the Black family. "In the environment I grew up in, I've heard that being anything but straight is 'something white people made up,'" May says, "and I've heard African Americans talk about how 'homosexuality was never in Africa before the Europeans.'"

It's a convoluted mix. The ace community can be racist. One Black woman, who asked to remain anonymous, told me about an AVEN thread a few years ago that discussed whether an upcoming conference should include a safe space for aces of color. Specifically, it let white aces respond to the question too, and some said no because the safe space would break up the community. When this woman protested that white people should not be deciding on this question, others accused her of being hostile and divisive. "I still don't really get the feeling that [the community] is a safe space for people of color, though maybe [it is] ever so slightly safer now," she says.

The Black community isn't free from prejudice either. There can be queerphobia, mixed with reasonable suspicion that comes from the long history of white people dominating Black people's sexuality. It would mess with anyone's head, and May wasn't sure what to believe. "I struggled with a lot of self-doubt," she says. "Did I believe I was asexual because of those stereotypes that I wanted to fight, or was it something that I truly felt?"

To suspect that one's sexual orientation is actually a reaction to racism is disconcerting. It feels false and fraught, traitorous. Asking these questions of oneself seems necessary, and asking takes extra psychological work that might not be necessary if people could look around and see others like them. White female aces who struggle with the perception of being repressed can turn to plenty of other white female aces for support. Aces of color can be far more isolated.

May's fears were assuaged when she found the work of Vesper, the Black ace blogger. Because Vesper wrote about their struggles as a Black ace, May felt more at ease identifying as ace too.

Like May, Vesper says that their asexuality—or rather, the way that asexuality is considered white—has made them feel alienated from both white and Black communities. Just as I observed that expectations tied to being Asian came both from outside and within my demographic, Vesper points out that both white American and Black American culture can sexualize Black people. Dominant images are easily internalized by minority groups and proliferate in many ways.

Vesper, who grew up in Las Vegas and for years was an English teacher in Japan, long ago absorbed the idea that Black people are supposed to be extremely sexual and also good in bed. Now, Vesper fears that other Black people who believe the same, or who believe that asexuality is a tool of white control, will be judgmental of their identity. "I feel more vulnerable with Black people than with white people because I fear that the second I meet another Black person, they can tell that there's something different about me, something that is unconsciously and invariably associated with whiteness," they say. Vesper has long been self-conscious that their hobbies and "that I'm not a Beyoncé fan or whatever" marked them as not Black enough: "There's already that foundation before I even open my mouth about anything sexuality related."

"I've often heard, 'Oh, you're asexual? I've only met white asexual people,' and it's the same disconnect that existed for me when I [only saw white queer characters on television and] didn't believe that was even an option for Black people," they continue. "There's a lot of shock. To not experience sexual attraction was just another way that people would say I was whitewashed. Literally, my sexuality was another thing that was whitewashed about me." White and Asian aces complain about being perceived as prudes but that's not something people say about Vesper. There is no prude accusation, only surprise that Black aces exist at all. Certainly, no one like Vesper is on television, and people's imaginations are not as strong as they would like to believe.

And so, old stereotypes and power structures persist and one type of ace experience is emphasized over others. Many aces do try to be welcoming, but the work of making any group truly diverse is difficult. Some signs, though, are hopeful. When I tell Vesper that May found their writing useful, they are delighted. It takes hard work to be so visible and fight other people's racism and your own internalized racism, all at the same time. Knowing that people like May find it helpful means that all that work is for something. Vesper has expanded the experiences that Black people can claim as their own.

· · · · · · · · · ·

Selena is no longer the person who worried about the trade-offs of gender and sexuality, who wanted to wear dresses and thought that doing so meant she was a gay man. She's ace and trans and Asian and can be all of these things, yet she still cannot talk about these parts of herself separately. A lot of thinking and questioning and talking have confirmed for Selena that she is on the ace spectrum, but how secure she feels in her aceness—and how confident she is that aceness isn't a reaction to prejudice—is connected to how secure she feels in her other identities. "It's impossible to be empowered with one aspect of my identity without also working to be empowered with all of the others," she says.

Once, when she was always aware of how others perceived her and insecure about those perceptions, sexual assumptions about what it meant to be an Asian man or an Asian woman strongly influenced Selena's experiences of attraction. Today she says that the key to feeling authentically ace is to do her best to clear her mind of those stereotypes and to stay away from the people who believe them. Race and gender and sexuality intersect, and the way for them not to intersect in a limiting way is to support the possibilities of every part.

It can be easy for Selena to feel culturally homeless, like she's too trans to be Asian or too Asian to be trans, leaving both identities diminished. When Selena is around people who don't respect her gender or race, who see "trans" and "Asian" and immediately have ideas of how a trans Asian person is supposed to be, her identity feels to her like nothing but an amalgamation of stereotypes. *Ace* then adds another layer, leading Selena to feel boxed in by how all the stereotypes fit together or are in tension, like whether it's weird that a trans person would not experience sexual attraction. (Being transgender is often associated with hypersexuality.) "With people I don't know really well, my sexuality itself feels like it's running on scripts based on *my* perception of *their* perception of what my identity should be, and it gets really messy," she says.

When Selena's Asianness and transness are affirmed as more than caricatures—when they're treated respectfully as part of her unique identity instead of ways to predict her personality or behavior—her ace identity feels more meaningful as well. Aceness becomes another part of her, not something that must confirm or violate the expectations of race or gender. If you don't have assumptions about what a certain race or gender should be like, there is nothing to confirm or violate to begin with.

Far from being seen as an emasculated East Asian man, today the judgment of Selena runs in the other direction. "To be honest, I dress in a way that is very attention-getting," she says, though this hardly needs to be clarified. Selena's Instagram feed is a salute to vanity, and I mean that in the best way possible. It features photo after photo of her posing, wearing all black, always. High boots, crop tops, black square glasses. Leather leggings. Chest-length straight black hair with an undercut, sometimes streaked through with bright colors, like cerulean blue. Mesh tops, dark lipstick. You get the idea.

The day we hang out in New York City, Selena is wearing skin-tight pleather pants and a knee-length coat. It is the middle of June and this might be one of her tamer outfits. "Everything about me is extremely visible and it's complicated because a lot of people now assume I'm a hypersexual person because I present myself like I want to be desired," she says. "People frequently assume that I want and will have sex with them, and my 'nos' are extremely difficult for people to deal with. Now it's like, 'If you're ace, why do you dress like that, why do you talk like that?'"

These are the same types of comments that people direct toward Yasmin Benoit, a model in the United Kingdom. Yasmin, who is also aromantic, grew up "Black and goth and asexual" in a white town. She realized that she didn't experience sexual attraction when she was nine, and that has never changed. Yasmin did question her asexuality—"I wondered if it was because I was insecure or awkward, but then I got older and I'm no longer insecure or that awkward"—but enough time has passed that much of the doubt is gone. It's clear to her, too, that asexuality is perceived as a white orientation, so Yasmin has been trying to do her part as an ace woman of color and a model.

That work unfortunately involves receiving messages from strangers about how she can't be asexual if she cares about fashion or posts provocative photos. "We still expect people to dress for other people and think that if a woman is making herself look good, then it's to attract someone else," she says. Tired of these responses, Yasmin started the hashtag #ThisIsWhatAsexualLooksLike to show that there is no single ace aesthetic. Despite this, people continue to claim that she's pretending to be ace to further her modeling career. It's not true. It's for herself.

It's how she is, it's how Selena is, and there should be no reason for the incredulity. "I like it when people give me attention! I like being interesting! And these are all things that our societal narrative attaches to sex," Selena says. For allos, sex is so natural an explanation for behavior that other reasons, such as wanting to dress creatively for its own sake and wanting to be seen just to be seen, can be hard to fathom. "I'm like 'I want you to stare at me, but I don't want you to fuck me, and they have nothing to do with each other,'" Selena continues. "And then allos are so funny because they just insist that *those have everything to do with each other*."

It is a conflicting thing to hold up Selena and Yasmin as forms of representation. Anyone who represents anything is no longer only themself, and placing that pressure can be disrespectful. Yet I don't want to deny that their versions of asexuality—one in which female aces of color can claim attention and claim their own desire to be desired—are powerful. I am uncomfortable with the insinuation that the only valuable forms of ace representation are the ones that bust expectations, but I want to acknowledge that much of my own resistance toward asexuality, and the resistance of many other aces, could have been ameliorated had we known more people like them all throughout our lives.

Neither are fantasy eunuchs or reserved white men who love science and shy away from emotions. Both are real, full humans, stylish and fashionable and funny and not afraid of difference. Each time someone is surprised by their existence, especially as women of color, another stereotype about the meaning of sex and who desires it and who doesn't is debunked. I am not surprised by their existence, yet being exposed to their attitudes feels like it changes me in real time.

. . . .

Talking to Selena and Yasmin highlighted my failure of imagination, which may be shaped by the narrow-mindedness of creators of culture but is also partly my own doing. I feared being perceived as passive, yet passively absorbed what others believe—about aces, about women, and about Asians—and accepted it, remaining uncomfortable instead of flipping the script or trying to shape my own. Other stories were available. I might have seen asexuality as a form of power that makes me impervious in a way others are not, or as an intriguing point of difference. It could be a neutral piece of trivia, something thrown out as easily as the fact that I like Russian novels and horror movies, or it could be a taunt to the kind of man who prides himself on how much women sexually desire him.

Yasmin, for instance, never assumed that there was anything embarrassing about being asexual. "I was a nonconformist anyway and so this was another weird thing to add to my long list of weird personality traits," she says. "Plus, I don't feel like I'm missing out on something enjoyable when you're watching your friends crying over a boy or crying over not having a boy. I don't feel like I need to be focusing on this on top of everything else in my life. That just sounds like extra effort in terms of existence."

In her view, being ace is the default. Everything else is extra effort. I, on the other hand, just felt sort of bad. In my view, being allo was the default. Everything else seemed somehow inferior, a source of frustration. Let's call it what it is, all these descriptions I've given of how I felt so ambivalent about being Asian, female, ace: internalized racism and misogyny, self-hating, always too eager to perform for the white gaze, the male gaze, the allo gaze, always caring too much about the approval of those who are least likely to understand and most likely to withhold.

The longer I grapple with identity, the more I realize that there is a fine line to walk between acknowledging the assumptions of the dominant power and centering ourselves, between being honest about our awareness of the white allo gaze and also taking time to consciously turn away from that watch. It is so natural to struggle with that double (triple? multiple?) consciousness and always be existing in relation to another reference group, a generalized other that is puzzled if not outright contemptuous. It has taken a long time, too long, for me to step away from my lazy masochism. Others stopped caring about that approval a long time ago; I am still working on it.

Toni Morrison, who knew as much as anyone about the power of stories, once proclaimed that from her perspective there are only Black people. "I stood at the border, stood at the edge, and claimed it as central," she said. "Claimed it as central, and let the rest of the world move over to where I was."[18] The first time I heard that line, I was very still for a long time. Of course Toni Morrison knew about racism and how white people think Black people are supposed to be. No matter. For a Black author to center Black people and not write for the white gaze should not be at all extraordinary, yet it felt like it was.

Aces can do the same. Asexuality truly does feel like baggage when all the other parts of our identity are treated as such, when we feel crushed by the stereotype layered on stereotype. If I had not internalized that racism and misogyny, being ace would not have felt like some kind of additional burden on top of being Asian and female.

Asexuality can feel less like baggage when aces reject the gaze that evaluates our identities so narrowly, even—especially—if that gaze is also our own. We can fight stereotypes, racial and otherwise, and also, as Selena said, try to spend time with those who see us fully. We can also step away from the masochism, try to avoid giving it so much due in our own minds, apply all the resources of our creativity and self-regard, and rewrite the story. Aces can look like ourselves and be ourselves— attention-getting and fashionable, nonconformist and awkward and shy, and everything in between. Aces don't need to experience sexual attraction to move through the sexual world on our own terms.

An inherent irony is present in this prescription. This book is partly an attempt to explain asexuality to allos, and many aces have thanked me and said that it's necessary. I hope that the explanation will reach its audience. I also hope that over time we will move closer to not feeling that any explanation is necessary and that we can shed the need to be understood by these others. Let these others think what they will. Our own attention, at least, can be turned more strongly to ourselves. Stereotypes are out there. In our own minds, many narratives of self can be spun from the same starting materials.

■ CHAPTER 6 ■

IN SICKNESS AND IN HEALTH

A WHEELCHAIR CANNOT BE HIDDEN. For Cara Liebowitz, a twenty-eight-year-old disability activist with cerebral palsy, her wheelchair is an obvious mark of difference, one of many such contrasts that began early in life. An individualized educational program. Having to leave the classroom "five minutes early so I wasn't trampled." Constantly being pulled out of lessons for physical therapy. Sexuality, too, is not the same for Cara as for her abled peers. "Nobody sees me as sexually attractive anyway," she says. Nobody, Cara tells me, thinks that a disabled woman in a wheelchair could be interested in having sex.

There exists no perfect, ironclad formula for understanding how sexuality and health interact, but that hasn't prevented people from believing an elegant but incorrect statement: people who don't want sex are sick, and people who are sick—that is, mentally or physically disabled or different in some way—don't want sex.

To outsiders, Cara, who identifies as ace, seems to confirm this mistaken belief. To people in the disability and asexuality communities, however, Cara is a contradiction. Her identity has put her at odds with both groups, each of which is marginalized in a different way with regard to sex. The disabled community has spent a long time fighting the idea that disabled people are, or should be, asexual. The ace community has struggled for as long as it has existed to prove that asexuality has nothing to do with disability.

A disabled ace woman complicates both these political agendas, and it is perhaps in a situation like this that the questions of legitimacy and in-group loyalty are most acute. Both communities are well-meaning,

85

but the groups "toss you between each other like a hot potato," says Cara, who knits while we Skype and wears a black shirt that says PISS ON PITY, "and you can't really find a place where you belong."

•••••••••

This is complicated territory, so let's first unpack the idea that people who don't want sex are sick. Doctors in the West have been worried about the "problem" of low sexual desire since at least the thirteenth century, when Pope Gregory IX wrote about the issue of *frigiditas*. Back then, *frigiditas* was considered a male problem similar to impotence, says scholar Alison Downham Moore, coauthor of *Frigidity: An Intellectual History*, in an interview. Frigidity wouldn't switch to being a more female-focused problem of psychological desire until the nineteenth century, and it's "a bit of a mystery" why that change happened, she adds.

Today, people who insist that low sexual desire is a form of medical dysfunction have a convenient ally in the *Diagnostic and Statistical Manual of Mental Disorders (DSM-5)*, the bible of psychiatric diagnosis in the US. Since 1980, the manual has included a diagnosis that was once called "inhibited sexual desire disorder" and, after changing names a few times, it is now most commonly referred to as hypoactive sexual desire disorder, or HSDD.[1] (In the *DSM-5*, the disorder is split into male and female forms, but let's stick to general HSDD to keep things simple.)[2] Because there is no biological marker for HSDD, the basic criteria sound quite similar to what they might have been when people were worrying about frigidity centuries ago: persistent lack of sexual fantasies and sexual interest.[3] It sounds like asexuality.

With a diagnosis like this in the books, it's no wonder that asexuality is widely considered a sickness to be cured. Long-ago treatments for *frigiditas*, like rubbing wine on the genitals,[4] seem laughable now, but the *DSM* enjoys the authority of modern medicine and the heft of the modern scientific establishment. Though the concern over low sexual desire would probably still exist if the *DSM* disappeared tomorrow, the existence of the HSDD diagnosis legitimizes and amplifies these worries. The officialness of the *DSM* encourages others to ask aces, and aces to ask ourselves, if we're *sure* we're not sick and if we're *sure* we shouldn't be cured.

And how the pharmaceutical companies would love to sell us a cure. The symptoms of HSDD are not uncommon, especially among women, who are primarily the ones diagnosed. One 2008 study of 31,000 women found that 10 percent could fit the diagnostic criteria.[5] Combine this with fears for relationship maintenance—not to mention the message that sex is necessary for a healthy life[6] and that being healthy is an individual moral duty[7]—and the company that has a fix is a company that will be rich.

The list of attempts to create libido-boosting gadgets for women is exhaustive and clever. (Little word exists on treatments for men, partly because sexual stereotypes mean that people are not as comfortable with the idea of boosting men's desire.) Companies have tried to target hormones; Procter & Gamble created a testosterone patch to treat low sexual desire in women, but the US Food and Drug Administration rejected it due to safety concerns.[8] Companies have tried to target the genitals by creating products like the EROS clitoral therapy device, a vibrator-like gadget designed to improve blood flow to the clitoris and external genitalia.[9] It is still around but never became popular. And companies have tried to target the brain. Viagra manufacturer Pfizer spent eight years studying three thousand women to determine whether the same drug that made men stiff would make women want sex. It didn't, and Mitra Boolel, who was then leader of Pfizer's sex research team, told the *New York Times* that the researchers were changing focus from a woman's genitals because the brain was the crucial sexual organ in women.[10]

In the past five years, the FDA has twice approved new libido-boosting drugs for women that act on the brain. In 2015, the FDA said yes to Addyi, a failed antidepressant[11] that was repackaged and remarketed as the "pink Viagra."[12] Addyi was supported by a pharmaceutical-funded campaign called Even the Score, which is a prime example of feminism being used to sell dubiously successful products. Even the Score argued that it would be feminist to approve the drug because it focuses on women's pleasure, never mind all the complications: Women had to take the pill daily, couldn't consume alcohol while taking it, and experienced side effects including nausea and fainting. After all that, it created only half of one more "sexually satisfying event" per month.[13] Happily, Addyi failed, though not necessarily because of an objection to desire drugs.[14] Poor effectiveness, drugmaker dysfunction, and the ban on drinking ultimately made it an unattractive option.

Now there's Vyleesi, a brain-targeting solution for women that the FDA approved in 2019.[15] Vyleesi doesn't have as many restrictions as Addyi, but it does require women to give themselves a shot in the stomach or thigh forty-five minutes before they think they want to have sex. It also causes nausea and it is once again unclear whether the drug works well. In total, taking Vyleesi didn't result in more "sexually satisfying events" in a statistically significant way.[16] That may be enough for the FDA, but it's not enough for a skeptic like me. Despite demand for a libido-boosting drug and despite desperation on the part of pharmaceutical companies to create this drug, no safe and widely effective libido booster exists. When there is, everyone will know, believe me. Pharmaceutical companies will make sure of that.

. . . .

Medical authority can be powerful even when it is imaginary. Doctors encourage aces to ask ourselves if we're sick and doctors also diagnose and make declarations without caring at all what an ace person might think. Perhaps nothing better captures the attitude that asexuality is a delusion of the unwell than an episode of the popular medical drama *House* titled "Better Half"—an hour of television so notorious among aces that it is colloquially known as just "that *House* episode," accompanied by a grimace.

Dr. Gregory House is, famously, not a sensitive man. Upon hearing about a coworker's asexual patient, his first response is to ask whether the woman is a giant pool of algae or extremely ugly. Luckily, the showrunners correctly intuited that people will think an ugly ace woman is lying to spare her pride and gave the patient all the markings of conventional female attractiveness—long blonde waves, curves clad in a clingy pink sweater—to deflect this very question. All these serve to signal that when a woman is blonde and pretty, asexuality simply is not possible.

House then bets his coworker one hundred dollars that he can find a medical cause for this woman's supposed sexual orientation. "Lots of people don't have sex," House says, but because sex is the fundamental drive of the species, "the only people who don't want it are either sick, dead, or lying."

As it turns out, House is two for three, and he doesn't even need to refer to the *DSM* to be right. The woman is not dead, but she is also not asexual. She is pretending to be asexual because she loves her asexual husband. The twist is that her husband isn't asexual either. His lack of sexual desire is caused by a brain tumor that can be easily treated, meaning that with the quick intervention of science the two can soon enjoy the heterosexual married sex that is their due. House wins his money and congratulates his coworker on having brought these patients to his attention and therefore "having course-corrected two people's wildly screwed-up world views." As he says, it's "better to have schtupped and lost than never to have schtupped at all."

First aired in 2012, "Better Half" remains one of the most high-profile depictions of asexuality on a major show. For many, it was their introduction to this "wildly screwed-up" orientation. Even today, when I tell people I am writing a book about asexuality, many allos will mention the episode, adding sheepishly that it confused them then and that they are still sort of confused now.

Any regular viewer of *House* knows that the character's arrogance is a feature of the show, not a bug. He is not supposed to be nice and no one expects him to spend much time worrying about other people's feelings. But House *is* supposed to be brilliant and authoritative, a genius who sees through the other, lowly people and calls them out on their bullshit. Smug aha moments are amusing when he is an expert in obscure signs of gold poisoning, but less so when his assumptions contribute to the idea that asexual people cannot be trusted to tell the truth of our own experiences. As such, the target of House's incredulity reveals the extent to which compulsory sexuality is accepted. House isn't real, but the people who wrote this episode are and they thought it was okay to approve this storyline, playing right into the idea that aces and the ace-adjacent need to be disabused of their notions. A brilliant doctor says so, therefore the rest of us should listen up and be suspicious. In his world, which is our world, asexuality does not exist; it is either a lie or sickness.

So what is the difference between HSDD and asexuality, or even HSDD and a "normal" level of low desire? Over the years, several attempts have been made to separate the two. One is the criteria of "distress" that was added to almost all *DSM* diagnoses in 1994.[17] The idea is that people who have low desire and feel bad about it have HSDD, but people with the same symptoms who feel okay about themselves don't. Then, in 2008, ace activists created a task force that recommended to a *DSM* panel that patients not be diagnosed with a desire disorder if they identify as asexual.[18] Since 2013, the *DSM* has included this so-called asexual exception.[19]

Both of these clumsy attempts to separate the medical problem of HSDD from unproblematic low desire are unsatisfactory. People experience distress over many conditions not because the condition itself is a problem, but because prejudice makes their lives harder. Gay people and trans people generally have worse mental health than straight cis people[20]—not because being gay or trans is a sickness, but because bigotry causes distress and takes a toll on mental health. The same is true for aces. As for the asexual exception, its existence requires twisting the mind in strange ways. Saying that someone has HSDD unless they identify as ace is like saying that someone who experiences same-sex attraction has a psychiatric condition unless they happen to identify as homosexual. Having the exception is better than not having the exception, but experiencing same-sex attraction, or no attraction, is not a sickness regardless of which words one might use to describe the particular experience.

The features that truly separate psychiatric sickness and asexual orientation are not the amount of sexual attraction or any biological marker or whether someone feels distress. Most of the differences are social, explains ace researcher Andrew Hinderliter in a paper on the topic.[21] HSDD and asexuality have separate intellectual origins, separate approaches, and separate interpretations.

Desire disorders come from the medical field of sexology, while the exploration of asexual identity has been rooted in queer studies and social justice discourse. Desire disorders are about top-down medical knowledge, with doctors being the ultimate authorities in diagnosing a disorder. Aces encourage personal exploration, emphasizing that people must decide for themselves if they are asexual. I have told others that their experience as described to me lines up with the experiences of other asexual people. I have never "diagnosed" someone as asexual or insisted that they must identify this way.

Most importantly, the difference lies in what people believe about the implications of having low sexual desire. Disorders of desire are about seeing difference and calling it a problem. Asexuality is about embracing variation and avoiding the language of disorder, even if being asexual can be inconvenient. I, and most aces, simply do not believe that there is anything wrong with low desire or lack of sexual attraction. We do not believe that there is any moral obligation to work on increasing sexual desire. Wanting sex should not be a requirement of health or humanity.

Going further, ace activist CJ Chasin criticizes the idea that people should accept being asexual (or having low desire) only if they can't be made more sexual. It's a common idea, even among ace-friendly researchers and therapists and aces ourselves. "But would you say this to someone who was lesbian?" Chasin asks. Would you say, *If she can be made straight, we'll do that, but if she can't be turned straight, we'll help her accept that she is gay?* "I would argue that it shouldn't matter if someone *can* be changed; we need to be unpacking the expectation that people *should* be changed, that it's better to want sex, that we should only accept an asexual identity if people can't be otherwise," Chasin continues. "It's the same with trans and nonbinary people; I reject the idea that we should accept people who are trans as whatever gender only if they can't be cis. That's nonsense."

Chasin is right that nobody should feel pressured to be more sexual regardless of whether that is possible. Still, personal choice is important and if a safe and widely effective libido-boosting drug existed, I would not try to ban people from accessing it—though it should be used only after plenty of education and sold without using the language of "cure." As sexologist Barbara Carrellas told *The Outline*, a drug like Vyleesi should be marketed as a pleasure-enhancing device, not as a fix for a medical problem.[22]

I am not categorically against diagnoses either. Diagnoses can provide community, as well as the insurance codes necessary to access specialized treatment. As it stands, however, the most helpful treatment for HSDD is usually plain old therapy, not any special pill. It is difficult for me to see the purpose of a diagnosis that is not very likely to connect you to useful services but that *is* likely to reinforce the idea that you are medically unwell.

Were I to start identifying as an allo woman with HSDD tomorrow, the main difference would be that I feel worse about myself. I could be prescribed Addyi or Vyleesi, but that process takes time and money and the drugs likely won't work. I could learn more about HSDD, but many online materials focus on how devastating the condition is, which does little to help an anxious mind that already worries about every imperfection. The HSDD diagnosis is of little use when an alternative and more affirming way of thinking exists, which can mean identifying as ace or simply thinking that having low sexual desire is not a sickness. Rejecting a medical diagnosis doesn't mean being forced to be happy about a situation, either. Again, it is possible to be distressed by something—plenty of aces are distressed about being ace—without the cause of that distress being a problem in itself.

Many aces were once allos diagnosed with a disorder (and prescribed hormones off-label) before they learned about asexuality and decided that they were fine as is. A change in perspective is all that is necessary to switch from one to the other, from sick to well, disordered to different. Indeed, criticism that HSDD is a social construct is far from new and the social nature of the division is borne out by research too. According to one 2015 study that compared self-identified aces with allos diagnosed with a desire disorder, in general, aces had less sexual desire than the HSDD-diagnosed group but felt better about themselves.[23] That's a pretty fuzzy distinction, which is unsurprising because fuzziness has always been a feature of the *DSM*.

Throw together some criteria, approve it by vote, and anything can become an official psychiatric disorder—which means that the manual has long been a mirror for biases that would horrify many people today. Fifty years ago, a man who wanted to have sex with other men would have been classified as mentally disordered, and this would have been supported by the *DSM*'s entry for homosexuality, which wouldn't be fully dropped until the 1980s.[24] Today, a man who has little interest in partnered sex is still considered to have a psychiatric disorder. Both diagnoses arise from narrow-mindedness.

• • • • • • • • • •

While aces have been fighting the idea that we're sick, disabled people have been trying to prove they're not asexual. To represent those who believe that people who are sick don't want (or shouldn't have) sex, I present six words: *Three generations of imbeciles are enough.* The legendary Supreme Court justice Oliver Wendell Holmes Jr. wrote this phrase, shocking in its bluntness, in 1927 to support the right to forcibly sterilize the "unfit."[25]

The "imbecile" in question, Carrie Buck, was the middle of these three generations, the child of a woman who failed to meet standards of respectability. At a young age, Carrie had been taken away from her mother, Emma, and sent to live in the home of the more distinguished John and Alice Dobbs. When Carrie was seventeen, she was raped by the nephew of her foster parents. The resulting pregnancy put John and Alice in a socially delicate position. To save their nephew, they decided to sacrifice Carrie—marking her as "feeble-minded" without evidence and though she was of sound intelligence and had never had trouble in school—and place her in the Virginia State Colony for Epileptics and Feebleminded.

Institutionalizing Carrie was not particularly hard to do, explains journalist Adam Cohen in *Imbeciles: The Supreme Court, American Eugenics, and the Sterilization of Carrie Buck.*[26] The changing racial demographics of this era stoked the fear of the wealthy whites in charge. Eugenics, or the idea that society could be improved if the unfit were banned from reproducing, appeared to be a perfectly rational solution to the perceived threat of a world overrun by the unworthy. It was an idea championed by top thinkers, taught at Ivy League universities, and it was even the subject of a song called "Love or Eugenics" that F. Scott Fitzgerald wrote as a Princeton undergraduate. ("Men, which would you like to come and pour your tea / Kisses that set your heart aflame / Or love from a prophylactic dame?") "Unfit," however, could mean anything that powerful people didn't like. It could simply mean "not privileged." For example, studies by top researchers suggested that up to 98 percent of prostitutes had "subnormal" intelligence.[27]

Following her commitment to the Virginia State Colony, Carrie would become the plaintiff of *Buck v. Bell*, representing the argument that no person should be sterilized against their will. The case made it to the Supreme Court. To Holmes, Carrie—young, unwed, supposedly promiscuous and mentally deficient—represented a vision of America that could not be allowed to continue, and so he ruled in favor of eugenicist John Bell, the superintendent of the colony. There was only one dissenting opinion, so Carrie was sterilized. The case was cited by the Nazis as they developed their own eugenics program.[28] The ruling has never been overturned.

· · · · · · · · · ·

Many who learn about *Buck v. Bell* for the first time are horrified that the Dobbses lied about Carrie's intelligence, but it does not matter whether she was actually "feeble-minded." Forcibly sterilizing her violated her bodily autonomy and the case would have been just as horrendous if she truly had an intellectual disability or epilepsy. *Buck v. Bell* is one of the most harrowing Supreme Court decisions, a continual reminder of the strain of eugenicism in the history of the United States.

People with disabilities are one of the groups that the world assumes to be asexual or tries to make asexual, never mind their own thoughts and desires. "Desexualization is a process that separates sexuality from disabled bodies, making it irrelevant to and incompatible with them because disabled people are supposedly undesirable in society and because disability is believed to lead to sexual incapacity," writes gender studies scholar Eunjung Kim, who has done important research on disability and asexuality.[29]

The desexualization of disabled people may seem to disprove compulsory sexuality, but it actually reveals a nuance of the way it works. Compulsory sexuality is the belief that it's "normal" to be lustful. The flip side is that groups that are *already* perceived as less than "normal"—like older people, people who are autistic, Asian men, the racist stereotype of the mammy, or disabled people—are desexualized, considered sexually unattractive to others, and assumed to have no lust of their own. Beautiful abled women may be told to remain virginal and shamed into chastity, but their bodies are still considered objects of desire, used as props in movies and to sell beer. The bodies of those with physical disabilities, however, are seen as deviant and ugly—and disabled people are considered to be eternally childlike and not ready for sex—so the idea of disabled people having a sex drive is repulsive. As disabled academic Tom Shakespeare told *The Atlantic*, images of disability and sexuality tend to show disabled people either as "perverse and hypersexual,"[30] as Carrie supposedly was, her sexuality so dangerous that she needed to be sterilized, or asexual.

Many abled people assume that physical disabilities take away sexual desire, but that's not always the case. One study of nearly a thousand women found that these women with physical disabilities reported very similar levels of sexual desire as a control group of women without disabilities.[31] Those who are intellectually disabled or autistic are desexualized too, assumed to be too pure or naive to experience sexual desire. As a result, disabled kids are frequently excluded from sexual education due to a reflexive belief that it won't be relevant to them,[32] and people with disabilities often start dating later than their abled peers.[33]

Stereotypes aren't the only obstacle preventing disabled people from exploring their sexualities. The bodies of disabled people are treated like objects and burdens by an unkind medical system, says Cara, the ace disability activist with cerebral palsy. At medical appointments, nurses, doctors, and therapists flung her legs around. She went through physical therapy and surgery and has scars. "I think disabled people, especially those who grow up with their disability, are not taught that our bodies can be a source of pleasure," Cara says. "It's a process every day to figure out how I'm going to do things and I do things differently than your average person. At least twice a day, I'm like, 'Why do I even have a body?'"

Similarly, Jo, twenty-eight, says that being in constant pain from a young age means she didn't have the same connection to her body that other people did. (Jo is one of the eleven disabled aces that University of Glasgow sexuality researcher Karen Cuthbert interviewed for a study on what it's like to manage these two identities.)[34] "Maybe that had something to do with how I view other people's bodies or physical interaction in general," Jo tells Cuthbert. A woman named Erin—who has joint hypermobility problems that come with "weird sensory issues"—says that sometimes she wonders if there's simply a disconnect between her mind and body and *that's* why she doesn't want to engage with anyone sexually.

Such questions aren't only limited to physical difference. Steff, who is twenty-two, told Cuthbert that she had assumed she didn't care about sex because she was on the autism spectrum. "I blamed my lack of interest in intimacy on my Asperger's," she says. "If I did not have Asperger's, I think I would have suspected I was asexual a lot sooner."[35]

It makes perfect sense that in response to all this—misguided and malicious beliefs, disrespectful doctors, and true violence sanctioned by the highest court in the United States—the disabled community would insist that people with disabilities have the same sexual desires and deserve the same sexual rights as the abled. The group Yes, We Fuck! has created a documentary focusing on disability and sexuality.[36] Podcasts like Andrew Gurza's *Disability After Dark* discuss the same topic.[37] The 2012 movie *The Sessions*, about a disabled man working with a sex surrogate, has brought attention to the issue, as have continuing political debates over the practice.[38]

Notably, disability scholars Maureen Milligan and Aldred Neufeldt claim that asexuality among the disabled is largely a myth, and a self-defeating, self-perpetuating one at that. "Physical and mental impairments may significantly alter functioning, but do not eliminate basic drives or the desire for love, affection, and intimacy," they write.[39] Milligan and Neufeldt argue that while people with disabilities might have fewer opportunities to have sex, that doesn't mean the desire itself is absent. The problem isn't the amount of desire, it's what other people think about their amount of desire and how defeating the whole situation can be.

• • • • • • • • •

Keenly aware of how she'd be perceived by abled people, Cara assumed she was a straight woman until her twenties. After she started dating, Cara began to wonder whether that was true. Sex wasn't upsetting or bad but, as she says, "You can have sex or you can watch Netflix and I'm going to pick Netflix." Certain sexual activities did feel pleasurable, but the pleasure didn't seem to come from sexual attraction. It felt good in the same way that brushing your hair or stretching a hamstring feels good, so it seemed right to identify as "somewhere on the ace spectrum." Ace identity matches what she knows of her life.

Not all aces have been welcoming of people like Cara. Members of the ace community, especially in early years, rejected disabled aces completely, insisting that they would delegitimize asexuality and make it impossible to prove that asexuality is not related to (or caused by) disability and sickness. Even the efforts to add the asexual exception to the *DSM* ended up being subtly ableist by focusing on how happy aces are. "Rather than challenging stigma against both mental illness *and* asexuality, it seeks instead to rid asexuality of the stigma of mental illness," writes Wake Forest gender studies scholar Kristina Gupta. "Such normalizing tactics may come at the cost of intersectional analyses and coalitional possibilities."[40]

That's hard. At the same time, Cara can also feel like she's a "bad disabled person" because she doesn't want to fuck. "I do feel sometimes that I'm just bowing to stereotypes," Cara adds. "You know, 'Of course the girl in the wheelchair doesn't want to have sex because who'd want to have sex with her?'" As to where her asexuality "came from," there's no perfect answer to that either. Some disabled aces do have the clarity of separation and of knowing the two are not related. For Cara, though, it remains unclear whether she is ace "just because" or whether cerebral palsy somehow played a role. "Is it because I was a little sheltered as a kid?" she wonders. "Did nobody ever teach me about those things?"

• • • • • • • •

There exists a vision of the perfect ace person, one who never needs to ask themselves these questions. The *gold-star asexual*, also called the *unassailable asexual*, has no doubt at all about their identity. (The term, coined by the blogger Sciatrix in 2010,[41] is similar to the term *gold-star lesbian*, meaning a lesbian who has never had sex with a man.) The gold-star asexual will be the savior of us all, the one who can prove that asexuality is legitimate simply because there is not a single other factor that could have caused their lack of sexual attraction.

Cara is not a gold-star ace. Disability is an automatic disqualification, perhaps one of the biggest ones. The other enormous disqualification is being a survivor of sexual abuse or sexual assault. "For a long time, a lot of the most dominant voices in the asexual community said over and over, 'I was not abused, I was not traumatized,' because there's such a desire to distance oneself from abuse or trauma being a cause of asexuality, as that would mean asexuality is a problem that could be fixed or cured," KJ Cerankowski, a professor of gender studies at Oberlin College and coeditor of *Asexualities: Feminist and Queer Perspectives*, tells me. "The result is that people with sexual abuse or trauma histories—who aren't sure how that relates to their asexuality—are dismissed."

The gold-star ace is healthy in all ways, between the ages of twenty and forty (since elderly people are assumed to be asexual anyway), and cis, as well as sex positive and popular, write Sciatrix.[42] The gold-star ace is beautiful so as to deflect accusations of being a bitter incel. They can't be religious because that would mean they're just repressed. They do not masturbate and have no history of sexual problems. Maybe they have tried sex before but, after that, never, ever changed their mind about being ace or felt the slightest bit of sexual curiosity. (Bonus points if they've been in committed relationships before.) The gold-star ace would never worry, as an autistic woman named Kate did, that she might make asexuality "look bad" if she didn't appear neurotypical enough. The gold-star ace would not be autistic to begin with. They would always fit in. More than fit in: be beloved.

The obsession with the origin of asexuality, this pressure that makes proving asexuality nearly impossible, comes from—you guessed it—the belief that every person should be sexual, whether that belief comes from the general public or is enforced within a particular community. When a preference or behavior is socially accepted, people don't care about its origins, even when the origin is similarly influenced by multiple factors. Scientists spent a long time trying to find the "gay gene,"[43] yet the same amount of effort has not been spent trying to find the straight gene. Straightness is considered the ideal, so people rarely bother to wonder whether that's nature or nurture, even though it's both and even though straightness, as Adrienne Rich made clear, is often conditioned instead of chosen. Being ace is not considered the ideal, so the cause of this abnormality becomes a point of interest, since understanding whether one could be otherwise is supposed to, as Chasin noted, guide the question of how accepting society should be.

Compulsory sexuality makes asexuality prone to double standards. A person's heterosexuality isn't considered fake if they were abused as a child, yet childhood abuse is often the automatic culprit for asexuality. Straight people can start identifying differently without their straightness being called "just a phase," yet aces—and all others who aren't straight—have less room to be fluid. Sensitive people who would never tell a gay man that he hasn't found the right woman think little of saying the same to an ace person. The parent who asks one five-year-old boy which classmate he wants as a girlfriend asks another five-year-old ace or gay boy how they can already know their sexuality. Straight people are rarely treated like they're close-minded for knowing their sexual orientation, but aces are assumed to be unsure and always on the brink of finding the person who will change everything.

So aces become afraid, closing ranks and excluding everyone who ventures too far from the gold-star ideal, who might raise too many questions and bring the rest of us down. The tally of requirements adds up, creating a long list of criteria that very few people can fulfill. In the desire to be respected, people become ableist and prejudiced, straining to present ourselves as happy and healthy when it should be fine to be ace and unhappy and unhealthy, like all the unhappy and unhealthy straight people out there.

Exclusion will not work. Those who are determined to dismiss asexuality will find a way regardless, using the *DSM* or the logic of reproductive fitness or the duty to have children or anything else. The dream of the ace community was to bring together people with shared experience, to help us find each other and create resources and feel okay. Trying to please those who were always going to be naysayers does not bring us any closer to these goals. When ace acceptance is conditional on how closely a person matches the gold-star ideal, anyone who doesn't fit tortures themselves with doubt. It excludes those who must be included and then makes us question ourselves too.

I have never met a gold-star ace. The gold-star asexual is a fantasy and a false promise. It turns our attention to placating others instead of helping ourselves and chasing the fantasy hurts the real ace people who are here, right now. Holding on to this ideal makes it the norm for people to ask, over and over again, the questions that have been threaded through these chapters: What is asexuality and what is cerebral palsy? What is the influence of patriarchy or the influence of shyness or of being sheltered?

What is the result of stereotypes or shame and what is not? How can we feel okay claiming asexuality when so many factors make it easy to doubt? And when are we allowed to stop questioning?

•••••••••

There is a short answer and there is a long answer. The short answer is personal and practical, about what individuals should do next and for how long we should wonder. Most of us will never have the luxury of an airtight answer to these questions, just as we'll never know how much any of our other preferences were affected by thousands of other factors. Interactions are too convoluted. As Cara and every ace person knows, questioning can be exhausting and futile. Experiences may change on their own later or they may not—so after a certain amount of effort, this work is no longer helpful and acceptance becomes more important.

Harmful social conditioning, whether that be the pressure to wear high heels or the pressure not to cry, is inescapable. The list of lessons to unlearn is nearly infinite but time and energy are not, and a person may decide that the question of sexual desire is not the most important issue for them to challenge and that focusing on other issues will bring greater rewards. All aces should be welcomed into the community. There are no gold-star aces among us, but we are not the worse for it.

The long answer is the societal one, about what must shift on a greater level. It truly is necessary to question the expectations that others hold for us and the purpose and origin of these expectations. Each person should explore who they are and what they want and how all that might change.

That goes for people who identify as ace too. There should be freedom to not identify as ace if it doesn't serve you, freedom to be ace and still be curious about sex, freedom to identify as ace and then change your mind. For example, Lucid Brown from the first chapter has begun identifying as demisexual after discovering that they do experience sexual attraction, albeit toward a single person. Lucid doesn't feel sexual attraction for anyone except their girlfriend, but that's enough for the shift and there should be no angst around the switch.

"I think people go in and out of heterosexuality and homosexuality and queerness in various ways, and why can't that also be true for asexuality?"

asks Cerankowski, the gender studies scholar. "There are different circumstances under which people might find themselves identifying with different sexualities, and I do think we have to allow movement and fluidity as we think more complexly about sexual identities." Age and health, for instance, may factor into sexual identity and experience and "taking this more fluid approach to sexual identity formation does not necessarily negate asexuality if it's not this essential lifelong thing; there are just different ways of experiencing sexuality."

Yet fluidity and exploration and unlearning of stereotypes will mean little if the encouragement only ever pushes someone to be more sexual. To get meta for a moment, the work of questioning and the target of the questions ("Am I secretly repressed? Bowing to stereotypes?") is often *also* a product of social control and conditioning, just from a different side. If the options asexual and allosexual are equally available—in visibility and in what people believe about what these identities mean—and a person chooses allosexual, that is reasonable evidence that they are allosexual. If the only acceptable option is allosexuality and a person chooses allosexual, it is far more likely that this choice is the result of the shame of being abnormal. People will deny their aceness and explore forever in the hopes of discovering that they are allo after all.

Exploration is impoverished unless it is paired with full societal acceptance of aces. Acknowledgment that all types of people can be ace and that asexuality is simply a different and not inferior way of being is paramount. Furthermore, it is not enough to merely say that it is okay to be asexual. People should actively be encouraged to decide whether they might be asexual and learn about the joys of an asexual life. Only then does exploration lead to more freedom. Everyone should be free to figure themselves out, but no one should take from this freedom the idea that being ace is wrong and that they have to keep trying to find a different answer.

• • • • • • • •

It is a moral imperative that both the disabled community and the ace community welcome disabled aces. The disabled community must welcome disabled aces because sexual variation exists and disabled people can be ace, and there is nothing wrong with being ace. The ace community must welcome disabled people because sexual variation exists and ace people can be disabled, and there is nothing wrong with being disabled— and because the power of the ace movement does not depend on purity of origin.

People want to reject asexuality not only because it might be the result of external control, but also because asexuality will supposedly ruin your life. Lack of sexuality means being dried up and tired. In addition to being associated with children, it is associated with being old, because old people supposedly never again feel "the rush of excitement that comes with the first brush of the lips, the first moment when clothes drop to the floor."[44] Others casually talk about their fear that they "will stop being a sexual being any second now" and that losing their sexuality means they will "disappear or evaporate into thin air,"[45] which can leave those of us who weren't particularly sexual to begin with wondering if we have already disappeared, already evaporated. Such comments are understandable; there can be real grief in lacking or losing sexuality. I am sympathetic and do not think these comments should be censored. They still reinforce a particular story that too often is the only story.

The asexual view of the world is important because it presents a rarely seen vision of a happy, asexual existence and says that this is (or can, or at least should be) possible. What is wrong with the message that people should be able to be happy in a variety of circumstances? In a variety of ways? The strength of this vision does not rely on the insistence that asexuality always comes from nowhere or that it is lifelong or never shaped or caused by anything else. Its power comes simply from showing a different life to those who might want it or need it for any reason. The fact that many forms and many causes of asexuality exist does not negate this.

You can be asexual if your disability caused your asexuality, and you can be asexual if sexual trauma caused your asexuality, and you can be asexual if you lose your sexual desire later in life. The asexual community should be there to help in all these cases. You don't have to be part of the asexual community forever, but the lesson that a happy life for aces is possible, regardless of origin, is one that is important and one that includes you too. It's for you even if you don't identify as ace. If asexuality is fine, so is every other form of low sexual desire or so-called sexual dysfunction. Anyone who has any form of desire or attraction lower or higher than "normal" can still be okay. Better than okay.

So many groups are ultimately fighting against the same thing, which is *not* not having sex but which is instead sexual normativity and sexual control. All these groups have the potential to be allies. The greater fight is to have everyone realize that there does not need to be "normal"—there only needs to be what we are comfortable with and the ability to decide what we like to do with our bodies and our stories and our lives. True sexual liberation means having many choices—no sex forever, sex three times a day, and everything in between—that all feel equally available and accepted, and that all can lead to happiness if they are right for you. Context matters, but there will be no sexual act that is inherently liberatory or inherently regressive, no sexual stereotypes of any kind.

Doing away with compulsory sexuality also means doing away with hypersexualization and desexualization. Many voices are needed. No more being thought strange for not wanting sex, or people being shocked if you do. We should ask people what they want and not be surprised, no matter the answer. And we should tell them that no matter their answer, we will work to make sure that life can be good for all.

PART III

OTHERS

CHAPTER 7

ROMANCE, RECONSIDERED

"I THINK I AM IN FRIEND-LOVE WITH YOU," says the narrator of a comic of the same name, written and illustrated by Yumi Sakugawa and published in *Sadie Magazine* in 2012.[1]

"I don't want to date or even make out with you. Because that would be weird," the comic continues across a series of panels, but the narrator does want·

the other person to think they are awesome

to spend a lot of time hanging out

Facebook chats after midnight

to email weird blog links

to swap favorite books

to @reply to each other's tweets

to walk to their favorite food trucks

to find the best hole-in-the-wall cafes together

to have inside jokes

but all "in a platonic way, of course."

I want to be close to you and special to you, the way you are to me, but I do not want to be sexual with you, this comic says. I want to be emotionally intimate with you and I want to be in love with you, but not *in that way*. Just as saying *woman doctor* implies that a doctor by default is male, clarifying this feeling as friend-love implies that love—the real thing, the romantic thing—is for sex. In truth, Sakugawa's descriptions of platonic friend-love are similar to what many aces would call nonsexual romantic love.

Nonsexual romantic love sounds like an oxymoron. Almost all definitions of the feeling of romantic love—separate from the social role of married partners or romantic acts like saying "I love you"—fold in the sexual dimension. People might not be having sex, but wanting sex is the key to recognizing that feelings are romantic instead of platonic. Sexual desire is supposed to be the Rubicon that separates the two.

It's not. Aces prove this. By definition, aces don't experience sexual attraction and plenty are apathetic or averse to sex. Many still experience romantic attraction and use a romantic orientation (heteroromantic, panromantic, homoromantic, and so on) to signal the genders of the people they feel romantically toward and crush on.

Intuitively, it makes sense that people can experience romantic feelings without sexual ones, and few are confused when I define romantic orientation as separate from sexual orientation. The understanding breaks down once someone asks what it means to feel romantic love for someone if wanting to have sex with them isn't the relevant yardstick. How is that different from loving a platonic best friend? Without sex involved, what is the difference people feel inside when they draw a line between the two types of love? What is romantic love without sexuality?

Once again, this isn't a question only applicable to aces. Allos might feel infatuated with a new acquaintance or be more attached to their best friend than to any romantic partner, yet they can deny the possibility of romantic feeling because of the lack of sexual attraction. Allos can wave their hand and say, "There are people I want to sleep with, and I don't want to sleep with you, so it's only platonic."

As convenient as it is that allos can use sexual desire to distinguish the categories, this is also a constricting way to evaluate the world, and allos can seem as bewildered by their feelings as aces. For them, emotional intimacy and excitement can be confusing or nonsensical if they don't include sexual attraction. Many allos have shared with me their puzzlement at feeling like they were in love with friends despite no sexual attraction on either side. The writer Kim Brooks published a long essay in *The*

Cut puzzling over how it could be that she has obsessive relationships with women despite being straight. Of her college roommate she writes, "the relationship was never sexual, but it was one of the most intimate of my young adulthood. We shared each other's clothes and beds and boyfriends."[2]

Aces know that sex is not always the dividing line that determines whether a relationship is romantic. We take another look and say, "Maybe you're in love with your friend even if you're not sexually attracted to her." Questions about the definition of romantic love are the starting point for aces to think about love and romance in unexpected ways, from new, explicit categories beyond friendship and romance to the opportunities (legal, social, and more) of a world where romantic love is not the type of love valued above all others. Asexuality destabilizes the way people think about relationships, starting with the belief that passionate bonds must always have sex at the root.

* * * * * * * *

For sixteen-year-old Pauline Parker, June 22, 1954, was "the day of the happy event." She wrote those words in neat script across the top of her diary entry, marking it as a much-wished-for occasion. "I felt very excited and 'the night before Christmas-ish' last night," she wrote underneath. "I am about to rise!"[3]

The happy event would take place as Pauline hoped, though the long-term consequences would not be what she intended. Later that afternoon, Pauline and her friend Juliet Hulme, age fifteen, took Pauline's mother for a walk through Victoria Park in Christchurch, New Zealand. As the three went down a secluded path, Juliet dropped a stone. When Pauline's mother bent down to pick it up, the two girls bludgeoned her to death with a brick inside a stocking, taking turns bludgeoning the woman to death and smashing her face almost beyond recognition.[4]

The teenagers had met a couple of years before, when Juliet—beautiful, wealthy, and from a high-class British family—was then new to the country. Pauline was less comely and less moneyed; her father ran a fish store and her mother a boardinghouse. The two became inseparable, often lost in their own rich fantasy world. The bond was threatened when

Juliet's parents decided to send her to live with relatives in South Africa. Pauline could come along if Pauline's mother would allow it, but everyone knew that this suggestion would never be approved. For the girls, the only way forward seemed to be the brick and escaping to a new life in America.[5]

From the murder to *Heavenly Creatures*, the Peter Jackson film it inspired, to the lasting fascination the case holds today, Pauline and Juliet have never been able to dispel the suspicion that they were having sex. Juliet has denied that the two were lesbians, but her denial means little in the eyes of a world that believes only specifically sexual love could inspire that type of mutual obsession.[6] This belief—that platonic love is serene while intense, passionate, or obsessive feeling must be motivated by sex—is common. It does not track with reality.

If you don't believe aces who say that passionate feelings can exist without any sexual desire, believe University of Utah psychologist Lisa Diamond, who says the same thing. (Diamond refers to the feeling of "infatuation and emotional attachment" as "romantic love," so I will too here. We'll return to the question of whether this feeling is actually romantic later.) Diamond theorizes that the two can be separate because they serve different purposes. Sexual desire tricks us into spreading our genes, while romantic love exists to make us feel kindly toward someone and willing to cooperate for long enough to raise those exquisitely helpless creatures known as babies. Romantic love can be more expansive than sexual attraction because heterosexual sexual attraction, while usually necessary for producing kids, is not required for successful co-parenting. To use ace lingo, sexual attraction and romantic attraction don't need to line up.

Diamond first noticed this conflation of passion and sex when interviewing women about how they became aware of their sexual attraction to other women. "So many [women] would tell these stories about having a really strong emotional bond to female friends when they were younger, and they'd be like, 'So I guess this was an early sign,'" she tells me. Close female friendships do frequently use affectionate, quasi-romantic language that can confuse burgeoning sexual desires. Sometimes though, the story can be more complicated, and Diamond, an expert in sexual fluidity, began questioning whether passion must always equal secretly sexual.

If sexual desire were necessary for romantic love, kids who haven't gone through puberty wouldn't have crushes. Many do. Surveys show that children, including ones too young to understand partnered sex, frequently develop serious attachments. I had elementary school crushes and so did many of my allo friends.[7] Adults have gone through puberty but their sexual desires don't always dictate their emotional ones either. In one study Diamond references, 61 percent of women and 35 percent of men said they had experienced infatuation and romantic love without any desire for sex.[8]

It is already taken for granted that sexual desire doesn't need to include infatuation or caring. One-night stands and fuck-buddy arrangements are all explicitly sexual and explicitly non-romantic. The opposite conclusion—that for some, infatuation never included and never turns into sexual desire—is harder for people to accept, at least in the West. The story is different elsewhere. Historical reports from cultures in Guatemala, Samoa, and Melanesia describe how these close, nonsexual relationships were acknowledged. Sometimes honored with ceremonies such as ring exchanges, these relationships were considered a middle ground between friendship and romance and were often simply called "romantic friendship," Diamond tells me.

In these cultures, marriage was often more of an economic partnership than a love match. The marital and sexual bond was not automatically assumed to be the most important emotional relationship, unlike in current Western culture. Romantic friendships were not considered a threat to marriage and it was easier for people to believe that a nonsexual relationship could be as ardent as a sexual one. Romantic friendships were passionate on their own terms because passion is possible in many types of relationships.

. . . .

Believing that everything containing a special, charged energy must be sexual is not only simplistic; it can also shift how a relationship is perceived in a harmful way. In an insightful essay for *Catapult* magazine, writer Joe Fassler responds to a *Boston Review* piece about the eroticism of teacher-student relationships[9] by describing how his high school teacher coerced him into having sex and warning about the dangers of co-opting the language of sexuality.[10]

"The authors [of the *Boston Review* article] are right to point out that passionate teaching can bring about a kind of heightened energy between people. In my work in the classroom, I've experienced that feeling too," he writes. "But falling back on a convenient shorthand—the language of romantic attraction—to describe that phenomenon seems to me, at best, misguided."[11] This is the same mistake that *The Cut* writer Kim Brooks makes when she uses the language of sexual infidelity[12] to frame her intense friendships and calls them "affairs," as if they must automatically be a betrayal, as if there are no other comparisons possible. This is the mistake all of us make when we casually sexualize language and forget that the sexualization is a lazy interpretation of a feeling and not the feeling itself.

Language betrays us by making sexual attraction the synonym for fulfillment and excitement itself. When describing different types of social energy and intimacy, like the mind-meld of creative collaborators or the trust between pastor and congregant, there are few metaphors that don't resort to the sexual. Wanting to be "intimate" with someone—even emotionally intimate—can seem lewd. Being in a "relationship" with a friend sounds sort of odd. A thesaurus search for *passionate* offers as synonyms *wanton, lascivious, libidinous, aroused, sultry,* and, well, *sexy.*

"Isn't what we need a better, more precise vocabulary to describe the intense bond between teachers and students—one set apart from the language of eros?"[13] Fassler asks. With training, he continues, well-meaning educators would learn not to mistake the "sparkle of mentorship" for something more, just as therapists learn to deal with the complicated emotions they can provoke in clients without assuming the relationship is romantic in nature.

It is more than educators and therapists who need to be concerned about this dynamic. It is everyone who lives in a world where language traps us into thinking there is only one kind of pleasure and everything else is derivative. The joy of learning and the emotional fulfillment of therapy, like the closeness of friendship, are all wonderful in their own unique way. Pay attention to these feelings, their weight and heft and experience, the way they enrich our lives and how each holds their own value. "I think people sometimes make sense of things as romantic crushes when really it isn't," CJ Chasin, the ace researcher, says. It's common for two close friends to be accused, even jokingly, of being romantically obsessed with each other and in denial about it. They themselves may wonder if their feelings toward each other are romantic. "Why can't that 'denial' go both ways?" continues Chasin. "Maybe you're just in denial about friend intimacy."

Developing and normalizing language that lets us talk frankly about emotional intimacy without it seeming like a come-on will help the world come into focus. Better language will protect us from confusing intention or misinterpreting emotion when that might be inappropriate, and it allows us to enhance the energy that is present without trying to turn it into something else. It will let us talk about relationships for what they are, not what they resemble.

· · · · · · · · ·

If sex isn't the dividing line between romantic and platonic love, what is? Academics have long tried to isolate the emotional components that distinguish different types of relationships. Though there can be endless moving parts, one commonly used framework, developed by anthropologist Helen Fisher, features three basic components. (Fisher developed her model to explain the components and forms of romantic love specifically, but I think it can be useful for analyzing all types of feeling.) There is the desire to have sex. There is infatuation. And there is emotional intimacy and caring, which psychologists often call the rather clinical-sounding *attachment*.[14]

These components mix and match to create the specific feeling that lives between any two people. In any loving relationship, there can be a lot of infatuation or a little, a lot of sexual desire or none, and so on. The difference in feeling is real, but the feelings do not always fit neatly into the mutually exclusive categories of "platonic" or "romantic." (Strangely, the word *platonic*, as used colloquially, seems only to be defined by what it is not: it is the union of nonsexual and non-romantic.) The same combination of emotions can be categorized many ways, as either platonic love or romantic love.

"Attachment plus infatuation," for example, is how the psychologist Lisa Diamond and many others define romantic love. To others, the identical combination of attachment and infatuation feels platonic, like being excited about a friend. Attachment alone, without infatuation or sex, is usually experienced as platonic love only for friends and family—but try telling that to celibate aces in long-term relationships, or even some allos who have stopped having sex over time. "Attachment plus sex" is also a hazy case. Though often considered romantic, these are also the components of a friendly casual sex arrangement.

In every case, this game of mix and match creates a multiplicity of possible—and often opposing—labels for each combination of emotions. "Romantic" and "platonic" are categories that people experience differently. In the absence of sex or sexual desire, Juliet Hulme and Pauline Parker may have experienced their love for each other as romantic or as platonic. Two other girls might have felt the same thing and named it differently.

A more detailed attempt at breaking down and classifying the categories comes from psychologist Victor Karandashev. In his book *Romantic Love in Cultural Contexts*, Karandashev reviews the social science literature and lists the most common criteria that people claim divide the two feelings. Romantic feeling, according to people around the world, typically includes: infatuation, idealization, wanting physical and emotional closeness, wanting exclusivity, wanting your feelings to be reciprocated, overthinking the other person's behavior, caring and being empathetic toward the other person, changing parts of your life for them, and becoming more obsessed if they don't like you back.[15]

It all sounds reasonable enough, but when I read Karandashev's list to Leigh Hellman, a queer ace writer in Chicago, they point out that every emotion that supposedly differentiates romance can be found in other emotional settings. Sensitivity, attachment, and caring are part of any healthy relationship. People who are polyamorous have multiple romantic partners without the desire for exclusivity. Infatuation might be the factor that aligns most closely with widespread ideas of what romantic love feels like, yet it's common to idealize a new acquaintance or feel possessive when a best friend becomes close with someone else, and romantic love doesn't automatically turn platonic once early energy wears off.

"I can be jealous, I can experience adoration and devotion toward my friends, all these intense qualifiers that we usually put toward romantic love," Leigh says. "In past relationships, I was like, 'Do I actually want a romantic and sexual relationship, or do I just have a really intense platonic love for someone and I wanted to have some sort of validation that I was significant in your life the way you are in mine?'"

• • • • • • • • •

While reporting this book, I asked everyone, regardless of romantic orientation, how they separated platonic and romantic love. People like Leigh did not and could not. Others claim that there is a definite difference but have trouble explaining what that difference might be. One person pointed to a difference in "touch attraction," which is not a desire to have sex, but a desire to be close in other physical ways, like holding hands or cuddling. Another man said that even though he doesn't feel sexual attraction toward anyone, he finds women and not men aesthetically beautiful and lets aesthetic attraction guide the romantic classification.

Simone, a grad student from Malaysia, says that though no one has been able to properly explain romantic attraction to her, she has accepted that she doesn't experience it. "I don't have any urge to have a relationship with someone that is more special than any of the friendships I have with my very good friends," Simone says. Still other aces say they want a devoted relationship that looks and is structured exactly like what many people consider to be a romantic relationship—in other words, they want someone to fill the social role of romantic partner—even if they don't feel romantically toward the other person.

Alicia, a soft-spoken scholar in her thirties, has been with her partner since her teens. She knows what it's like to be romantically attracted to men and women. She knows what it's like to look at her boyfriend and admire how good-looking he is and not want to have sex with him at all. "And I know what a friend crush feels like," Alicia adds. She's familiar with that feeling of infatuation, of hoping that the other person reciprocates and likes her too. She still feels something different when it comes to her partner. She pauses, looking frustrated. It is impossible for her to describe anything more.

To try and answer this question myself, I mentally compared my romantic love toward my boyfriend, Noah, with my platonic love for my friend Jane, and found that much of the contrast stems from different expectations and all the heavy, complicated emotions that go with such. To isolate romantic feeling, I asked that we peel away social role and performance, but the differences seem partially created by both. "Platonic" and "romantic" are types of feeling while "friend" and "romantic partner" are social designations, and the latter molds the former.

As much as I love Jane, she lives a few states away and I'm lucky if I see her twice a year. Our lives long ago diverged; there's little chance they will intersect again in the future and little expectation that we will work together to make that happen. In a conventional romantic relationship like mine and Noah's, the assumption is that we will stay together for the rest of our lives, and that brings new anxieties and a greater shared dependency.

Shallow as it is, each of Noah's choices feels far more personal because they reflect more on me and my own social value. Small habits and considerations have more consequences too, and emotions are accordingly turned up. Hating Jane's eating habits would be an annoyance but not at all hard to endure the few times I see her. Hating Noah's eating habits would raise the question of whether I can endure this forever, whether I should have to endure this forever, why can't he be exactly the way I want him to be, why can't I be less uptight, and on and on. Tiny annoyances snowball. Everything is harder to bear when you might need to bear the situation every day for the rest of your life.

Such distinctions seem situational more than innate. If Jane and I committed to living together indefinitely, the same mix of emotions and expectations might develop too. If I knew that we would be seeing each other daily for the next five decades, Jane's eating habits might take on a more ominous implication as well. I might scrutinize her choices more closely, not only because I care about her, but also because I care about what they'd mean for me and for us and our life.

Differentiating emotion, like figuring out whether someone experiences sexual attraction, is a problem of phenomenology. No one has invented a way to perfectly compare if my experience of a bitter taste is the same as yours, or whether we're feeling the same thing but you call it romantic love and I call it platonic love because of how we have been socialized. Or whether the emotion we feel toward different people is the same, but we change what we call that feeling based on the role someone plays in our life. I am infatuated with Noah in a way I am not with Jane—but this may partly be because it is common and expected to continuously praise your romantic partner and the same is not true for friends. Perhaps, over time, the emotions grow to be different because of the different ways we reinforce them, having been taught to praise and feed in one case and to benignly neglect in another.

Don't get me wrong. I am not claiming that romantic and platonic love are secretly the same; there can be any number of small factors or combination of factors that differentiate the two. There are, after all, reasons that Jane and I have not committed to living together indefinitely. I am aesthetically attracted to Noah and not Jane. Both are dear to me, but Noah is currently about the only person on earth I would sleep with.

Nor am I claiming that romantic love is platonic love but deeper somehow. Shallow romantic obsessions exist without being love at all, as do profound, loving friendships that trump romantic bonds. I am saying that people think of romantic and platonic love as two distinct categories, but, frequently, there is overlap and no clean separation, no one emotional feature or essential component that makes a relationship one or the other.

There is attachment, and there is the desire to have sex, and there is infatuation, and it all can be felt in all sorts of circumstances and all types of relationships, shaped by different expectations and called by different names. "Romantic attraction, much like sexual attraction, is something that you know it when you feel it or you don't," says Chasin, who identifies as aromantic. "Which isn't very helpful. There isn't going to be a checklist. There isn't going to be a set of necessary or sufficient conditions because once you get into classifying kinds of relationships, there are just going to be blurry boundaries and that's okay. That's the landscape."

For Leigh Hellman, the writer in Chicago, recognizing the blurriness of these categories provided a new opportunity. Accepting that overlap made it possible to use language in a new way, to brush away the ease and baggage of old assumptions and shape outer experience to more closely match inner feeling.

. . . .

Leigh came out as queer at sixteen, half a lifetime ago. "I spent a lot of time being single," they say. "I'm 6'1", I'm not a skinny supermodel, I'm a lot of person. And before I understood my gender identity, that was also at odds with the ideas of traditional femininity."

Leigh moved to Korea on a Fulbright scholarship after college and met the man who would become their husband. After five years in Asia, Leigh decided to return to the States for grad school and knew that if the two wanted to stay together, a spousal visa would make it easier to emigrate. So they got married. It was weird, Leigh says. Not bad, just unexpected for someone long used to being alone and who sometimes thinks they're panromantic and sometimes thinks they're aromantic.

Back in the US, Leigh started studying creative writing and spending time with artists and met Taylor. Leigh liked that Taylor was extroverted while Leigh was introverted and that Taylor had a practical streak and got shit done. "A lot of people sit around and want to do something and they don't do it," Leigh says. "Which I get! Things are hard and life is hard and you're tired, we're all tired. It's not a judgment thing, but it takes a particular type of person to be like, 'I want this, what do I have to do to get it?' And Taylor was like that."

Leigh, who had until then identified as queer and allosexual, was starting to understand their asexuality. Taylor realized they were aromantic through talking with Leigh. The two became close friends and then decided that they wanted their relationship to be something different.

In another time, this relationship might have been one of the romantic friendships that psychologist Lisa Diamond writes about, passionate and effusively affectionate without being sexual. It was a relationship of that same mold, existing in the Western world but not legible or easily understood here because for so long there has been a lack of vocabulary and concepts. In this era, Leigh and Taylor use a different term, one of the few explicit titles available to describe the social space between "friend" and "romantic partner": *queerplatonic partner*.

The idea of queerplatonic partners (or QPP) originated in ace and aro communities. "We developed [the concept] out of frustration with a world where romance is the center of how people relate," says s.e. smith, a journalist who coined the term with fellow writer Kaz in 2010.

It is undeniable that culturally, romance trumps friendship. Romance is higher on the hierarchy of importance and is portrayed as more interesting and essential. Casual phrases like "just friends" and "more than friends" relegate friendship to something less special and less whole. Frustration over the devaluation of friendship is not new; the term QPP is.

The bond between queerplatonic partners is not sexual, nor does it necessarily seem romantic to the people in such a partnership. Some people feel differently about their queerplatonic partner than about either a friend or a romantic partner. For others, a queerplatonic partnership is less about a unique feeling and more about acknowledging each other's importance in a way that is rare for relationships that aren't explicitly romantic. These relationships transcend the bounds of what is typically found in friendship alone, even when "romantic" as a descriptor seems wrong. The *queer* part is not about genders, but about queering that social border. Mutuality is key: smith plays an active role in the life of a friend's child, but none of the adults involved view the relationship as queerplatonic, even though others in the same situation might describe the relationship differently.

"Queerplatonic" is an attempt to develop more precise language to fit the range of roles that people can occupy in our lives, roles more varied than the few words available. Social labels provide information; they are signals and instructions. Labels carry emotional weight, whether for the people who are dating, but it's "not really a thing" or for the monogamous couple who refuse to call each other boyfriend and girlfriend because that would take the relationship one step too far.

The simplest way to capture a meaning of queerplatonic may come from the medical melodrama *Grey's Anatomy*. Coworkers Meredith Grey and Cristina Yang were never sexually or romantically involved, but their relationship contained a level of trust and commitment not typically seen between colleagues or even many friends. In the pivotal scene, Cristina tells Meredith that she put her down as an emergency contact for an abortion procedure. "The clinic has a policy. They wouldn't let me confirm my appointment unless I designated an emergency contact person, someone to be there just in case and help me home, you know . . . after,"

Cristina says. "Anyway, I put your name down. That's why I told you I'm pregnant. You're my person."[16]

"You're my person" has worked its way into popular culture, inspiring listicles in the vein of "10 *Grey's Anatomy* Quotes That Remind You of Your Person"[17] and an entire ecosystem of You're My Person merchandise (mugs, shirts, jewelry) wherever kitschy goods are sold. It has become a shorthand stronger than best friend, a gender-neutral way of saying "soul mate" or "the one I trust most."

"You're my person" isn't tied to official romantic relationship status. Meredith isn't Cristina's person because Cristina can't find someone to date. The women didn't abandon each other once they found boyfriends. Their importance to each other is of a different tenor. Explaining her relationship with Meredith to her boyfriend, Cristina tells him this: "If I murdered someone, she's the person I'd call to help me drag the corpse across the living room floor." *She* is, not him.

• • • • • • • • •

The way Leigh and Taylor treated each other didn't change much after they became queerplatonic partners. The two were already so close, and besides, Leigh was married, so their talks didn't focus on logistics like how often they'd see each other. "It came down to explicit discussion of our emotional commitment to each other," Leigh says. "How do we see the way our relationship works and the way we want to define ourselves and be defined by others?"

For Leigh, a QPP was not about proving that their feelings for Taylor were the most important of all, stronger than their feelings for anyone else. It's not like a QPP is like a special friendship—if that were the case, then friendship itself goes back to being more casual and less devoted and Leigh, who is one of the most thoughtful people I have ever met, has no interest in denigrating friendship yet again. Their QPP was about action and attitude more than entirely unique feeling, in the same way that traditional romantic relationships often work because of an explicit commitment to the partner and the bond. Leigh was extending an invitation to Taylor to, together, create a set of norms and a container for their feelings. The QPP was about being vulnerable and boldly asking for something back, about that intense relationship and the security of explicit validation that Leigh had often thought they wanted.

Precisely because social labels provide signals and instructions, they also constrict. *Queerplatonic* resets from the unspoken expectations of either *friend* or *romantic partner* and forces the relationship into a new place, with the ability to build new obligations and new expectations together. The switch to *queerplatonic* is a change in both language and thought, a relational example of what the Russian literary theorists called defamiliarization, or taking something and trying to see it anew and then noticing what you might not have seen before.

In friendship, Leigh explains, it can be unclear where you stand. Conversations about emotional commitment are uncommon, and if you don't know where you stand, you don't know your place. In a QPP, these questions have been tackled already, their answers cocreated. It became possible to voice opinions and preferences on a more even ground. Everything became freer. Taylor told their mom about Leigh. Leigh called Taylor their partner in queer spaces and "my really good friend" in situations where *partner* might bring up questions that would take too long to answer.

Leigh's other partner, their husband, knew about the "intense friendship" with Taylor but didn't exactly understand the concept of a QPP. Nor was he interested in delving into the specifics. His concerns were primarily about sexual fidelity, and once it became clear that Leigh and Taylor were not sleeping together and had no intention of doing so, any worries and further curiosity vanished.

Do you consider yourself poly? I asked Leigh. Unsure. Leigh's husband didn't consider their marriage to be open and Leigh and Taylor's relationship wasn't exactly romantic. On the other hand, as Leigh says: "I don't know if my feelings were really different for my husband and QPP. If you're in the small group of people I care about, I feel pretty much the same about all of you. That's just how I do relationships."

· · · · · · · · ·

It can be eye-opening to look more closely at the meaning of *romantic* or *platonic*, but it is not necessary to litigate semantics. It is meaningful to separate romance from sex and puzzle over the term *queerplatonic*, but I am more interested in changing the way people behave around relationships than in forcing everyone to change the words.

Language is shared with others and policing word choice can backfire. I wouldn't demand that Yumi Sakugawa rename her comic "I Am in a Non-Sexual Romance with You," or insist that her feelings are truly romantic. I would not point to two close friends and tell them their relationship is not friendship but actually queerplatonic. Telling people what their relationship actually is or insisting that people cannot use *friend* and *romantic partner* to describe conventional social roles is not the road to progress. That way lies a rabbit hole of definitional confusion and linguistic tricks. Plus, it's disrespectful. These new ideas are meant to provoke, not to prescribe.

I am, however, curious about what would happen if everyone more carefully considered the distinction we make between friendship and romance, and the way we treat them differently and why. Many people are hesitant to say "I love you" to friends, much less ask, "How do you feel about time? What are we to each other?" As Leigh noted, outside of romance, there is no "defining the relationship" talk unless something has already gone wrong. Couples therapists usually focus on romantic couples, and no advice industry is available to help people recover from the loss of a friendship, though friend breakups can be as devastating as the romantic kind. The looseness of friendship and lack of official obligation is a delight for many, but as a general rule, people tend to treat casually that which is less important.

This doesn't have to be so. As queerplatonic relationships show, we can borrow from the language and norms of romantic relationships to structure other types of feeling. Queerplatonic partners take a type of relationship that is usually taken lightly and decide that it is important enough to merit unusual and potentially awkward conversations. Relationships of many kinds can be important enough to risk those talks, to set expectations and dig in.

Instead of letting labels like *romantic* and *platonic* (or *friend* versus *partner*) guide actions and expectations, it is possible for the desires themselves to guide actions and expectations. More effective than relying on labels to provide instruction is skipping directly to asking for what we want—around time, touch, commitment, and so on as David Jay wrote—regardless of whether those desires confuse hardline ideas of what these two categories are supposed to look like. When the desires don't fit the labels, it is often the labels that should be adjusted or discarded, not the desires. If everyone is behaving ethically, it doesn't matter if a relationship doesn't fit into a preconceived social role, if it feels neither platonic nor romantic or if it feels like both at the same time.

Taylor and Leigh broke up a year after they got together, for reasons that had nothing to do with sexual identity or labels. That's important to note too, Leigh says. Queerplatonic partnerships shouldn't be infantilized or idealized as these "too pure, too good" relationships protected from emotional storms. They may be subversive; they may challenge entrenched hierarchies; but they are still relationships between people and people are always flawed. The emotional components supposedly unique to romantic love can be experienced in other contexts, and so the challenges and struggles of romantic relationships can be experienced in other types of partnerships too. And though the relationship with Taylor ended, working through the relationship together helped Leigh recognize what they wanted and deserved in a relationship and helped Leigh leave their abusive marriage.

Love and caring are precious and appear in contexts beyond the romantic; they are not necessarily the most powerful in romantic contexts either. One group of people feels this truth especially acutely: those who are aromantic, or aro. They know that elevating romantic love ends up harming everyone. They're waiting for others to catch up.

• • • • • • • • •

"Only someone in love / has the right to be called human," wrote the Russian poet Alexander Blok in 1908.[18] A century later, the pop singer Demi Lovato had a similar message: "You ain't nobody 'til you got somebody."[19]

So long as there is no romantic partner in the picture, others will think the picture incomplete. To say that only someone in love—and the poem suggests Blok is referring to love for a romantic partner—has the right to be called human implies that our humanity depends on circumstances largely out of our control: other people, the way the world works, sheer luck. It is ghastly to believe we are only human when we can experience one specific emotion or when others feel that way about us. Regardless, the desire for romantic relationships is often necessary to prove one's morality, and so aros are judged, their humanity denied.

David Collins, for instance, loves romance novels, loves his friends, and for a while wondered whether he was a sociopath. "There is an idea that this—caring about people but not romantically—is what bad people do," he says. "It really made me feel like, 'Okay, I'm not a good person, I can't relate to people, this is some shit that [fictional serial killer] Dexter Morgan does."

The aromantic community is connected to the asexual community, but not everyone who is aromantic is asexual. David is not. He's pansexual and experiences sexual attraction but doesn't know what it's like to want a specifically romantic relationship. His story hits many of the same points that I have heard from aces: As a kid, David, who is now in his twenties, saw others partner up and assumed that he'd grow to want romance like everyone around him. Despite having relationships from age fourteen onward, the hoped-for change never happened. It was hard to shake the worry that deep down, he was a sick, selfish person who wanted to use people for their bodies.

Around the time David was eighteen, a friend told him about aromanticism. He first dismissed it as an "incel thing." Then David decided it might be a made-up term for people with depression or for people in denial about some obscure psychological problem.

A few months later, walking through Times Square with his girlfriend, David was forced to reconsider. As they passed through that tourist trap, his girlfriend turned to tell David how passionately she loved him. This was a woman David could relate to on every level. Both studied computer science, agreed on politics, loved horror movies and analyzing pop culture and writing fan fiction. They supported each other, enjoyed each other's company. Yet the only thing David could think was that he could not return her words. He cared about her and wanted her to be happy and wanted to treat her well, but he did not feel the same way about her as she did about him. Something, some ineffable feeling, was missing.

Whatever she felt toward him, whatever she was describing, he had not experienced—not with her and not with anyone else.

"That's probably one of the few times in my life where I literally sat down and said to myself, 'What is wrong with you?'" David says. "'We gotta figure this out right now.'" A lonely year followed as he began to wonder if it was true, that as much as he might love people, he would never want the kind of relationship he was supposed to aspire to—and because of that, he might always be seen as cold or amoral. The people he saw like him in the media were killers. The stories available about lives without romance were few and far between.

· · · · · · · · ·

The ubiquity of romantic plotlines first came to my attention when Tired Asexual wrote to *Slate* advice columnist Dear Prudence asking for suggestions for books without romance.[20] Helpful readers responded with a short list, many from young adult fiction.[21] Surely, I thought, the list of eligible novels had to be much longer.

For my own version of the test, I developed the following criteria:

- The novel is not young adult fiction or science fiction/fantasy. (There are plenty of YA books without romantic subplots, both because intended readers are younger and because recent YA authors are more likely to incorporate characters along the sexuality spectrum.)
- The novel is not about romance, and romance—or yearning for romance—isn't a major plot point even if it's there. Maybe there's a couple, but their relationship is taken for granted and the book doesn't focus on its evolution. Maybe someone goes on a date, but dating doesn't move the story forward.
- The novel has no explicit sex scenes or sexual themes (including sexual assault).
- The novel doesn't present romantic love as necessary and central to flourishing. This last requirement is crucial. Even if there are no sex scenes and nobody goes on a date, if the main character is constantly thinking about how they should be dating, the novel is disqualified.

Go ahead, see what you can come up with.

It is only when forced to provide these examples that it becomes clear that it shouldn't be this hard. And though it's easy to understand why it would be frustrating for someone who is aromantic to be surrounded by books implying that life is pathetic without romance, this state of affairs is harmful no matter how one identifies.

Culture may not always create the desires for the things it valorizes—sex, romance, money—but having a single story about what these things signify can amplify them and make them seem necessary. If the vast majority of stories posit romantic love as the ultimate goal and unpartnered people as losers, people are unlikely to think outside those narrow lanes. If accurate representation matters when it comes to class and race and gender (and it does), representation also matters when it comes to storylines, the narratives that are present about what matters, what people want and should want, and what is necessary for a good life.

Hunter wanted to feel like a hero, and he learned from *American Pie* that the easiest way to become one would be to have sex. I want to feel deeply, and the story I see all around is that the easiest way to do so is to stir up romantic drama. Lauren Jankowski, the aro-ace fantasy writer, wants to write about friendship, but has been told by literary agents that asexuality and aromanticism won't sell because they're not compelling enough. "Why can't we just have a narrative where you have two best friends fighting for each other, fighting to protect each other?" she asks. "Why can't we have a group of friends going off on adventure? It's like, unless they're attached to somebody, why would that be a story?" To Lauren, the answer obvious: "Because it's fucking interesting."

The ubiquity of romantic subplots, even in books that aren't romance novels, suggest that only stories with romance can involve big emotions and that romance is automatically more interesting than almost all the other strands of human experience. What if books focused more on the emotions that are generated from friendship, ambition, family, work? What if that intensity were just as elevated?

· · · · · · · · ·

There are books that meet the criteria of my test. Albert Camus's *The Stranger* and *The Plague* and many works of Knut Hamsun fit within the parameters, as do surrealist novels from Borges, Calvino, and Markson. Historical and family stories are also a good bet: Per Petterson's *Out Stealing Horses* and Harry Mulisch's *The Assault* deal with complicated family dynamics during World War II. More contemporary selections include Marilynne Robinson's *Housekeeping*; Catherine Chung's *Forgotten Country*, about family secrets, the Koreas, and immigrant experience; Chaim Potok's *My Name is Asher Lev*, about individual desire versus community expectation. The story that has moved me most in recent months—Duncan Macmillan's play *People, Places, and Things*—chronicles an actress's repeated attempts at rehab. Cormac McCarthy's *The Road* is bleak and dystopian; in that universe, the most important love is between a father and a son.

The catch is that almost all these selections fit into a secondary genre. All are acclaimed and considered literary, but they're also usually described as philosophical novels, or Holocaust novels, or immigrant novels; they're pegged to something else. You need always to be looking for something that makes the novel "other." At the core, as one friend pointed out, the nuclear family and romantic love are key parts of the genre of serious literary fiction without needing to add another descriptor.

Some of the books I mentioned may still feature romance. I lack the time to reread them all and so fully expect to discover that some include a romantic subplot or fail my criteria in another way. Others who helped me brainstorm encountered the same problem. Again and again, friends would respond with a suggestion, only to see someone else chime in and point out that, actually, *Watership Down* and *East of Eden* do have romantic and sexual themes, you simply forgot. Romance is so taken for granted that we often don't register it, the way we rarely register if all the characters in a novel are white. This message affects our values and our hopes, all while fading so cleanly into the background that it's barely even evident.

• • • • • • • •

Rice University philosopher Elizabeth Brake calls this undeserved elevation and centrality of romantic love *amatonormativity*, from the Latin word for love, *amare*. She coined the term in her book *Minimizing Marriage: Marriage, Morality, and the Law* to describe the assumption that "a central, exclusive, amorous relationship is normal for humans." Not simply normal, but preferable. Not only preferable either, but ideal and necessary—better than being polyamorous, better than having a strong web of family, better than having a close-knit group of friends.[22] A good that we should universally work toward and are incomplete without.

It is not difficult to find examples of amatonormativity, points out psychology writer Drake Baer. As philosopher Carrie Jenkins says, even well-intentioned phrases like "You're so lovely, I can't believe you're single"[23] imply that single people are lacking somehow. Supreme Court Justice Anthony Kennedy's much-applauded opinion in favor of same-sex marriage stated that being denied the right to marriage meant being "condemned to live in loneliness."[24] Lyrical court opinions and throwaway comments alike can make it difficult to figure out whether you truly want a relationship or just believe that without one you will always be pitied. Amatonormativity is also responsible for a lack of research on single people, Baer adds. Social scientists assume that everyone wants to be in a relationship, creating a missed opportunity to learn more about people for whom this is not true and what their perspectives could teach everyone else.[25]

Amatonormativity, like every kind of normativity, erases variation. The erasure of variation means the erasure of choice and the triumph of stereotype and stigma. If someone is not in a romantic relationship, they are to be pitied or mocked. If someone doesn't want a romantic relationship at all, they are heartless like a serial killer. The spinster becomes a pathetic creature, a strange and unwanted woman. The bachelor is either closeted or emotionally stunted. If he's hot, he's irresponsible and a rake. If he's not, like South Carolina senator Lindsey Graham, there may be something more seriously wrong. When Graham tried to run for president in 2015, he faced scrutiny over his bachelor status and had to defend himself as "not defective,"[26] even joking that if everyone were so desperate for a First Lady, his sister could do the job. Graham should be disqualified from presidency because of his policy proposals, not because he has little interest in romantic relationships.

A person's value and humanity—regardless of their political views or attractiveness or gender—should never be dependent on either their familiarity with the very particular emotion of romantic love or their ability to inspire it in others. Yet "people immediately think that if you can't relate to someone on a romantic level, you are mentally malformed," David says. They will ask if he's autistic (a negative, ableist stereotype). Other Black people have told him he's gay and in denial about it. "Depression" and "you're an asshole with no feelings" are two commonly suggested explanations.

The stereotype of the sociopathic aro is so common that Simone from Malaysia has started embracing it. "It's not an identity, exactly," they say. "It's a character that I sometimes play facetiously. I pretend to be an alien observer who doesn't really understand how humans function and I'll jokingly be like, 'Ah yes, *how fascinating*, these humans and how they press their fleshy bodies together and have feelings.'"

Simone is the Tin Man without a heart, or an alien in the world of romantic love. It's part performance and part coping mechanism because there is an uneasy balance between joking about being a robot and the genuine feeling of being perceived as robotic for being aromantic. "I think that's why I'm interested in concepts like post-humanism and trans-humanism," Simone adds. "It's appealing to think that, 'Well, if I can't feel like this and if I have to feel less human because I'm aromantic, I am just going to be human differently.'"

· · · · · · · · · ·

Being both human and judgmental, I am not immune to a form of amatonormativity myself. I found it easy to sympathize with nearly everyone I interviewed. Asexual and aromantic? I get that. Same with women who were aromantic but not asexual, like Elana, who is in her twenties and lives in rural Ohio (but says her greatest wish is to leave the state). "I won't feel terrible if I never have someone in my life that I can spend the rest of my life with," she says. "It's not necessarily a priority for me." A boyfriend broke up with Elana over text right when she finished reading *The Fault in Our Stars* and she was "more upset over the fact that a book character had died than that I had been dumped."

Yet, the one group I felt knee-jerk skepticism toward were men like David, who are aromantic but not asexual. I am a woman who has spent a decent chunk of my life listening to friends' horror stories about men, many of them jerks who wanted nothing but sex. Part of me remained suspicious that "aromantic but not asexual" was a cop-out for an immature man trying to justify bad behavior.

Intellectually, I knew this suspicion made little sense. If people can be asexual and not aromantic, they can be aromantic and not asexual. There's also no reason why only women could be aromantic and allosexual. It was always clear that my beliefs—that an aro-allo woman was independent while an aro-allo man was a fuckboy—were gendered stereotypes I should disavow. Still, it was hearing David talk about how these same stereotypes hurt him that changed the situation for me emotionally. Because he's male, people will say he's "just a horny guy" and a monster, he tells me, even though he really does care about others. "The friendships I have, I try to hold that close," he says. "Human connection is important and I think there are way more people who crave human connection than crave romance, if that makes sense."

Little doubt exists that someone will end up using aromanticism to defend cruelty. Don't fall for this. Callous behavior is a problem on its own terms, regardless of any kind of orientation. Lisa Wade, the Occidental sociologist and author of *American Hookup*, writes that the problem with hookups is not the casual sex itself but the culture that has developed around casual sex, which encourages people to treat each other coldly to show they don't have feelings. It is entirely possible to be clear about boundaries, to want sex without romance and treat others with kindness and respect.[27] That's not "using people for their bodies," it's communicating and entering a consensual agreement and it's the route David wants to go. He makes it clear from the beginning that he's not interested in dating but will do his best to be attentive, check in on others, and care for them.

Now, David is in a friends-with-benefits arrangement that seems, as he says, pretty much perfect. He enjoys giving relationship advice—"I feel like I can be more impartial"—and spends time on the aromanticism subreddit helping others who wonder whether they're aromantic or late bloomers or afflicted with emotional baggage and likely to change. Change is certainly possible, and fine too (though the existence of happily single people at every age suggests it's not inevitable). Just as with asexuality, the possibility of change should not justify disbelieving what someone says is their experience or being overly concerned that they might miss out on a part of life they currently don't want.

David has even started reaching out to people from the Men Going Their Own Way community. The societal expectations around romance that hurt him are the same ones that make incels feel lonely and isolated, so "being there to help them deconstruct romance as a concept has actually been fairly decent in terms of getting them to open up," he says. As for other people who think they might be aromantic, "the biggest piece of advice I always give is to just wait, you'll have [a sense of your identity] in time," David adds. Don't believe that you're sick for not wanting a romantic relationship. You're probably not going to find the answer on a Reddit thread, he tells them, but whatever you are is fine.

．．．．．．．．．．

Amatonormativity permeates more than TV shows and books. It is woven into our legal rights, creating forms of discrimination that become more and more apparent as people age. Romantic love within marriage confers privileges that other forms of devotion cannot, including over 1,100 laws that benefit married couples at the federal level. Spouses can share each other's health insurance, as well as military, social security, and disability benefits. They can make medical decisions for each other.[28] Companies grant bereavement leave for spouses, no questions asked, but there will be more hesitation if leave is requested for a mere friend. It is possible to marry a stranger and give them your health insurance but not possible to give health insurance to a parent.

Marriage, in its ideal form, is a promise of love and mutual responsibility, a declaration of importance in the eyes of everyone. That such a promise is celebrated and comes with legal benefits and special standing can make sense. That such a promise can only be made and legally recognized in romantic and sexual contexts does not. In debates over marriage, people on all sides "share an assumption that our most important non-blood relationships must be with people we have, or at least have had, sex with," writes philosopher Julian Baggini in *Prospect Magazine*.[29]

Criteria based on sex made sense when the main purpose of marriage was to merge fortunes and produce children, but today, as Baggini points out, marriage is more about a match of devotion than a match of trade. In many cases, the point is no longer to create an heir and a spare. Plenty of married couples don't have children (or sex, for that matter), and bad marriages with little caring are common.

One particularly poignant example of what happens when romance is required for rights occurred in 2012. That year, the Canadian government deported seventy-three-year-old Nancy Inferrera, an American woman who had lived with her eighty-three-year-old friend Mildred Sanford. The two had moved to Nova Scotia several years earlier and pooled their money to buy a $14,000 mobile home together. They were described as "inseparable," and Nancy helped take care of Mildred, who had dementia.[30] "Such a friendship serves one of the primary purposes of marriage—mutual long-term caretaking and companionship," writes Brake of the case. "As such, it deserves legal protections similar to those in marriage."[31] Yet, a couple in an abusive marriage would have received more protection from deportation than Nancy and Mildred did (though, seven years later, Nancy did finally gain permanent Canadian residency[32]).

Offering legal and social benefits only to the romantically attached suggests that the mere presence of romantic feeling elevates the care and deserves special protections, even though friendship and other forms of care, which can come with less obligation, can include more love, more freely given. Therefore, the legal and social privileges of marriage should be extended to all mutually consenting adults who wish for them.

Baggini advocates for allowing siblings or just very close friends to "have the same rights as those in civil partnerships."[33] Reed College political scientist Tamara Metz has argued that the state should recognize and support "intimate care-giving unions"[34] even if they are not sexual or romantic in nature. And Brake adds that extending these privileges will have a big effect in other areas too. "In terms of policy, marriage law really reaches into all areas of law, like tax and immigration and property," Brake tells me. "It doesn't matter if it's different-sex only or same-sex marriage, so long as we restrict marriage to romantic and sexual partners we will ensure amatonormativity." Reforming marriage law by abolishing it altogether or extending marriage-like rights to friends (to small groups or networks) is one way to eradicate discrimination.

· · · · · · · · ·

Jo the Australian policy worker originally identified as homoromantic. Even in the ace community, she explains, there's a narrative that romantic aces can have relationships and regular lives but aromanticism is one step further from normal. Using the label of homoromantic felt less confrontational and easier for both others and herself to accept. Today, Jo identifies as aromantic and is realizing that she will need to contend with amatonormativity for the rest of her life. Amatonormativity extends well beyond marriage, compounding and affecting the very fabric of society and our chances of flourishing in later years.

In the West, couples often pair up, marry, and then seclude themselves into a new, separate unit, sometimes retreating from their prior community of friends and family. With this as the norm, it becomes harder and harder for aros to build the social network they need. Milestones become bittersweet, like when Jo's best friend moved out to live with her boyfriend.

"I can't begrudge her for this, of course, and I am happy for her because she is happy," Jo says. "But it was hard because we had this really good thing going but I have now been deprioritized. This will probably keep happening for the rest of my life because that tends to be what people do. Their primary romantic relationship takes precedence over friendships and sometimes their family." Jo won't be the one moving out to live with a romantic partner, and that makes her both value friendship more and become frustrated when others don't value it as much. In the past few months, two of Jo's other friends have gotten engaged, emphasizing the lack of options for those who aren't interested in traditional romantic cohabitation.

"If only we could bring back Boston marriages," Jo says, referring to the arrangements of adult women living together in the late nineteenth century.[35] The term comes from such a relationship depicted in Henry James's novel *The Bostonians*, and though some in Boston marriages were lesbians, that was not always the case. Boston marriages were not glorified roommates but true partnerships that provided structure and companionship, which is what Jo wants: a non-romantic, cohabitating relationship, the "kind that would last for a lifetime."

Instead, amatonormativity makes Boston marriages uncommon and contributes to the problem of care in old age. When the nuclear family is the ideal, it is commonly assumed that members of the family (the children, the spouse) will act as unpaid caregivers later in life, leading to questions like, "Who will take care of you when you're old?"

"It's a pretty intense thing to worry about," says Julie Sondra Decker, who is aromantic and in her forties. Julie emphasizes that a romantic partner is not a perfect guarantee of future security. People get sick. People get divorced. "I think even if you're looking at having this sort of built-in support from another person, you need to look at your wider networks and other resources," she says. "It takes a lot of effort to maintain friendships and take them seriously, to understand how much you can give to other people. Sometimes I worry I cross the line into giving too much to someone, but I also know that those people will be there for me if I ever need anything, so there's no way I will be alone in this world."

Julie is right that it is possible to build a chosen family for support in later years. Justice Anthony Kennedy was wrong when he wrote that those who aren't married are "condemned to live in loneliness." It is still unfair that people worry that not having a romantic partner means they can't take care of themselves in old age. Amatonormativity and the assumption of free familial care have made it easier to ignore the necessity of changing welfare and labor laws to make eldercare more financially accessible and also to compensate the caregivers more fairly. When the infrastructure of care work and eldercare changes, it will help those who are aromantic, as well as everyone who has this worry—including the many people in the so-called sandwich generation, who have a nuclear family but drain their financial resources caring for ailing parents as well.[36] Many policy changes are necessary to ensure fairness for anyone who doesn't have, or doesn't want to have, a spouse and kids and a picket fence.

It is connection and personal fulfillment that count, not received ideas of what different types of relationships should look like or which forms of relating are superior. Life can take so many shapes and look like so many things, like devotion to family, friends, a cause. It can look like strong feelings for others even when those feelings don't slot neatly into categories, and falling in love without sexual desire. Simple stories—about passion equaling sex or passion reserved only for romance, about needing to be validated by the love of others and about friendship not being as important as that fuzzy category of romantic love—all distract. The effect of these stories is powerful. The disadvantages they can bring are real. But look a little closer, and the authority can begin to crack.

CHAPTER 8

THE GOOD-ENOUGH REASON

IF SOMEONE CANNOT SAY NO, any yes that is given is meaningless. The tricky thing is that James, an Asian programmer in Seattle, would have told you that he did feel like he could say no to his girlfriend. At the time. He remembers the constant conversations about why he didn't want to initiate sex though "that's what men are supposed to want," the arguments that ended with him giving up and having sex anyway, the shame at feeling that he was denying her. "But if I just went back and looked at the day after all these examples, I would have concluded that I did give consent," he says.

In his mind, as in many people's minds, it's okay to say no to a partner if you're having a bad day or have come down with the flu, if your job is especially stressful or if they're a bad partner who is hurting you. Those are some of the good-enough reasons. Not a good-enough reason? "I don't want to."

You see, if all humans have a baseline of sexual desire and nothing is currently wrong, saying no on a beautiful, happy day to a beautiful, happy partner means you are selfish and intentionally withholding. You don't want to be that kind of person and you love your partner. So you say yes.

"Now I feel more coerced," James says. After learning about asexuality, he knows that he could have said no forever, and that saying no didn't make him a bad person. New information paints the relationship in a different light and makes him think that the yes he gave before was compromised. The facts remain the same, but the interpretation has shifted. "Looking back now, I feel mad about it, like that's not anything that she had any right to do. I feel like I should have resisted more," he says. James's experience is an example of the worst outcome of overlooking the ace perspective in consent, which is that the likelihood of sexual coercion—and sexual violence—is elevated for everyone who has not yet learned about compulsory sexuality, a presence that is rarely challenged.

That doesn't mean James wants to go back and accuse his ex of sexual assault. The situation is more complicated. It means only that James now has another way to process and analyze his history. Before, when he was working from the premise that there are good reasons to refuse sex and bad reasons to refuse sex, he was experiencing what the philosopher Miranda Fricker calls "hermeneutical injustice," or the harm caused by being denied crucial information.[1]

All of us have had the experience of learning something and wishing that we had known it earlier. It can be as simple as *If I had known that my college roommate was in town, I would have tried to meet up with her.* Fricker's concept of hermeneutical injustice, however, is not about the fact that you missed a useful social announcement. That's individual bad luck. Hermeneutical justice is a structural phenomenon. It is about marginalized groups lacking access to information essential to their understanding of themselves and their role in society—and these groups lack this information precisely *because* they are marginalized and their experiences rarely represented.

It is, as Fricker uses in one example, *If I knew about the concept of postpartum depression, my experience would have made more sense and I'd have felt less guilty and not blamed myself so much.* It is, in another classic example, *If I had known about the idea of sexual harassment, I could have more easily interpreted and explained what was happening.* Hermeneutical injustice is present in stories like the one that James shared, which is itself a template for experiences that I have heard again and again from aces.

In these cases, coercion doesn't look like stereotypical images of inadequate consent. It's not fraternity parties or strangers at bars after heavy drinking. It can seem, to all accounts, completely normal, like the committed couple who get along well and are good for each other. Here, common assumptions that underlie most discussions of consent—that sex with strangers is never necessary, but sex in relationships is a requirement—fall short. Messages that everyone wants sex *sometimes* make people feel like they have to say yes *sometimes*. If you have to say yes sometimes, better to say it to a partner, because sex is supposed to be good when you're in love.

So coercion looks like being told that you would have sex if you really loved someone. It feels like being afraid to see your partner because you don't want to keep denying them sex. It feels like, as activist Queenie of Aces writes, making a list of all the reasons you shouldn't have sex now (not old enough, haven't been dating long enough, birth control access could be a problem) but never knowing that the real reason—that you don't want to—is the only one you need.[2] It feels like wishing that you were religious so you could at least use religious celibacy as an excuse. It feels like being hurt by having to have sex and learning that you shouldn't have had to have it because there's nothing wrong with not wanting sex ever—and looking back and revoking consent, in your own mind if nowhere else.

Guilt and shame and anger: Shame at saying yes, anger at not knowing you didn't have to say yes, shame at not standing your ground and saying no, anger at partners for not telling you to say no, guilt at being angry because no one knew better. And in so many cases, the same conclusion, one that ace blogger StarchyThoughts summed up beautifully:

> I blamed my ex for a while—why did he push it when I said no so many times before? why did he enjoy it when I was clearly disinterested?—but that didn't feel quite right. I said yes multiple times, and people can't read minds. So then I was back to blaming myself. Perhaps if I truly felt so strongly that I didn't want to have sex, I would have said no every time. But that doesn't encapsulate the pressure and feeling of brokenness that I felt—the unspoken social norm that because I didn't have a "good" reason to "deny" him, saying yes was a given. The problem is that I was left with no way to explain my hurt. On the surface, it shouldn't have been a big deal: he said yes, I said yes, therefore everything was consensual. The problem is, *had I known about asexuality*, I would have said no. It felt like a wrong had occurred, even though there was no one to blame. And that is hermeneutical injustice.[3]

· · · · · · · · · ·

Nearly everyone agrees that there's no reason to have sex with a stranger if you don't want to. Add the context of a relationship and this rule is suddenly weakened. Consensus is gone. It's easier to support the person who always says no to a stranger than the person who always says no to a spouse, but understandings of consent won't be complete unless we grapple with the realities of negotiating with loved ones. Aces can and do feel pressured to have sex with strangers, but it is within relationships that the guilt can be strongest and setting boundaries the most difficult. Within relationships, the desire to have sex and the desire *not* to have sex are so often treated unequally because of the common belief that entering a relationship requires giving up a measure of consent.[4]

Typically, this means the woman giving in to the man because of the idea that men need sex and women need to serve male desire. The logic is sometimes based in traditional gender roles, sometimes in economic or religious ideas. The notion is not a relic of the far past. The 1962 US Model Penal Code, an influential text that helped legislators revise criminal law, specified that rape was forced sex against someone with whom one is *not* in a relationship.[5] The belief that marital rape is acceptable is so widespread that when reports surfaced that Donald Trump's ex-wife Ivana had accused him of rape, Trump's attorney Michael Cohen defended his client by saying that "you can't rape your spouse."[6]

Marital rape is illegal, but it took a long time to get to that point. In 1979, then California state senator Bob Wilson jokingly posed the following questions to a group of female lobbyists: "If you can't rape your wife, who can you rape?"[7] Lawmakers in the state of Virginia didn't make it possible for someone to be prosecuted for spousal rape until 2002. During that debate, Virginia politician Richard Black made a speech against criminalizing spousal rape, arguing that it would be impossible to prove that rape had happened when the husband and wife are sleeping in the same bed and "she's in a nightie."[8] Today, several states still treat spousal rape and non-spousal rape differently.[9] In all these circumstances, the message is that it's not *really* rape when it happens in the context of a relationship.

Never mind the law. Culturally, there is no consensus on sexual rights within relationships. Conservative lawyer Phyllis Schlafly, for example, has said that "by getting married, the woman has consented to sex, and I don't think you can call it rape."[10] Phyllis Schlafly may be famous for being anti-feminist, but here she is expressing a doubt that many people across the political spectrum have felt. Articles in mainstream magazines like *Essence*[11] and *HuffPost*[12] answer questions about whether having sex is a duty in marriage. People post the same question on sites like Quora[13] and MetaFilter,[14] wondering how far their obligations extend.

The questions don't always stem from a sense of ironclad external duty either. They can arise from our desire to do well by those we love and who love us. The stranger at the bar whom we reject can find someone else, curse us in their mind, and get over it. A partner will feel the pain far more acutely. Rejection is more personal, especially if they believe that we are saying no for no good reason. If we're monogamous, they can't have sex with someone else. Their unhappiness is real and enduring.

· · · · · · · · · ·

And still, aces reject the idea of the good-enough reason. Every no is good enough, and that goes for every person. If we believe that people shouldn't have unwanted sex with strangers and that strangers are not entitled to sex, we should believe that people shouldn't have unwanted sex with partners and that partners, no matter how loving or good, are not entitled to sex either. As long as people don't know about asexuality—hell, forget about the label, so long as they don't know that saying no forever and for any reason and in any context is okay—sex education, sex therapy, and popular depictions of sex are incomplete and people don't have the relevant information to fully consent.

Sexual rights should not be assumed and self-determination must never end upon entering a relationship. You can give a no with zero caveats in each and every situation, full stop. You can say no if someone loves you and you love them back. You can say no for the rest of your life. Loving another person should never mean forfeiting bodily autonomy.

It is common for one partner to want to regain or enhance their sex drive; working toward that goal is fine. It is also common for one partner to feel pressured to do that work while the other partner does nothing. That is not fine.

Low desire is not the problem. Just think: if both partners had equal levels of low desire, it would be no issue. Incompatibility is the problem, and incompatibility is a shared problem that will require a shared solution. Aces say, over and over, that it is not morally correct to automatically privilege the preferences of the person who wants to have sex. If one person wants to have sex just as much as the other person wants *not* to have sex, the desires are equal, and one desire should not trump the other. (Not to mention that, when it comes to strangers, most people are quick to agree that it's more important to respect the wishes of the person who doesn't want to have sex than those of the person who does.)

Yet it is so easy to unconsciously adopt an attitude of being a burden, of one's needs mattering less. Hermeneutical injustice can be the norm, and unspoken social rules are powerful in their invisibility. Asking a person to work on themselves to have more sex seems natural and intuitive, but imagine asking the allo partner to be celibate. It's barely thinkable. Pharmaceutical companies want to sell libido boosters, not develop a drug that can lower libido. In an interview with *The Cut* about helping couples with sexual problems, a sex therapist says that it "really boils down to the person who feels the aversion."[15] And as sociologist Thea Cacchioni has extensively studied, women especially feel so much individual responsibility to work on their sexuality and make sure their shared sex life is great.[16]

Alicia, the feminist scholar with an allo partner, didn't necessarily think that she was broken, but she cycled through medications for years, trying to "fix" her uninterest in sex. "I had enough confidence in the back of my mind the whole time to ask myself, Is this really a problem?" she says. "But without asexuality—the language, the community—I didn't know what else to do. I was trying to fix *something*. Discovering asexuality has freed me from that."

Of course, just as one person has the right to say no forever, the other has the right to prioritize their own sexual needs. For the higher-desire partner, the difference between setting boundaries and being coercive is the difference between saying that you respect preferences but sex is a deal-breaker and saying that your partner is wrong and sick and would have sex if they weren't wrong and sick. The higher-desire partner has the right to know what to expect and they're not in the wrong for leaving because of sexual reasons. For what it's worth, I do believe that sex can be a justifiable deal-breaker in any direction. (The next chapter will discuss how ace-allo couples work together.) I have watched allo friends go to therapy because of a sexual mismatch, try to work it out, and hold on; I have seen how they remained miserable and counseled them to end the relationship. Differences in libido can be a source of shame for both sides, and claiming that sex shouldn't matter at all or judging someone for wanting to leave is not helpful. If sex is important, let sex be important. It's okay to leave and have sex with someone who wants to have sex with you. Just remember that leaving for sexual reasons does not mean the other person was wrong.

• • • • • • • • •

Narratives about the ubiquity of sexual desire do more than make it hard to say no; when oversimplified, they also make it hard to speak honestly about sexual experiences. Compulsory sexuality lurks behind the popular slogan "Rape is not sex, it's violence," an idea popularized by the feminist writer Susan Brownmiller in her groundbreaking 1975 book *Against Our Will: Men, Women, and Rape.* The book, which brought the problem of rape into national consciousness, argued that rape was often symbolic, motivated by desire for control instead of desire for sex, and is a way for men to control women and keep them in "a state of fear."[17] The publication of *Against Our Will* helped kick off a wave of anti-rape activism and laid the groundwork for modern understanding of rape culture, supporting the claim that victim-blaming arguments about a woman sexually tempting the rapist are nonsense.

As a slogan, "Rape is not sex, it's violence" quickly pervaded popular culture and has been a rallying call for decades. Gloria Steinem called the phrase a truism.[18] The idea that rape is not sex has been mentioned in *New York Times* articles from 1989[19] to 2017.[20] In 2016, a consent pledge created by behavioral scientists trying to reduce sexual assault on campus included the words "non-consensual sex is not sex, it is violence."[21] The heyday of the exact phrase has passed but the idea has not, and many people repeat similar ideas, almost always with good intentions.

It is true that rape is often used as a political tool. It is true that arguments over what a victim was wearing are specious and a distraction and that rape is underreported.[22] It is right for people to protest upon seeing headlines like "Fifty-Five-Year-Old Man Accused of Having Sex with Ten-Year-Old." A ten-year-old cannot consent, so what happened must be called rape, not sex. Rape and sex are not interchangeable terms. I cannot emphasize this enough.

But the idea that rape is not sex at all—and that rape is completely distinct from sex—is inaccurate as well. The tacit extension of "rape is not sex" is "rape is bad and sex is good." "Rape is not sex" therefore tries to rescue sex because if rape is forced and violent and bad and it is *not* sex, then sex itself must be *not* forced and *not* violent and good. "To say 'rape is violence, not sex' preserves the 'sex is good' norm by simply distinguishing forced sex as 'not sex,' whether it means sex to the perpetrator or even, later, to the victim, who has difficulty experiencing sex without re-experiencing the rape," wrote Catharine MacKinnon in a 1989 journal article on pleasure under patriarchy. "Whatever is sex cannot be violent; whatever is violent cannot be sex."[23] The world does not work this way. The result of such an attitude is that, as MacKinnon summarizes in a different article, "so long as we say that [rape, pornography, sexual harassment, sexual violence] are abuses of violence, not sex, we fail to criticize what has been made of sex, what has been done to us through sex, because we leave the line between rape and intercourse, sexual harassment and sex roles, pornography and eroticism, right where it is."[24]

Sex describes a type of encounter. It can be good and it can be bad and forced and unforced and everything in-between, including forced and unforced within the same encounter. "Rape is not sex" creates a binary, but sexual experience and consent are not binaries. There are different types of sexual experience and different types of consent, so a two-part framing is inadequate. In many cases, a clear line cannot be drawn between rape and sex and trying to do so does not serve us. "Rape is not sex" makes it easy for everyone to agree that this separate, scary, forced sex called rape is bad without dealing with the dynamics that drive the enormous spectrum of sexual encounters that are at least partially consensual and also violent, consensual and also damaging, consensual and also coerced.

Most people don't know about asexuality, so people who might otherwise identify as asexual are especially vulnerable to sexual pressure. Aces say yes to sex we don't really want. So does almost everyone else. In one

2005 study, 28 percent of women said their first sexual experience was consensual but not exactly wanted."[25] In another study of 160 college students in relationships, more than a third reported having consented to unwanted sex within a span of two weeks.[26] The existence of all those questions about the "duty to sex" in marriage shows that this is also a common problem for people who aren't young college students. "Multiple times I have given explicit consent to partners, but mentally I didn't want to do that," says Sebastian, the model from Canada. "Even if somebody had picked up on my body language, I would still have said, 'No, it's fine, keep going,' because then you deal with feelings of guilt and shame for not wanting it." In all of these cases, there is some form of yes and some form of no.

A simple platitude, "Rape is not sex" cannot take into account all these subtleties and instead leads people to wonder how to process a consensual, negative experience and how they're allowed to feel afterward. It doesn't provide a way to think about how much force (physical, cultural, or emotional) is necessary for the designation of rape and how to think about the meaning of coerced sex that falls just shy of that mark. If you said yes but your body language didn't seem particularly enthusiastic, then is it not rape but sex, which is good? Then why didn't you feel good? Did you forfeit your right to have regrets and your rights to feel bad and to claim harm?

I'm simplifying, of course, but mostly because the binary is too simple. Being forced to decide between violent rape and pleasurable sex can require going around in circles. In reality, adding some amount of pressure or violence can simply turn sex into more violent sex—but not forced or violent enough that anyone, including the person who had sex, would be comfortable calling it rape. It is also possible to feel violated when you said yes, or violated because of trauma from past encounters, even if the other person did nothing wrong in the present.

A broader perspective is necessary to account for these realities. Rape is not interchangeable with sex, but it is a form of sex and the lines can blur. Rape is terrible and violent. Sex can also feel terrible and violent even if nobody thinks it was rape, even when there are good intentions and no grounds to prosecute. Harmful, consensual sex happens and people should be allowed to speak freely using those terms. Those who have been harmed by sex deserve support regardless of whether they consented. Everyone should acknowledge the other side too, that we can hurt someone even if we did not mean to and even if we checked in and tried to do due diligence.

An attitude that sex is good also ignores the needs of ace survivors of sexual violence. Organizers of the group Resources for Ace Survivors have worked with sexual violence hotlines to teach volunteers how to help this group. Members of organizations like GLAAD and the Rape, Abuse & Incest National Network obviously mean well, activists tell me, but counseling often veers into the territory of "This wasn't sex, sex is beautiful, and you will love it again." Such a message is comforting for many but doesn't suit the needs of people who didn't care for sex before and don't need to enjoy it again or be told that something that hurt them is beautiful.

It is not necessary to prove that sex is inherently good. It is not. For some, it is never good and never wanted, no matter how seemingly ideal the circumstance or how caring the partner. Mixed experiences, mixed layers of agency, and mixed attitudes toward sex all exist, and honoring these is more important than clinging to the idea that sex is by default nice, or that there always exist conditions under which it can be wonderful. Sex is complicated, and accepting what happens and how people feel—even if it transgresses expectations of how things are supposed to happen and how people are supposed to feel—is the first step toward healing.

• • • • • • • • • •

Because "Rape is not sex" is a false binary, so is "No means no" and "yes means yes." These popular models of consent offer only two options: yes and no, which map onto sex and rape. An overhaul to thinking about consent will require many changes in perspective, beginning with the necessity of breaking this binary of rape and sex and thinking instead about different levels of willingness. One useful tool is a framework created by sex researcher Emily Nagoski, author of *Come As You Are: The Surprising New Science That Will Transform Your Sex Life*, and amended by aces. Nagoski suggests using the categories of enthusiastic, willing, unwilling, and coerced consent, although the last two are consent mostly in the extremely literal sense that someone did not yell out "no."

ENTHUSIASTIC CONSENT:

When I *want* you

When I don't fear the consequences of saying yes OR saying no

When saying no means missing out on something I want

WILLING CONSENT:

When I care about you though I don't desire you (right now)

When I'm pretty sure saying yes will have an okay result and I think maybe that I'd regret saying no

When I believe that desire may begin after I say yes

UNWILLING CONSENT:

When I fear the consequences of saying no more than I fear the consequences of saying yes

When I feel not just an absence of desire but an absence of *desire for desire*

When I hope that by saying yes, you will stop bothering me, or think that if I say no you'll only keep on trying to persuade me

COERCED CONSENT:

When you threaten me with harmful consequences if I say no

When I feel I'll be hurt if I say yes, but I'll be hurt more if I say no

When saying yes means experiencing something I actively dread[27]

Nagoski's model is better than "no means no," which assumes that someone is saying yes unless otherwise stated. Unlike models that emphasize enthusiastic consent ("yes means yes"), it doesn't imply that aces who can't give enthusiastic consent are unable to consent at all, which would wrongly place us in the same category as children and animals. It expands the "yes means yes" slogan by pointing out all the possible varieties of yes.

Nagoski's model has been popular in the ace community because it makes room for sex-indifferent or sex-favorable aces and takes into account the practical realities of aces in relationships with allos. The balance between willing and unwilling can be delicate, but distinguishing the two is imperative. "I'm not horny, but I'm glad to have sex to feel closer to my partner" and "I'm not horny, but I said yes so you'd stop pressuring me" both have elements of being consensual but unwanted. Neither is a perfect yes or a perfect no. Nagoski's model marks them differently, making room for the exceedingly common experience of maintenance sex, or sex for the sake of a relationship.

For aces who do have sex, the difference between willing and unwilling is not one of action but one of intention and agency. Willing means choosing to have sex with someone because you love them and will get something out of it. Unwilling means believing you have to have sex with someone because you love them, even if doing so harms you. As Hunter, the man who grew up in a religious household, said, having sex for his wife's sake was completely fine—the awful part had been the pressure he put on himself to have sex and the constant questioning about why he didn't love sex for its own sake.

Rethinking consent doesn't require reinventing the wheel. Another useful idea comes from the kink community, which has long been ahead of the curve when it comes to best practices. Kink, in the popular imagination, is all about sex, sex, sex; kink for aces can be about everything but. It is about power and emotion, role-play and interesting sensations and about getting away from the pressures of sex, sex, sex. In fact, kinky aces say that community norms help them negotiate consent in a supportive way that leaves more room for saying no.

In the vanilla community, sex is usually assumed to be part of any romantic relationship. If two people fool around and one becomes aroused, the other person (usually a woman in heterosexual contexts) can feel responsible for helping the other person "finish," lest they be considered a tease or killjoy. One thing is supposed to naturally lead to another, then to sex. A lack of consent is built into the system, and saying no is a burden that comes with a price to pay.

Play partners, on the other hand, don't assume that sex—or anything—is a given. In the kink community, everything is negotiated (or at least is supposed to be) beforehand. "In a scene, I can say, 'I don't care if you get hard, I don't care if you get wet, as long as you don't expect me to do anything about it, or only do certain things about it,'" says Cassie, the ace therapist in Chicago, who adds that they've found the kink community to be safer than the vanilla community. Such changes provide automatic structure and boundaries that are frequently missing in the vanilla context. Acts are more sequestered, not part of a domino effect that ends up requiring something that a person does not want to do. It is clear that consent is conditional, meaning that yes to kissing doesn't automatically mean yes to oral sex as well.

It's not just that someone *can* negotiate, but rather that negotiation is the standard, so people feel less hesitant for trying to do so. Negotiation is considered less of a libido-killing ritual and more like a sensible, taken-for-granted practice, so much of the burden of no is lifted.

Formal precautions are wise, but consent cannot always be perfectly hashed out beforehand. Desires can be hard to predict and frequently change in the moment. Nothing is foolproof, but, ultimately, true consent is an attitude of respecting what the other person might want to do with any part of their body at any time. It is the mindset that it's not okay to progress unless there's approval, but that approval (and disapproval) can be signaled in the moment and in many forms. A shifting process sounds trickier to navigate than a contract or preset rules, but it can be more intuitive and safer. As scholar Meg-John Barker explains in their book *Enjoy Sex (How, When, and If You Want To)*: "The idea [of consent] is to really tune into yourself, the other person or people and the experience, rather than just doing something from habit, doing something 'to' another person, or—on the other hand—talking about it without actually having a sense of the experience and the ongoing process."[28]

For those who have sex, these ideas—breaking the binary of yes and no, norms that encourage discussion—must be combined with always checking in. Checking in doesn't mean stopping for a five-minute discussion in legalese. It requires paying attention to—and wanting to pay attention to—all forms of information. Nonverbal communication in particular is important because social pressures can make it hard for some to speak up and verbally say no. "I'm autistic and people are always telling me that 95 percent of communication is nonverbal and tell me it's important to make efforts to understand that," says Lola Phoenix, a writer in London. "And then when it comes to consent it's suddenly like, 'Why didn't they say something? No one is a mind reader!' That's really hypocritical."

Paying attention to nonverbal cues can provide a much fuller picture. Enthusiastic consent for kissing at the beginning can turn into willing consent for touching later on and then withdrawn consent, all signaled in different ways. It may also be helpful, as those in the kink community do, to consider fluid, expansive concepts like harm and trust. Regardless of intent, did the other person harm me? How much trust did they take the time to build and how much do I trust them now and how does that change our relationship? The more trust there is, the less explicit negotiation may be necessary, and evaluating the amount of trust between two partners beforehand and how both felt afterward can be more fruitful than evaluating whether one person should have said something else.

The process of consent should be more like developing a friendship than signing an employment letter. Friendship takes many different forms and is not given by one person to the other. It is mutual and reciprocal and created over time. We don't assume that if someone says yes to getting coffee that they'll also say yes to attending an amateur improv show or that both people need to know (or can even know) beforehand exactly how the friendship will change and grow. We don't think that being open to friendship means someone is obligated to be a friend forever, or that others are equally enthusiastic about every part of friendship.

Thinking of consent as a shifting process makes it easier to understand how it might work in long-term relationships, for aces and allos and everyone. Consent matters after ten years just as much as after ten days, but it rarely looks the same after a decade as it did on the third date. Checks and balances that are crucial earlier on become unnecessary for both people now that they know each other better and can read each other's cues. The forms consent takes will change, but the right to say no always must remain. If someone never wants to have sex, that is okay forever. For people who do decide to have sex, it is a choice each time, not a set of ossified obligations that are impossible to challenge or change.

■ CHAPTER 9 ■

PLAYING WITH OTHERS

WITHOUT REALLY BEING TAUGHT, most of us know what a romantic relationship is supposed to look like: heterosexual, often; monogamous, usually; sexual, pretty much always. Relationships are like an escalator, and a successful relationship is one that goes up and up and up, from a romantic relationship to marriage, then having kids. Running parallel to the relationship escalator is the escalator of touch, or, as they are commonly known, the sexual "bases": hand-holding to feeling up to oral sex to penis-in-vagina intercourse (a "home run"). Sex is the reward and the ultimate destination on the journey. Anything else means getting stuck.

I knew all this, though I couldn't have told you exactly how I learned or been able to point to who shared this knowledge. I also knew people who didn't follow these rules exactly, yet their relationships still highlighted the existence of the rules because they so often felt the need to justify any deviation from the expected. The exception proves the rule, even when the rule is mostly unspoken and unquestioned.

Selena, the Bay Area workplace consultant, also believed that relationships should look a certain way, that they had to come prepackaged and ready-made. Selena might have spent her entire life believing this—if not for the fact that the first time she had sex, freshman year of college, she found herself inspecting her fingernails and then wondering why she was thinking about her manicure when she was supposed to be in the throes of passion.

It's possible that it was just bad sex, but Selena's girlfriend, Georgia, was "all glowy" and happy afterward. A few more experiments made it clear that sex wasn't what Selena had expected it to be. Selena wanted to want, but it wasn't enough. And if sex wasn't what Selena had expected it to be, the relationship itself would not be what the two of them had anticipated. So Selena and Georgia began to talk, setting out the terms and asking questions where before they had operated from an assumption. They asked each other: How much time did they really want to spend together? What types of physicality and touch were okay and what didn't do it for one or the other or either? Did they want to have sex?

Georgia's answer to the last question was yes. Selena's answer to the last question was no.

. . . .

Aces are not the only ones who can have very particular requirements for dating and relationships. Take the Amish and Orthodox Jewish communities, for example. Their cultural rules around dating might seem unusual by the standards of liberal culture, but they solve this problem by dating other members of their communities. Aces, however, don't cluster in geographical enclaves or have our own long-established dating traditions. The numbers aren't on our side, either. Keeping in mind the official statistic that aces are about 1 percent of the population[1]—not to mention that being asexual isn't usually the most important factor in romantic compatibility—most end up entering the wider dating pool and trying to make a relationship work with an allo partner.

The truth is that if aces were forced to have traditional relationships, many of us would end up alone, or partnered but unhappy. To avoid this, it becomes necessary to challenge the conventional wisdom of how relationships are supposed to work, starting with the ur-belief, the one that can be found at the bottom of almost everything else: that sex is one of our most primal instincts, as natural and automatic as breathing.

This is wrong. We don't have sex purely from instinctive drive. Biology does play a part—it can create the feelings and urges—but biology alone does not tell us what those urges represent and what they lead to. Human physiology provides "a set of physical possibilities unlabeled as to use or meaning," writes sex researcher Leonore Tiefer in her 1995 essay collection *Sex Is Not a Natural Act*.[2] Culture—like books and movies and what parents say and what we see everyone else doing—then teaches a story to attach to these sensations. Individual psychology and context also play a part. A beating heart and sweaty palms can be interpreted as anxiety or excitement. In one famous psychology experiment, men were asked to walk across either a swaying bridge or a sturdy bridge. All were approached by a pretty woman who asked them to fill out a survey and told them to call if they had any questions. The men on the swaying bridge were more likely to call the woman, because they interpreted their physical fear from the surroundings as attraction to the researcher.[3] Sensation plus story.

In the sexual realm, even basic acts can signify very different things. Remember the masturbation paradox and how it's odd that aces who masturbate are considered to lack a sexuality? Some of the aces who masturbate consider it sexual, but others don't. To them, masturbation is like any other bodily quirk, no different from scratching an itch on the arm.

Kissing is another example of the slipperiness of the sexual. In most Western cultures, kissing is considered a non-negotiable step on the road to a romantic relationship. Yet when groups as diverse as the Mehinaku of Brazil, the Thonga of South Africa, and the Trobriand Islanders first encountered the act, they perceived it as disgusting instead of a mark of affection.[4] Today, romantic kissing is still not a universal human act. In one 2015 study, anthropologists surveyed 168 cultures and found that fewer than half of them engaged in what they called "romantic-sexual kissing."[5] Kissing can be a learned act, not something done by everyone around the world and throughout time.

Similarly, the concept of sex itself is constructed. The word conjures up images of penis-in-vagina penetration, even though that's a limiting way to think about sex and the many other ways of having sex and being sexual. "We tend to think that sex is immune to social forces," Lisa Wade, the sociologist at Occidental College, tells me. "We fetishize sex as this unique asocial, ahistorical, acultural force, just something that bubbles up from inside of us and is completely primal. But that of course is not true."

Rather, social context colors almost every situation. A woman visiting the gynecologist does not consider herself to be engaging in sexual behavior with the gynecologist; she thinks she is undergoing a medical exam. Giving a backrub to a romantic partner might be the same physical action as giving a backrub to a relative, but the intention and feelings provoked are very different.

Society teaches what sex is, how to have sex, how much sex to have, how to feel about that sex, and what a good sex life is. It provides sexual scripts and rules to follow. Sex advice books, which frequently push the narrative of sex as a primal act, socialize us too.[6] They teach what sex means for relationship health and what types of sex are good and bad—and in doing so, amusingly, disprove their own claim about sex as an immutable drive. If sex is completely natural and biological, why does anyone need this industry of sex experts at all? Why are there sex manuals dating back centuries?[7] Why do we need *Cosmopolitan* to tell us how to do it, when we far more rarely see guidebooks for how to digest and how to breathe?

· · · · · · · · ·

The scripted nature of sex and relationships became clear to James, the Seattle programmer, once he started dating an ace woman. For the first time in his life, James realized that he didn't know whether he liked kissing. In previous relationships, he kissed without thinking, mostly to signal interest and keep the relationship moving forward. Romantic relationships involved kissing; that was a rule.

Since James is a man who dates women, another implicit rule—the expectation that men take the lead—gave him a good amount of control over when or how quickly he initiated sex. The initiation itself, though, always felt non-negotiable. "I definitely feared losing attention," James says. "There's an expectation that after a certain number of dates that if some things haven't happened, you're not interested." There was a sense that feelings "were not really real unless we're doing certain things," he adds. Without the steady infusion of sexual attention, the woman might think that the relationship was off or that it was a bad sign that he couldn't be like everyone else and follow the rules. Kissing was so mandatory that it no longer even registered as mandatory. James never thought to question whether kissing brought him any pleasure.

As she's explored her own ace identity, James's girlfriend has found that she doesn't want to do anything beyond cuddling. Along the way, James has had to unlearn some of what he has been taught about how physical intimacy is linked to emotional intimacy and how dating is supposed to progress. "A lot of the things that I would do, I really don't need to do anymore and in fact shouldn't do here," he says. Behavior that would have been a red flag for others turns out to be what she prefers. The first few times they hung out together, James caught himself planning how he would break the touch barrier, a step that would usually be necessary a couple of dates in at the latest. It felt odd to not have to worry about that, and it was a little disorienting to notice how he was so used to always strategizing the next move. "Now I've become a little more comfortable with letting whatever happens, happen," he says. "I have to perform less."

Romantic relationships without kissing aren't normal in American society, insofar as *normal* means *common*. Sleeping in separate beds or living apart or swinging aren't normal. All these choices face stigma because of the power of normal, but normal and widespread matter far more in relationships than they should. *Normal* is often treated as a moral judgment, when it is often simply a statistical matter. The question of what everyone else is doing is less important than the question of what works for the two people in the actual relationship. It matters that everyone's needs are carefully considered and respected, not that everyone is doing the same thing.

Relationship rules are laws of nature. Natural law cannot be defied. Gravity will pull you back to the ground no matter how much thinking and questioning you do about physics. But though sex and relationships have biological and physical components, they are also interpretations that come from our mind and the minds of others, so it is possible to reframe and start anew. Relationships should always be a game of mix and match, not a puzzle that you have to perfectly snap into, or a Jenga tower that will collapse as soon as you try to wiggle one block out of place. Customizability is the best part, yet most people try so hard to make their relationship stick to its premade form, a one-size-fits-all shape. Many people don't take advantage of their own freedom.

But they can, and this is good news for aces. Aces, along with other queer communities, have been questioning sexual and relationship scripts for a long time. You have to, when your starting point is on the outside of most scripts. This is good news for allos too, who may be happier opting out of default patterns even if they can fit in. Ace-allo relationships, like all relationships, take creativity, patience, and vulnerability and require both partners to investigate and then violate the lessons we are taught about sex, to interrogate and reframe their own beliefs and desires and beliefs about desires.

• • • • • • • • • •

Sex, in addition to being primal, is supposedly non-negotiable. "It does not seem to be enough to take reader interest in sex for granted, rather sex has to be promoted as absolutely vital," observe the authors of *Mediated Intimacy: Sex Advice in Media Culture*, an academic study of popular sex advice. It is not just vital for a person, but also absolutely vital for any relationship.[8] Sex, according to this popular advice, is the glue that holds people together and keeps relationships from collapsing. The *Mediated Intimacy* scholars quote from sex advice books that tell people that they "owe it to themselves" to leave if there's no sex and to declare the lack of sex a deal-breaker.[9] Other problems can be endured but sexual problems, apparently less so. Without sex, it seems, the health of the relationship and the feelings between partners are always doomed.

Such is the lesson being taught to the masses. Specialized sex therapy books for professionals echo many of the same ideas,[10] according to ace blogger Anagnori, who is studying to be a therapist. Well-meaning guides usually point out that sexual norms are too rigid and that everyone would be happier if we stopped worrying about having sex exactly like everyone else. However, almost no books go on to say that it's okay if someone doesn't want to have sex at all. Constrictions need to be loosened, but not too much. The underlying assumption is that sex in relationships is imperative and everything else—the amount of sex, the number of partners, the positions, the toys—follows from that axiom.

Accordingly, sex therapists and other relationship experts like to focus on the social factors—for example, sex feeling like an obligation or one person's sexual pleasure being prioritized over the other's—that can often be responsible for low sexual desire, especially for women. It is true that these factors often play an enormous role. But accepting asexuality requires accepting that these social factors are not always the cause. It is true that sexuality and attraction are social and psychological, as well as biological. It is also true that, sometimes, changing one of these factors cannot fully override the influence of the others. Sometimes, changing the relationship or thinking about sex differently won't change the level of sexual desire. Sometimes, as in the case of Kendra, the Black ace writer, everything else can be great and someone just doesn't want to have sex.

Kendra was a virgin when she began dating her boyfriend. Years later, when she told him she was asexual, his first response was that maybe it was because of him, that she needed to try other people because he doesn't do it for her sexually. "I had to make him see that wanting to have sex wasn't about him at all," and had nothing to do with his attractiveness, she says, "and when he finally grasped that, it was like a light bulb went off." Her low sexual desire was not a reflection of him or the quality of their relationship.

The logical implication of these messages about the necessity of sex is that asexuality is an existential threat to any hope of a lasting relationship. Asexuality begins to feel like a twisted, reverse version of the scarlet A, a modern brand that now stands for *ace* and *alone*. It's no wonder that people hate the idea that they might be ace, if not wanting sex for any reason is a death sentence for romance. Tellingly, this cultural lesson has power even if neither person in the relationship actually wants to have more sex.

Brian and Alison are a couple who haven't had sex in twenty years.[11] He's fine with it. She's fine with it. They don't feel fine about the fact that they feel fine, because "sexless marriage" is an extremely negative term. It's all too easy to be haunted by the worry that a relationship without sex is broken, or is about to be, even if the members are happy. Maybe the two people don't know it yet. Brian and Alison, who were profiled in *The Guardian*, can keep their sexless marriage secret from others, but the interpretation of that phrase still bothers the couple themselves. Brian and Alison are not their real names.

Both questioned their own experiences and their own happiness. They joined a support group for celibate couples. "It did worry me that I didn't want anything more than kisses and cuddles, and even when we had sex I knew 'nice' wasn't the word most people use to describe it," Alison told *The Guardian*. "But I don't want other people to know because sex seems to be such a big thing to everyone else. I don't have to justify our marriage to other people, but it's almost like I have to justify it to myself."[12]

Far more common than celibate relationships are ones where the partners do have sex, just not as much as one person would like. Though this situation is frustrating, the reality is that a mismatch can be inevitable—the question is how much and for how long. According to the 2013 National Survey of Sexual Attitudes and Lifestyles (NATSAL), a major survey in the United Kingdom that comes out every decade, among those in relationships in the past year, about one-fourth reported not having the same amount of sexual interest as their partner.[13] A mismatch should be treated as an expected issue, not like one person's fault or a mistake. Sex advice in books and magazines can create the impression that no one should settle for anything less than an amazing sex life, but in the long run it might be more helpful to emphasize how common mediocre sex is, rather than portray it as a terrible embarrassment.

I do believe that certain aspects of relationships, like mutual respect and trust and kindness, are essential rights. I don't believe that a great sex life always needs to be part of this list. Or rather, I believe that people should decide for themselves what matters in relationships regardless of what others say.

The sex writer Lux Alptraum, author of Faking It: The Lies Women Tell About Sex—And the Truths They Reveal, remembers when a college friend got engaged and insisted that her fiancé was the best sex she'd ever had. This had to be the case, the friend said, because she would never have agreed to marry someone who provided merely okay sex. "That left a huge mark on me, until I started thinking, 'What does it even mean to have the "best sex"?'" Alptraum says to me. "What does sex even mean and is the 'best' sex the most exciting sex or the softest and most comfortable? You get to realizing that your life partner realistically needs to be so many things and sex doesn't have to be at the top." Rarely does a perfect correlation between sexual chemistry and relationship quality exist (or last), and the people with whom Alptraum has been most sexually compatible haven't necessarily been those that were the best for the relationships she wanted. "For me, there's a baseline of pleasure and there are so many other things about a person that makes them worth it," she says.

Sexual incompatibility is challenging. So are many other parts of relationships. Every relationship is strained by so many factors—over the eternal return of the same serious fights over spending money, raising children, or taking care of aging parents—yet sexual problems can seem pathetic in a way that is not true of these other situations. Sex can be a reason to leave, but it doesn't need to automatically be more of a reason to leave than any other important issue. One ace woman who has been with her partner for years simply told me, "It's a problem for us." The two fight about sex often, just like they fight about other things too. They still think it's worth it to stay together.

The idea that it is okay for sex to be lackluster, or an ongoing source of tension if other aspects are worth it, is freeing for some ace-allo couples I know. It can be a relief to decide that a shared love of rock climbing or the same sense of humor is more important than sexual compatibility. Making this decision doesn't have to be settling. It can be practical and wise and affirming, a sign of critical thinking and an expression of firmly held intention and values.

For her part, Kendra says that all the messages about the special importance of sex and the special torture of not having sex made her feel like a burden. She and her boyfriend will decide to have sex a few times a month but don't reach that goal most of the time. Then, the guilt comes from both sides: from her because she doesn't want to have sex, and from him because he does and doesn't want to pressure her. In these situations, all the other good things about her relationship don't feel like enough. "I've given him so many outs, told him he should leave and find someone else," Kendra says. "The last time I did it, he was like, 'Do not ever say this to me again, I don't want to leave, I don't want you to feel like I should leave. Stop telling yourself this. I'm not looking for anyone else.' So it's never been a question of when we're going to break up, it's a question of how we can change our relationship."

Stay with anyone long enough and that will always be the question. It is more than merely acceptable to pick and choose and then adapt; it is necessary. Tiefer, the sex researcher, is critical of what she sees as a relentless pressure to improve in every aspect of our lives. "You're not supposed to be tolerant of just 'doing well.' You have to be wonderful in all areas, you have to optimize," she says. "People think that you have to be able to have everything but you can't. You focus on what's important.

"I learned that from my mother," Tiefer continues. "She was an intellectual, political, musical creature and she knew that to gain mastery you have to give in some areas. She didn't care about cooking. She didn't think of herself as a sexual creature and never thought of sex as something important to her. Aren't there studies showing that you can only hold seven things in your head at once? One of them doesn't *have* to be your sex life. It can be there, but it doesn't have to be."

• • • • • • • • •

Sex was important to Georgia, but not to Selena. Selena, who would soon start identifying as ace, said no to sex but yes to everything else. Yes to still dating Georgia, yes to spending the same amount of time together, yes to being affectionate and sleeping in the same bed.

The process of questioning and answering set the stage for how Selena would relate to others and approach relationships going forward. "Relationships and sex were a black box, and we were starting to take it apart," she says. "Our conversations really stripped the complex parts from what I saw as this machine that I could never crack." The back-and-forth had made it clear that a traditional relationship—monogamous, sexual— would not work for them, but that something else might.

So the two decided to open their relationship. They discarded monogamy and the relationship escalator and belief that any relationship that wasn't exclusive and didn't progress toward marriage was a failure. They stopped having sex but rejected the idea that a relationship without sex had to end or be emotionally impoverished. Both remained dedicated to each other and also started looking for new partners, and Selena became immersed in the kink scene. She threw herself into play parties, learning "so, so fast" about bondage, impact play, dominance, submission, how her body worked, how she didn't want her body to work, what she liked in a partner and what she didn't like, as well as what she liked and didn't like in people generally.

"Now I could actually communicate about what I wanted," Selena says of that period of exploration. "I could say, 'I'm looking for this and

I don't want this,' and that space brought me into real dating instead of treating everyone like this black box that I had to accept on a trial basis. I could be like, 'You're very attractive, but that's not what I'm looking for, though we should hang out,' whereas before I'd be like, 'You're so attractive, let's just try it,' and it'd be a couple months of shit."

One funny thing: At most of the kink parties Selena went to, no one was doing anything that seemed to her to be sexual. People would say, "I'm tying someone up, that's sex," but much of the time it didn't seem to feel sexual and nobody could explain how this made sense. Was tying someone up really sex, or was it a rope and some trust? Selena didn't care about sex, but she did love rope, so it was unclear what exactly was happening here, and what she actually wanted.

Intimacy, as it turns out. Selena cared about intimacy, and kink was a way for her to be intimate with others. Intimacy and sex are not the same. Intimacy can be in service of sex or sex can be in service of intimacy, or they can be completely separate. People were mixing up intimacy and sex, just as they mixed up sex and what they want from sex. Sexual desire is frequently about ego and not libido. In this, there is an opportunity.

· · · · · · · · · ·

At a workshop many years ago, back when I cared more about self-improvement, I learned a technique called *goal factoring*. I sat at a table with other young people who all wanted to optimize ourselves to our limit. Each of us wrote down a goal at the top of a piece of paper and circled it. Mine was to run a half-marathon. Next, we asked ourselves why we wanted to achieve that goal, then wrote those answers in boxes lower down on the piece of paper, with lines connecting to the original goal. We kept asking ourselves why, why, why.

When it comes to sex, many people don't ask why enough. Casting sex as a primal, biological need often hides the fact that, as Selena noted, it is just as often motivated by emotional desire. Sexual incompatibility can be challenging precisely because it is connected to so many emotional needs that, when unfulfilled, create distance and dissatisfaction. These can include everything from the desire to get to know a new person to the desire to use someone else's desire as a barometer of your own self-worth. Though people do want sex only for the sake of physical release, in so many cases people want sex as a shortcut to something else, sex as a tool and a means to an end—a certain feeling—and not necessarily the end itself. Sex serves many purposes, but without more emotional excavation, it can seem like the why of sex is only to orgasm. And even when someone realizes that the purpose of sex is to reach a feeling, it can seem like sex and its lead-up are the only possible routes.

James believed that you couldn't enter a relationship and enjoy that bond without touch and kiss. Others think that the bases track neatly onto emotions so that holding hands is a little bit intimate and kissing more intimate and having sex the most intimate thing of all. Reality is rarely this neat or linear. Sex can be boring and impersonal, while a brush of the hand can be thrilling. One person can feel close to another from far away and the same person can have penetrative intercourse and not feel much of anything. Touch doesn't have to be a hierarchy, and sex doesn't have to be the only, or even the best, way of achieving intimacy. When I polled my allo friends, many pointed out that holding hands felt like a bigger deal than making out or said that they didn't like kissing either. People want to experience an emotion and get stuck on the known way to reach it. Yet there are many ways to reach a feeling, if you can figure out which feeling you're searching for.

Back at the workshop, my reasons for wanting to run a half-marathon were seemingly obvious. I wanted to get in shape and do something that seemed hard and impressive. The others kept asking me: Why did I want to get in shape? Because I wanted to look good and be healthy. Why? Because I wanted to not be tired and sluggish. Why else? Because I wanted to be hot, okay? They continued: Were there other ways to achieve all that? Fitness classes, perhaps, that wouldn't require me to spend a lot of time outdoors in the winter cold? Anything besides running, which I had said that I hated anyway?

To this day, I have not run a half-marathon. It turns out that the reasons that made people push back against this plan were the same reasons that I am probably never going to run a half-marathon. The goal-factoring exercise was a bit corny, but I frequently return to that experience when I think about goals of any kind. It is easy to commit to a goal. It is easy to stop at the obvious first level when asked about the motivation—to say that you want to run a half-marathon to get in shape—instead of digging further and thinking about why you want to get in shape, why it might be worth it, and how else it can be achieved. Being questioned really did help me refocus my attention on what I truly wanted to feel, not on the goal that seemed like it would get me there.

The same can be true for sex. Cassie, the therapist in Chicago, wouldn't use the term *goal factoring*, but they would do a similar exercise if a client said they might be ace and still wanted to have sex. At the end of the day, goal factoring is really just goal questioning. Cassie will ask about the client's definition of ace and their definition of sex, what else is going on and what purpose everything holds. *Who's in the room here?* they'll ask. *You're in the room, I'm in the room, but who else is speaking? Is this coming from your mother who expects you to have babies? Is this coming from just sitting in the societal soup where we're all expected to love and enjoy sex constantly, but just not too much? Do you want to keep your partner—is that where this is coming from? Do you want to explore? Do you want to feel sexy?*

In the chapter on romance, I suggested that we skip the labels and go directly to asking for what we want. In relationships, one option is to go directly to figuring out what sex is supposed to bring. When people stop viewing sex as the end-all be-all of an encounter, when sex loses its dominance as the most important and intimate thing that could happen, when it becomes feasible to ask directly for what is desired, more ways of relating and connecting become clear. "I'm starting to suspect that the greatest insight the ace spectrum has for sex therapy isn't identity labels," writes Anagnori, the ace blogger and therapist, "but making therapists re-examine their assumptions, and expanding their ideas of what 'intimacy' and 'pleasure' really mean."[14]

• • • • • • • • •

Re-examining desires is not easy for anyone. I, for example, have never had an ace partner or been on an ace dating app. Partly because there aren't enough people on those apps and I thought I could easily compromise with an allo partner. Partly because, for a long time, I just didn't want an ace partner. I didn't particularly care about the physical feeling of sex, but I craved the thrill of being, specifically, sexually desired. I didn't experience sexual attraction myself, yet I wanted others to have that desire for me.

The hypocrisy is not lost on me. I have always known that I want to be sexually desired because I want emotional reassurance and a sense of my own power. Sexual desirability is one of the greatest assets that a person can have, a form of privilege and protection that makes it easier to move through life itself, a quality that people can covet even if we don't feel the symmetrical desire toward others. (As aro aces say, not being romantically or sexually interested in others doesn't protect you from being treated badly if you're deemed romantically or sexually unworthy yourself.) Being the target of sexual desire felt like an extra form of ammunition against being left and balm for my insecurities about my looks, which were really insecurities about my ability to get what I wanted in life.

Lust in the popular imagination is involuntary and unendorsed, and that very fact about its nature—that it is disruptive and hard to control—can make it seem stronger than all the platitudes about love being a choice. Choice and intention and reframing and work all seem less powerful than obsession. The flip side of love being a choice is that someone can choose to stop loving you, whereas the compulsive thoughts and obsession that people associate with lust are harder to snuff out. I wanted something strong, something not easily controlled, something—ah yes—primal. Being emotionally desired seemed to be a cheaper thing, sad and second-rate.

An attitude like mine is common. James has sometimes told past partners that he's willing to have sex but "you have to understand that while I get intimacy out of it, the actual form is for you." Partners don't like this, just as they don't like willing consent. Anything short of enthusiastic, "I want sex for physical reasons" consent can feel like a blow to self-worth, puncturing the wished-for self-image of being someone who can inspire lust despite any and all obstacles. I know people are suspicious of emotional desire for sex because they like to ask me whether it feels good when non-repulsed aces have sex. The question stems from curiosity, but also from worry that the lack of sexual attraction means that all sex is automatic pity sex, endured instead of enjoyed.

The answer to the question of whether sex feels good for aces is sometimes yes and sometimes no, just like with allos. Many people, ace and allo alike, don't feel a spontaneous desire for sex, but they start to feel that mental wanting once (consensual) physical touch is initiated and their body becomes aroused. This process, called responsive desire, is a slow warming-up, an "I know I'll get into it once I start."[15] It's common and often at the core of willing consent. Sex can feel good on a physical level without attraction; I've heard it described as "superior masturbation." For others, the fact that the appeal is emotional or intellectual does not diminish its power. Jessica, a writer in New York, doesn't experience sexual attraction but did enjoy having a friend with benefits. Jessica's rule for her own body is "nothing below the waist," but she finds other people's sexual desires and sexuality endlessly fascinating. "It's so *intellectually* stimulating and that's fun for me," she says. "It's a game, like, okay, if I do this and this and *this*, what happens? What about *that*? It's kind of taking apart the person and seeing what they'll do and what makes sense, and what pleases them."

The biggest difference is that it usually requires much more effort for sex to feel good for aces compared to allos and much less awkwardness for sex to feel boring or uncomfortable. To return to a food metaphor: Imagine the difference between eating when ravenous and being full but willing to share a snack. People can enjoy eating when they're not hungry, but when the food itself is not satiating hunger, the social aspects need far more care and have to be just so.

Not being desired in the right way feels frustrating, and stepping away from this story takes work. But desire of other kinds can be just as heady, its grip just as hard to shake. Willing consent and other forms of emotional desire can be a gesture of caring, a starting point from which to explore and have fun too. The things people do from choice are meaningful and the effort that they take is a sign of a great love, even if they're not pushed by an uncontrolled, intense physical passion. Few things are more romantic than someone trying hard because they want to make you happy. That is what this is.

A switch in perspective requires elevating emotional desire for sex and seeing work as romantic. It also requires everyone paying attention to what we want emotionally instead of just physically and finding new (or other) ways to fulfill those needs. This challenge can be the start of knowing others more fully, in multiple dimensions. There is often more leeway in relationships than people fear.

Zee Griffler, a filmmaker in Colorado, initially believed that they couldn't be in relationships at all. After three relationships ended over sexual incompatibility, it seemed futile to even try. Avoiding relationships entirely was preferable to trying, becoming emotionally entangled, and having it end painfully. "If a relationship that was otherwise perfect resulted in me throwing it away because I didn't want to have sex, why bother?" Zee says. "I had already gotten the data that I needed and there was no reason to replicate that experience if I was just going to keep hurting people."

After years of refusing to consider relationships, Zee became open to dating again precisely because they learned about asexuality. The existence of asexuality helped answer the long-standing question of why they were different, and the stories of other aces in relationships made it seem like relationships could be possible for Zee too. "That was a revelation," they say. "It made me intrigued, like, 'Oh, maybe I should give this another shot on my own terms, rather than with the cultural narrative terms.'"

Zee met their current partner at a party. ("Everything about that sentence is very different from who I am," they assure me, but it was a "post-election-sadness house party.") The two started hanging out and were together within a day. For Zee's girlfriend, sex is a way of reaching others. For Zee, sex goes from "vaguely amusing" to "deeply chore-like" after the first two weeks of a relationship. Sex isn't repulsive, but it's a hobby other people have that Zee doesn't care for, like bowling. "If you have someone who loves to go bowling all the time, that's great," they say, "but I'm not the kind of person that wants to go bowling more than maybe once every couple of years, and I'm not going to buy the shoes for it."

Acknowledging this didn't magically lift the guilt of feeling that they were unfairly denying their girlfriend and not fulfilling her needs. "I had to work through that and basically stand up for myself," Zee adds. "I finally got to a point where I was like, 'This is how I feel and you're going to have to be okay that I will probably never be sexually intimate from this point on. It could happen, maybe, but probably not.'"

The two are in an open relationship, but that isn't a panacea. The person who wants sex can have sex with someone else, but confusion and resentment can still develop, and conversations about desire and need and want are necessary to remain close. "In [my girlfriend's] experience, one of the only ways to be intimate with people was sex and otherwise they wouldn't be intimate at all, so it took a fair bit of reorienting and negotiation," Zee adds. "She's said to me that 'I feel like I need less sex around you because we're so intimate in other ways." Intimacy for them looks like a lot of cuddling, hand-holding, "being close without necessarily having to be unclothed."

Honesty, better communication, and reframing needs have helped many aces and their partners discover how many options there can be to connect. "I realized there were simple things I could do—like touching him nicely or not being on my phone while talking—to help my partner feel recognized that weren't just sex," says Alicia, the scholar who has been with her partner for over a decade. It is only in recent years that they, as a couple, have realized that sex is the gateway to all sorts of issues, related to his need to be strong and respected and her fear of male anger. It's easy to say that sex is important and it's harder to be vulnerable enough to say that sex is important because a lack of sex creates fear and insecurity. It's that "why" and that "because" that have led the relationship to a more vivid and honest place.

· · · · · · · · · ·

My personal curse is that I do question incessantly yet serve as a cautionary tale that knowledge alone can have hard limits. This sad state of affairs is sometimes called the *insight fallacy*, or the mistaken belief that understanding a problem will solve it. As Zee said, knowing about asexuality was a first step but not a quick fix. It did not prevent Zee from feeling that their partner was entitled to sex with them. Writing an entire book about asexuality has done little to assuage the anxiety that sometimes underlies my relationship.

For my boyfriend, Noah, our relationship was the first time he had been friends with someone before sleeping together. For me, our relationship was the beginning of a strange period related to sex. Previous relationships had all been long-distance, but instead of living a few states away, Noah lived across the park, close enough that on a good day he could run straight through and be at my place in ten minutes. His availability unnerved me. More importantly, this was the first relationship I had entered identifying as ace. We initially had so much sex that I started wondering if I was really ace. Then we started having less sex. Specifically, I started wanting less sex and a new era of my sexual worries began.

Sex plateaus in nearly every relationship, and I never felt any explicit outside pressure, from Noah or anyone else. What I needed to manage was not sexual desire but the pressure I put on myself. Sex can be a symbol, and I watched myself turning it into a symbol that mattered too much. If I didn't want to have sex, I wondered about what that meant, as if it needed to mean anything at all. If I had sex and the slightest thing was wrong or I didn't enjoy myself, I was sure that the relationship was headed downhill. I felt agitated if we didn't have sex for a week, even if neither of us wanted to. I could name the traps, but I was falling into them anyway.

Soon, I found myself navigating the ways that identity labels and knowledge influence interpretation; the result was not always comforting. Before I knew about asexuality, if my desire for sex waned, I would have shrugged and said, "It'll come back soon like it does for everyone. It'll be fine." Now, I found myself becoming strangely essentialist, wondering again if this was who I truly was and feeling bad, and then feeling bad because I should know better than to feel bad. That's a one-two punch all too familiar to me.

The time I was most fearful and least inclined to have sex was likely related to a yearlong depressive episode related to my mother receiving a diagnosis of early-onset Alzheimer's, compounded by the stress of office politics and writing this book after hours. All of this is plausible, even reasonable. It's still a form of mental gymnastics designed to reassure myself that, deep down, I will always want to have sex in some form—and at the core of that reassurance is the tug of compulsory sexuality. Everyone else is fine if they never have sex again, but I, personally, really need to or something bad will happen.

My fear went beyond concerns over relationship maintenance. Noah has said that if I decided that one day I never wanted to have sex again, we would talk about it and consider an open relationship or some other compromise. He has told me again and again that nobody wants to have sex all the time, that it is nothing to worry about and he only wants to have sex if I do. I believe him, but it isn't enough. I am lucky that my relationship's existence isn't pinned to libido, yet I still want to want more.

For most people, our lives are a series of insight fallacies. When I was with Henry, I understood that my insecurity and fears were hurting the relationship. I was willing, and I tried, but no matter how hard I pushed, I could not quickly rid myself of years of emotional baggage. It is the same here. Little of what I learned—about compulsory sexuality, consent, or the ways we privilege sex and how that is culturally ingrained—made a dent in the fear. For all that I am steeped in ace discourse, I would sometimes feel terrible late at night and burst out that I hated being ace, that I wished I were "normal," that if I could choose, I would choose to be otherwise.

Let me tell you something: When writing this section, I struggled to be honest. I found myself wanting to add in defensive caveat after defensive caveat about how often Noah and I did still have sex. I cut long sections about how my partners tended to comment on how sexually open-minded I was, about how I visited sex clubs, about how I am definitely, absolutely not a prude. I struggled with a dilemma that I knew was silly. If I told the truth—that despite being open-minded, I am indifferent to sex most of the time—I would come closer to proving myself to be a real ace person. If I obscured the truth and emphasized all the parts that I wanted, I would come closer to presenting myself as I wanted to be seen.

I wanted to obscure the truth for Noah. I felt protective, worried that if people knew this about me, that they would feel sorry for him, even though I am far more bothered than he. And I wanted to obscure the truth for myself. I believe I am right when I think about compulsory sexuality and its negative effects, but self-righteousness is not as useful an emotion as I once believed. It's not an adequate buffer against the other ideas that float in the air and that I have ingested over my life. When it comes to the personal, I frequently lack the courage of my convictions.

The greatest help here has been Noah himself. Noah doesn't immerse himself in gender and sexuality studies like I do. He is a straight white man from the Northeast who went to private schools and, as a kid, spent summers in France visiting relatives. I am the one who spends time reading about sexuality and consent; he is the one who calmly tells me everything is okay.

Understanding compulsory sexuality does not always let someone stand up for themselves, just like understanding racism doesn't prevent people from being unconsciously racist. Remembering that it is not "normal" that matters but instead what people want—and that what they want may go deeper than they believe—doesn't strip those expectations of all their power. That sex is often a metaphor does not mean there is nothing left when all that symbolism is stripped away, or that we symbolic creatures can ever fully strip away that symbolism, no matter how much we might wish to. There is no guarantee that being able to name and recognize scripts will solve the problem and save the relationship. However, *not* talking does guarantee that the scripts will retain their power. Talking may not be sufficient, but it is necessary.

Advice to talk and question everything does not sound radical, in relationships or in any other part of life. I know. I spoke to many experts and scholars, wanting one of them to share with me one weird trick for fixing everything, preferably a quick tip, but I would accept a novel technique too. Instead, therapists and other experts told me this obvious piece of advice over and over again, and the more that I learned, the more I realized just how much no one wants to do it.

People will pay money to avoid talking. This became very clear when, in my day job as a science journalist, I was pitched a $250 suction-like device that promises to help women want more sex, essentially by simulating foreplay on their genitals. Because the device was geared toward women in relationships, I asked the CEO why the customer couldn't ask her partner for real foreplay, which is free. I was told that no one had asked that question before. The answer is that women didn't want to ask their partners. They felt pressured. They'd rather pay money for a gadget than talk.

Or they'd rather discreetly have an affair. In a widely read *New York Times* Modern Love column titled "What Sleeping with Married Men Taught Me About Infidelity," Karin Jones describes the state of these married men. "After our second night together, though, I could tell this was about more than sex for him; he was desperate for affection," she writes. "He said he wanted to be close to his wife but couldn't because they were unable to get past their fundamental disconnect: lack of sex, which led to a lack of closeness, which made sex even less likely and then turned into resentment and blame."[16]

It seems plausible that lack of sex might worsen a lack of closeness, but it is less clear to me which causes which. I wonder whether addressing the lack of closeness in another way could help with the lack of sex, or at least with the ability for both to speak about the lack of sex and other options. Communicating honestly and openly—in a way where both people feel free and able to talk—is uncomfortable and painful. It's unfair too, because it's easier for some people to speak up than others. But a life of being understood without any uncomfortable conversations does not exist for anyone. Talking and listening are the only sure ways to make intentions clear. The more I've researched and consulted, the more I've accepted that no one weird trick exists, and that the only way out is through.

Selena has realized this too. Selena is still with Georgia and has found other partners as well: a man named Daniel with whom she's in a dominant/submissive relationship, and some people that she and Georgia both date. She has sex with some partners and not others. It all depends on the person and the context. "I think something that continues to strike me through all these relationships is how non-important sex can be, and how awesome it can be, but how insignificant it is compared to all of the other things," Selena says. "I see sex as one of several hundred intimate things you can do, and just like every other one of the intimate things, it has its pros and cons and it's certainly nowhere near the highest on the list. I prefer hair pulling over sex any day of the week, but that doesn't mean I dislike sex if it's done right. If it's bad sex and no one knows how to do it, that's not as enjoyable; it's like getting whipped by someone who doesn't know how to use a whip."

She's grateful to have had those early conversations with Georgia and for the chance to learn all this about herself and others. She knows now that the people in the relationship get to decide how important sex is, and whether this is a challenge they can handle, and what they really care about in life and love. For Selena, sex can be unnecessary or it can be a way to enrich the relationships. It is never the goal.

CHAPTER 10

ANNA

AFTER TWENTY YEARS AND TWO KIDS, the marriage ended. Meredith had left. The boys, eleven and fifteen, were only around half the time now. Alone in her own space and with her own thoughts, Anna—though that wasn't her name yet—decided that she would do as she wished. Privacy was no longer a luxury; finally, there was no one to answer to.

First, Anna decided to dress how she wanted and for so long could not, in skirts and dresses. Next, a trip to the doctor to say *enough*. The testosterone was not working. It did not increase her sex drive as it was supposed to, and it did not make her any more of the man that other people told her she needed to be.

Anna asked whether she could try estrogen instead, to balance everything out. Her doctor said that was an option, so Anna thought about it for a few months before coming back and saying yes. She started using the estrogen cream, then stopped using it, then started again. It was on and off, then on again, until one day she looked in the mirror and saw the beginnings of breasts.

This was not an outcome that Anna had considered. The physical change had started without her full awareness, but it was happening regardless and presenting a decision Anna would need to make. Reverse, continue. Changing nothing would mean making a choice as well, and Anna did not want to be passive this time.

· · · · · · · · · ·

For most of her life, Anna didn't know what she wanted. Her family knew what she was supposed to want, and told her. Her religious leaders knew, and told her. The confident women she dated knew, and told her. Anna listened. She looked around and noticed what others wanted and tried to imitate them.

Many of us learn to desire by watching other people desire. We learn to desire George Clooney because *People* magazine says he's the sexiest man alive; we want a beach body because of the constant marketing telling us that summer is only a few months away. In theory, mimetic desire can be perfectly fine. In practice, the world is not a neutral place. We are rarely surrounded by many types of people who represent many visions of life, free to pick the one that fits best. If you don't know who you are or what you want, the world will decide for you. It will show you a couple of options and tell you those are the only ones. As so many people throughout this book have said, it takes active work to step back, to create even enough space to take a breath and admit that maybe you don't know what you want, but what has been offered has never felt right.

Anna is rueful when telling me about the ways that the world chose for her. She emphasizes, with a certain amount of self-recrimination, how it was her instinct to cooperate, only making decisions when she couldn't ignore the problem any longer. It was easier to accept the scripts she was handed, even if their meanings were sometimes opaque, than to engage with complicated questions whose answers might threaten what she already had. Her descriptions of her passivity come with anger and wistfulness too, some questioning of how things might be different if she had pushed back more openly all those years she was wondering inside.

I understand why she blames herself. Yet when I speak with her, I think only that I am often passive too, and that's with the advantage of being born three decades later and growing up in a liberal, secular culture far more encouraging than the environment of her childhood. Many people are passive, and all of us are immersed in instructions and expectations—not just when it comes to sex and relationships, but in every area of life—that feel overwhelming. It's especially difficult to reject scripts when it's unclear what they should be replaced with or when we haven't seen others do the same.

Anna's story is about asexuality and also family and religion, gender and age and relationships. It's not a neat narrative about how good intentions can make things work, or that finding a new identity will tie up all the loose ends. It's about how desire and identity meld and shift, about looking at what is expected and starting to wonder if that's what you want, about decades of fitting experience into a category and wondering what all of that was for and starting over.

·········

Anna was born in the 1960s in Utah, assigned male at birth. The grand-daughter of a sheep rancher, she had a proper Mormon family and was expected to be a proper Mormon boy. Instead, she was sensitive and anxious, the target of a father who would scrutinize her and then criticize her for crying.

Mormon children were separated by sex from a young age, with the boys preparing for their eventual missions and going to Sunday meetings to learn to lead the women and the family. Girls practiced for weddings and learned how to keep house. It was clear where Anna should fit, but by age four she was already asking herself where she might *want* to fit, though it was hardly a decision in her power to make.

It didn't feel like she belonged with the boys, not when she was bullied for being fearful and bad at sports, not enough like them. The girls weren't an option either; that was a different, closed-off world. A memory: First grade, watching the girls sitting in rows and playing with each other's long hair. Anna wanted to be in that world, *of* that world, and knew that she would not be granted access.

The rules of childhood turned into the rules of puberty, which felt even more like instructions that did not make sense, a series of changes that seemed to be happening to somebody else entirely. Anna knew that she was supposed to date and she knew how to date. Get the car ready. Pick someone up in the car. Take her out to dinner. Pretend to hesitate over the goodnight kiss.

The steps were clear, but the motions did not feel meaningful. The car and date and kiss never seemed to bring Anna any closer to the type of bond she wanted. "Looking back, I can see that the girls were assuming there was this sexual desire coming toward them, from me, that they had to protect themselves against," she says. No such urge in her existed, at least not for bodies and touching. For her classmates, the carefully choreographed moves may have helped them reach a wished-for goal. Not so for Anna. She stopped dating altogether.

There was one girl, though. Maria. Her last name was Solis, pronounced "solace." Maria was Mexican, unlike most other people in Utah, and also Catholic, which was then, as Anna says, "quite exotic." When Anna went to church with Maria to see what it was like, her parents became worried about her dabbling in Catholicism.

No physical intimacy existed between them, nor any movements that gestured toward that. Instead, Anna and Maria shared an emotional closeness that couldn't be sorted or categorized, though it was *felt* as the two talked on the phone for hours. "She could meet me," Anna says. "She could meet in this intense place where I like to sit and struggle. I like to just go to the hardest stuff." Perhaps the easiest way to explain is that most people are actually many different people, and Anna believed that she was her truest self with Maria.

Today, that bond might be called a queerplatonic relationship, or nonsexual romance, or simply love, but when it was happening, it didn't look like any form of friendship or romance that Anna had seen modeled by others. It did not look like holding hands in the hallways, and it did not look like getting the car to go to dinner, and it did not look like casually hanging out with friends either. "She's been in my consciousness forever," Anna says of Maria, who remained as a memory of a strong, rich connection, even after Maria herself got pregnant, married, and dropped out of high school. "I grieved so much after she vanished from my life."

Decades later, when Anna was in her thirties, living in Montana with the woman she would marry, Maria called. After having three kids, Maria had divorced the man she married in high school. Single again, a mother now but no longer a wife, Maria was trying to remember who she had been before all those other roles took over. Maria had asked herself where she had left off, with whom she had last felt like Maria first and foremost.

You, Maria told Anna. *You were the last person I was myself with. I felt the need to talk to you because talking to you was connecting with my old self.*

How strange and how powerful, this shared time-travel. Not just Maria talking to Anna now, but Maria talking to Maria's old self and squaring that with the Maria of today, and Anna today falling straight back to that same feeling of intense longing. "I had to have this real boundary around that conversation," Anna says. "I couldn't open that up too much given where I was in my life at the moment, but it moved me so much because I always had this feeling of *my* longing being really big—but was she in it, in that way?" Yes, Maria said, and it had been a gift.

· · · · · · · · · ·

Senior year of high school, Anna took a sociology class at the local college with a professor who was a bit of a perv. For the final assignment, the students were required to write about their personal fantasies of social deviance, a task that seemed designed to gratify this man's non-intellectual curiosities.

Hoping to avoid the professor's voyeurism without failing the class, Anna decided to write about the deviant fantasy of celibacy. Her solution was clever, but it was not a lie. She did fantasize about a world without sexual intensity and sexual surveillance, where she didn't have to meet with bishops who would ask whether she masturbated and questioned her about other sexual inclinations. The lascivious jokiness of "we know what you want" felt uncomfortable when she knew she didn't want it at all.

A celibate life represented a form of freedom. Being a monk would be a dream, though Anna didn't exactly understand what a monk was since no such thing existed in Mormonism. Her project became simultaneously a rebuke to the professor and a confession of being lost. She did not want what she was supposed to want. She had not copied others well enough. Anna was not a proper Mormon man and she needed to get out.

The escape was Swarthmore College in Pennsylvania. It was thousands of miles from Utah, it was a liberal arts college, it was her ticket out of the Mormon Church, and it was the 1980s. What had not been okay in Utah City could be given a pass here, and Anna began wearing skirts and dresses. To others, she said that the clothing was a feminist act that expanded gender expression for men. To herself, she admitted that it was simply what she wanted to do and what she had secretly tried in high school out West. Freedom was the best feeling, but it had a cost even at Swarthmore. At one on-campus event, a male professor gave Anna a look of such disgust that in that moment she knew that she could dress like this here and now, but not in the wider world and not forever.

Ruth from California attached herself to Anna freshman year. Unafraid of being forceful and sure of what she wanted, Ruth was comfortable telling Anna how to have a relationship and comfortable telling Anna when it was time to have sex. That Anna was terrified didn't matter, until it did. The first time they had sex, Anna broke down. She left the room immediately and walked for hours in the neighborhoods around campus and beyond.

The physical sensations had been overwhelming and they didn't connect to a place of wanting. "That breakdown was just for so many reasons, but the deepest place of it was, this didn't make sense to me," Anna says. "I didn't understand this experience and I was doing something without an anchoring place in me that I wanted. I didn't feel a sense of self around sexuality, and I went into a panic attack and I couldn't make sense of what was going on." The sensations were happening to her with no narrative, no structure or container that helped the bodily experience mean anything. The instructions were gone.

. . . .

In her late twenties, Anna decided to pursue writing. At a fellowship program in Massachusetts, she met Meredith, a super-fast talker and super-sharp woman. *Come over to my place*, Meredith said, *and I'll make dinner.* The two drank Scotch, but Anna could not relax. When Meredith made a pass, Anna said no.

The two eventually had sex, but Anna, self-conscious and unable to relax, felt removed from the experience. Older now, and having had other relationships since college, Anna knew what she had to do, and she did it. Anna could say no, but not indefinitely. Afterward, she pretended that it was wonderful, like Meredith had introduced her to a level of good sex that she had never experienced before. Meredith was the sexual teacher eager to share her wisdom and Anna the willing student, and the two played those roles for a long time.

The fellowship ended a few months later, and the two decided to move away together. Both wanted to go out West and chose Montana, where they were married a year and a half later. Anna studied to be a therapist while Meredith continued to write. Meredith wanted kids, so two sons followed. "There was so much that was powerful and strong and good about that relationship," Anna says. "We really connected on a deep level. We fell hard for one another, and if it weren't for the sex part, we might still be together honestly."

• • • • • • • • •

Sex was the problem from the beginning, apparent even early on. Once, Meredith had said that everything, no matter what, was actually about sex.

Anna was shocked. *What are you talking about?* she said. *No, it's not!*

Meredith was shocked in return, and she asked Anna what she meant and how she could not see that sex was everywhere. To Meredith, the presence of sex suffused the world. It was a vital energy that helped everything else make sense. To Anna, nothing was about sex. As a therapist, she was intellectually interested in sex and enjoyed talking about sex with her clients. Personally, she did not feel the presence of sex anywhere at all and never considered sex when making decisions. Anna thinks about that conversation often, as a moment that revealed her asexuality, though she didn't know it at the time. It's become an explanation for what is different for her and others, why she can't recognize when people are coming on to her: "I'm not in on the code."

This gap in experience became more and more clear. Over time, Anna stopped being able to pretend. Pleasing Meredith was great, but she could not generate desire for its own sake. "I struggled with that a lot because I was still trying to manufacture it and it was woven into masculinity and gender," she says. "I was trying to create the masculine sexual self that I thought I was supposed to be. I could have sex, but she didn't feel me desiring her and that was a deep place of identity for her."

Meredith was the woman who pursued and was pursued, whom nobody said no to, who took the initiative and invited Anna over to drink Scotch and then made a pass. She was the woman who always got what she wanted, who Anna let believe was a great sexual teacher who had taught Anna all she knew. The point of sex was not just to have sex. It was to know that she could inspire sexual desire in others. Sex was connected to who she was and who she needed to be. Sex held different meanings for Anna and Meredith, and it did not seem like the difference could be reconciled.

Couples therapy. Individual therapy. The therapists supported Anna taking testosterone and told her to work harder to rise to the level of desire of the other person, even though Anna had spent her entire life doing that and had "experienced so much direct pain from it and harm" from that.

The two decided to try an open relationship, but Meredith became afraid when Anna began dating a close friend, and Anna realized that she was not free to do what she truly wanted, which wasn't to have recreational sex but to love other people. Soon, they were sleeping in separate rooms. Finally, Anna, looking through the mail one day, found a notice about a new bank account Meredith had opened.

She thought, *Oh my god, what is happening?*

Meredith said, *I don't want to be in this relationship anymore.*

· · · · · · · · · ·

"I would have stayed in it," says Anna. "I don't like saying that about myself, but I would have. That's just how I'm wired. I would have kept paying the cost that I was paying in order to keep things together." But Meredith didn't stay.

After the divorce, in the middle of crisis, Anna began searching for answers online. Was she bigender? Was that a thing, was that even a real word? What did the low sexual desire mean about her? During one of these searches she found AVEN and read and wept. "It was like, oh, this shift from this weird thing in my experience, a way that I'm weird and broken in the world to thinking this might be something I can share with other people in a constructive way," she says. "There was this sorrow that I'd had to be alone all this time without having this name, this identity, this community. There was a sense of loss woven into it."

Finding asexuality was all mixed together with exploring gender. Anna began wearing skirts in the house. She started taking estrogen and it made her feel calm and at peace, finally comfortable in her body. Anna looked in the mirror and saw the beginnings of breasts and made the decision to move forward, to ask for the full dose of estrogen and go, *Oh, this is me, this is who I am.* The divorce turned out to be the push she needed and self-discovery was its unexpected gift. Maybe Anna could have come out without the divorce. Maybe she could have asserted a new identity from within her marriage. She doubts it.

It has taken a lifetime to reach this place. In Utah a half-century ago, nobody seemed to be ace or trans. All those years of struggle were experienced long before Anna knew about the option to transition and before there was AVEN. So many of these questions have been around for so long. Now, at this different stage of life, Anna's concerns are different in some ways from those of younger aces, but similar in that she too is still figuring out how romance and love and sex and self fit. She has stepped back from what the world chose for her, even when that leaves her in uncomfortable, un-pioneered territory.

"I'm still so puzzled. I have so many big questions," she says, including questions about her new body and how it might affect her desire. As she started transitioning, everyone said that her asexuality would change once she was further in the process or once she'd had surgery. "People really want me to find a path to sexuality, and they try to leverage my gender identity in the service of that goal," she says. Without a place for asexuality in the culture, those who love her were distressed about her asexuality in a way that they never were about her being trans. "I really stayed open to that," Anna adds, "and I still kind of try because I want aspects of that, but no, it's all pretty much still where it was."

Romantic or aromantic—none of that is figured out either. Anna has a "crushy friend" living with her now and it's the most wonderful thing, she says, like living in a dream. The relationship has energy and intensity, and sometimes Anna asks herself whether it's sexual or romantic and then decides no, probably not. "I cannot figure that out," Anna tells me. "But also, I'm more and more okay with not knowing" and not forcing herself to figure it out. "There's not a known structure, but I've spent my whole life letting other people define these structures and trying to fit into what they experience the structure of a relationship to be." It's better to accept the questions without demanding answers, to exist in the "open-ended lived experience" of the moment, one where she can just be.

CHAPTER 11

WHERE ARE WE GOING, WHERE HAVE WE BEEN?

"HERE IS A LIST OF THINGS I like more than having sex," begins poet and scholar Cameron Awkward-Rich in his slam poem "A Prude's Manifesto": "reading, lying flat on my back staring at the ceiling, [. . .] cheap whiskey, riding my bike away from parties."[1]

What about the joy in all of that? What about the pleasure and richness that can be found without sex—not as a consolation prize, but as equal to, or even greater in, its power?

Ace activists want to build a world where everyone can find their answers to these questions. We want to expand the potential for what pleasure can look like. If asexuality—which is often conceptualized as a lack—is negative space, we must consider that negative space can be more than an absent image, more than just not having sex. It can be an image in itself, an optical illusion where the picture flips back and forth. Two faces or a vase. A penguin or a man with hair. A woman's face or a man playing the saxophone. The experiences of aces do more than outline the constrictive structures caused by compulsory sexuality. They can also reveal, or at least give permission to embrace, other forms of eroticism and other ways of living that may be just as fulfilling.

Gender studies scholar Ela Przybylo is the one who showed me Awkward-Rich's poem, which she used herself in her book *Asexual Erotics*, an academic exploration of intimacy beyond the carnal. The word *erotic* today is interchangeable with *sexual*, but that was not always so.

In Plato's *Symposium*, "eros surfaces as a love for the good, a desire for immortality—a mytho-spiritual plane touching with but not bound to sexuality," Przybylo writes. It was through the work of Freud that the erotic became bound to the sexual, but Freud himself admitted, and other scholars confirm, that "it is not easy to decide what is covered by the concept 'sexual.'"[2]

Against Freud, Przybylo (and I and many others) offers Audre Lorde. In "Uses of the Erotic: The Erotic as Power," Lorde defines eroticism as "the sharing of joy, whether physical, emotional, psychic, or intellectual." The erotic is an inner resource, a vitality. It is a force that compels us to be close to each other, one that "forms a bridge between the sharers which can be the basis for understanding much of what is not shared between them and lessens the threat of their difference."[3] This energy—of connection, creative fulfillment, and self-expression—is not limited to the realm of sexuality, even though "we are taught to separate the erotic demand from the most vital areas of our lives other than sex."[4] It is a feeling that can suffuse many areas of life.

Such a definition of the erotic, as a profound force greater than the carnal, is crucial to how aces think about all that life has to offer, and Awkward-Rich's poem is a powerful way to reclaim this different form of eros. Awkward-Rich's list of "things I like more than having sex" is familiar to many aces. The twist is the lack of shame when elevating other activities. It is a manifesto, not an apology.

That acknowledgment of this possibility was slow to unfold for James, the programmer in Seattle. At first, realizing that he was ace caused a profound sense of loss. "I felt like there was a fairly central part of human existence that I really didn't understand and wouldn't participate in," he says. "I'd like to have a life that works, so intuitively the most straightforward way would be to have a 'normal' life."

A hole had opened up and he would need to fill it. "People feel that sex is so central to them, and it made me think, 'What can I feel similarly about the way allo people feel about sex?'" he says. "How can I find that feeling actively?" Cooking is one way. James will take a recipe and find its best form, making a dish like Swedish meatballs over and over until he arrives at "the perfectly optimal way." The ability to be creative and fill that hole, to still live a life that he likes, has helped James become less attached to the importance of "normal." Three years ago, he might have chosen to be allo if given the choice. He would not make that choice today.

Julie Sondra Decker, the writer, offers another perspective. "I prioritize other things in my life—I'm creative and active and connected in my community—but not as a reaction to 'not having sex,'" she says. Her life has always been complete. When allo writers ask Julie for advice on creating ace characters, she warns them not to write the character "like a 'typical' person but without the sex part." Aces aren't a puzzle with a missing piece. Everyone is their own full puzzle.

Difference can be a gift. Being ace can mean less interpersonal drama and more freedom from social norms around relationships. It is an opportunity to focus more on other passions, to be less distracted by sexuality, to break the scripts, to choose your own adventure and your own values. Zii Miller, the trans man from Florida, jokes that while he might be missing out on a part of life that many cherish, everyone else is missing out on the joys of not spending time worrying about whether others are sexually or romantically interested. A different Zee—Zee Griffler from Colorado—says that asexuality gave them a "cheat code" through life, just like what Hunter's friends said when they learned how easy it was for him to resist lust. To say so is an inversion of the common ace complaint that we are the ones who lack special knowledge. "Asexuality is just a different way of seeing on what terms we want to be with one another. It's a way of getting very honest about how humans see each other and the different ways that we place value on relationships," Zee says.

The lack of understanding around asexuality did create angst around romance and the question of how people could stay together. Asexuality also helped Zee build more intimate friendships, unburdened by the subtle expectation of sex. The path toward asexuality forced them to reject the idea that two people who were close should automatically try to date and have sex, as if that were a superior way of relating. The ace perspective offered a celebration of other types of intimacy. It fostered both the imagination and the will necessary to build a life on one's own terms.

· · · · · · · · · ·

Being asexual can provide these powerful new perspectives, but the frameworks have limited power when they are still so hidden. Learning about and claiming asexuality can be transformative, but the world won't be a safe and positive place for aces—or for anyone—until compulsory sexuality itself is dismantled. We do not dismantle compulsory sexuality by waiting for each person to catch up and then starting over again. We do it by fighting for structural change.

Fighting compulsory sexuality does not mean that everything must be desexualized but rather that the rights of the other side must be prioritized too. It means, as Wake Forest scholar Kristina Gupta writes, "challenging the unearned privileges that accrue to sexual people and sexual relationships and . . . eliminating discrimination against nonsexual people and nonsexual relationships."[5] It means resisting pharmaceutical companies that sell desire drugs by using the language of sickness. Creating more books and movies with diverse ace characters and themes. Teaching therapists and doctors not to assume that a lack of sexual attraction is a sickness (while also not holding ableist beliefs about sickness). Getting rid of amatonormativity in marriage law. Asexuality should be discussed in sex education, which can be as simple as teaching students that never developing sexual attraction is fine. The ace perspective on consent must be a universal concern.

Ace activism has been growing over the past decade. The first Asexual Awareness Week took place in 2010, organized by Sacramento-based activist Sara Beth Brooks. Sara Beth had been engaged in her early twenties but knew she didn't want to have sex with her then-fiancé, a situation that landed her in therapy and taking hormones to increase her sex drive. The hormones didn't work. One night, while googling ways of ending a wedding ceremony without kissing ("Maybe we could fist-bump?"), she came across AVEN and stayed up all night reading and crying. It changed her life.

Sara Beth, who had come out as bisexual as a teenager, was already involved in LGBTQ+ activism and had organized marches against California's antigay marriage legislation. Reaching out to other sexual minorities seemed to be a natural extension of this work. It was also a practical matter of sharing resources with ace kids who had nothing but a website.

Partnering with other LGBTQ+ communities, which had more experts and brick-and-mortar buildings, could bring support to ace kids too.

Today, Brian Langevin, executive director of the nonprofit Asexual Outreach, coordinates a national network of local ace and aro community groups and provides resources and trainings to schools and LGBTQ+ organizations. Langevin also developed the *Ace Inclusion Guide for High Schools*, a tool for teachers, student leaders, sex educators, and other school staff. Meanwhile, Sebastian Maguire—legislative director for New York City councilmember Daniel Dromm and one of the only out asexual people in politics—helped pass legislation that adds asexuality as a protected category in the city's human rights law and includes asexuality as an option on survey forms.

Despite this progress, compulsory sexuality is not a ubiquitous term and there is more to do, both inside and outside the community. The ace community needs to be more welcoming to people of color and disabled aces and anyone who does not have a gold star. Diversity of ace experience is a strength, and diversity of other types of experience and identity will only be more so. Reaching out to older aces, and thinking more about issues that older aces might face, is another way to enrich the community and the lives of people who may benefit. Older people are more likely to be unaware of asexuality entirely, and even the ones who do identify as ace frequently feel like they don't belong in either the online or offline groups.

In the world at large, "*asexual* in the biological term is still more well-known," says Sara Beth, who thinks that aces are waiting for what she calls "an Ellen moment" or "a Laverne moment." Aces need someone people already know and love—a celebrity—to champion the cause, she says. Then activism can move beyond the basics of ace 101 and toward the more ambitious projects of changing society to be better for all. Until then, many victories will be more personal.

・・・・・・・・・

For as long as he can remember, AVEN founder David Jay has been surrounded by kids. Two years old when his sister was born, David couldn't yet read, so he memorized books that adults read to him and then "read" them to her. Being the oldest of twelve cousins on one side and third-oldest of twenty-four cousins on the other meant that family events always featured him taking care of "mobs of babies."

One day, shortly after college, David was riding Bay Area public transit when he saw an ad for queer-friendly adoption services. He was hit with this knowledge that he wanted to have kids, but had no idea how to get there. It was difficult to imagine aging, and life itself, without kids. It was equally difficult to imagine how he would have them.

The problem was never how kids are made. The problem was that David didn't know how to enter a relationship committed enough to support the lifelong project of child-rearing. A teenager when he started AVEN in the early 2000s, David was quickly marked as the poster boy and the face of asexuality, and his choices have long provided a template for younger aces. Like it or not, he is the closest thing many have to an elder who helps lead the way—but all this time he was, of course, also navigating his own life too, without an elder of his own. As he, and the ace community, grew older, each new stage brought new questions, this time no longer about the basics of sexual attraction but about parenting and family life.

"At that point," David says, meaning his early twenties, "all of my relationships were being supplanted by romantic and sexual relationships when they came along." Many friends who discussed plans of long-term partnership would quickly abandon those promises, falling easily into the amatonormative script that Elizabeth Brake criticizes. David, who is "somewhat aromantic," was left "very aware that I wanted to be able to have relationships that were stable and that I could rely on, and that my relationships functionally weren't that." If relationships alone were such a challenge, parenting felt unreachable. Fostering and adoption were options and David was willing to be a single parent, but first he wanted to try finding people with whom to raise a child.

• • • • • • • • •

When David's friends Avary and Zeke married in 2014, they asked him to play a role similar to that of an officiant. David had met Avary, a non-profit founder, at a social impact conference four years earlier. Both were obsessed with the question of how to build better communities and had long talks about what that work might look like. Through her, David came to know Zeke, an expert in energy and climate science, someone who started diving into public climate data sets for fun and wound up at the forefront of the field. "I felt so much professional and intellectual alignment with them," David says of this thoughtful pair.

Though David moved to New York from San Francisco, where he had met Avary and Zeke, the three remained close, and he ended up flying back a few times a year to visit. During one visit in 2015, Avary and Zeke told David that they were thinking about starting a family. "We really want people to be involved," they told him, "and we want you to be involved most of all."

It was to be an unconventional plan: a cohabitating, co-parenting arrangement with three people. David was not part of Avary and Zeke's marriage, but he would be part of their family—a parent just as equally, and legally too, because three-parent adoption is legal in California. On New Year's Day in 2017, Avary learned that she was pregnant.

That May, David moved back to California and in with Avary and Zeke. He attended the birthing classes and was in the delivery room when Octavia, or Tavi for short, was born in August. All four live in a beautiful home near San Francisco's Panhandle Park, with a lush, plant-filled backyard. When I visited in early 2018, David showed me a collection of photos he's taken of his daughter: one every month, with Tavi in the same position, posed next to a Cornelius, a stuffed narwhal she's had since birth. In the family room, Tavi (who calls Zeke Daddy and David Dada) stumbles from Avary to David, who picks her up and puts her on his shoulders.

Life is different now, but on the whole, parenthood for David feels easier and more flexible than he expected. Avary, Zeke, and David share their calendars and have a weekly planning meeting that David calls "20 percent checking in and appreciating one another and 80 percent logistics" about cooking, childcare, and cleanup. Having a third person to shoulder the work of child-rearing is convenient, and explicit planning makes childcare more equal than arrangements between straight binary parents, which can often slide, undiscussed, into gendered roles and unequal division of labor.

Now, David often hears from people interested in alternative parenting, whether because they're single or poly or want to raise kids with someone regardless of romantic or sexual attraction. Many aces reach out to him too. "There are a lot of people who had strong feelings but didn't see a path to it, and a lot of people who wanted to be parents but didn't talk about it," David says. "It's not a new conversation by any means, but I think it's new as a conversation in our community."

These early years building up the ace movement taught David to break the script and explode the frame. All his life, unable to follow the typical routes, David had taught himself to be creative and find other options. He wanted connection but didn't care about sex. He wanted children but didn't want a traditional relationship. He got a version of all of it anyway.

· · · · · · · · ·

Adrienne Rich wrote that compulsory heterosexuality rendered lesbian possibility invisible. It made lesbian possibility "an engulfed continent that rises frequently to view from time to time only to become submerged again." It will take courage for straight feminists to question the natural state of heterosexuality, but Rich promises that the rewards will be great: "A freeing-up of thinking, the exploring of new paths, the shattering of another great silence, new clarity in personal relationships."[6]

These are also the rewards of working toward ace liberation, because compulsory anything is the opposite of freedom. *Ace liberation* is a complicated term. Asexuality is not inherently politically progressive. Not everyone who is asexual identifies as politically progressive, and that does not make their asexuality any less legitimate. But the goals of the ace movement are progressive, and the potential of the ace movement is greater than aces being more visible in the culture and more important than aces proving that, except for this one thing, we're just like everyone else. As CJ Chasin, the activist, has said, aces push the envelope. Once it is okay for aces to never have sex, it becomes more acceptable for everyone else who isn't ace too. Ace liberation will help everyone.

It comes in rejecting sexual and romantic normalcy in favor of carefully considered sexual and romantic ethics. The meaning of sex is always changing and the history of sexuality is complex. Compulsory sexuality and asexuality have changed across time and place; they can, and will, change again. The goal, at least to me, is that one day neither the *DSM* criteria nor asexuality-as-identity will be necessary. It will be easy to say yes or no or maybe—to sexuality, to romantic relationships—without co-ercion, without further justification, without needing a community to validate that answer. Sexual variety will be a given and social scripts will be weakened; sex will be decommodified.

The goal of ace liberation is simply the goal of true sexual and ro-mantic freedom for everyone. A society that is welcoming to aces can never be compatible with rape culture; with misogyny, racism, ableism, homophobia, and transphobia; with current hierarchies of romance and friendship; and with contractual notions of consent. It is a society that respects choice and highlights the pleasure that can be found everywhere in our lives. I believe that all this is possible.

THANK YOU

THANK YOU TO MY AGENT, ROSS HARRIS. Thank you to my Beacon editors, Rakia Clark and Rachael Marks. Thank you to the entire Beacon team: Marcy Barnes, Perpetua Charles, Susan Lumenello, Raquel Pidal, and Isabella Sanchez. Thank you to Carrie Frye for your wonderful editorial guidance. Thank you to every person who agreed to be interviewed for this book. Thank you to everyone who helped me brainstorm, who read drafts, and who supported me as I finished this project.

Thank you to Zonia Ali, Hayley Bisceglia-Martin, KJ Cerankowski, CJ Chasin, Aadita Chaudhury, Jessica Chen, Wei Chen, Charlotte Christopher, Alice Chou, Nicole Chung, Lilly Dancyger, Deena ElGenaidi, Rose Eveleth, Helena Fitzgerald, Jaime Green, Sara Ghaleb, Jessica Leigh Hester, Sabrina Imbler, Jeanna Kadlec, David Jay, Julie Kliegman, Morgan Jerkins, Kea Krause, Isaac Lu, Megha Majumdar, Tim Manley, Allison McKeon, Smitha Milli, Sulagna Misra, Kelsey Osgood, Ela Przybylo, Jaya Saxena, Cory Smith, Nina St. Pierre, Rachel Uda, Zachary Watson, Margaret Yau, Jess Zimmerman, and Sara Zoeterman.

Thank you to Noah, whose love changed everything.

I could not have done it without you all.

FURTHER READING

HERE IS A SELECTION OF BOOKS that will be of particular interest for those who want to learn more about ace-adjacent topics.

Asexual Erotics: Intimate Readings of Compulsory Sexuality by Ela Przybylo

Asexualities: Feminist and Queer Perspectives, edited by KJ Cerankowski and Megan Milks

Asexuality and Sexual Normativity: An Anthology, edited by Mark Carrigan, Kristina Gupta, and Todd G. Morrison

Big Pharma, Women, and the Labour of Love by Thea Cacchioni

Boston Marriages: Romantic But Asexual Relationships Among Contemporary Lesbians, edited by Esther D. Rothblum and Kathleen A. Brehony

Celibacies: American Modernism and Sexual Life by Benjamin Kahan

Frigidity: An Intellectual History by Peter Cryle and Alison Moore

The Invisible Orientation: An Introduction to Asexuality by Julie Sondra Decker

Mediated Intimacy: Sex Advice in Media Culture by Meg-John Barker, Rosalind Gill, and Laura Harvey

Race and Sexuality, by Salvador Vidal-Ortiz, Brandon Andrew Robinson, and Christina Khan

Sex Is Not a Natural Act and Other Essays by Leonore Tiefer

The Sex Myth: The Gap Between Our Fantasies and Reality by Rachel Hills

Sexual Politics of Disability: Untold Desires, edited by Tom Shakespeare, Dominic Davies, and Kath Gillespie-Sells

Understanding Asexuality by Anthony F. Bogaert

NOTES

CHAPTER 1: ARRIVING AT ASEXUALITY

1. The Asexuality Visibility and Education Network, https://asexuality.org/.

2. Abigail van Buren, "Dear Abby: Condolences Better Late than Never," *Monterey Herald*, syndicated in *Maui News*, September 16, 2013, https://www.montereyherald .com/2013/09/16/dear-abby-condolences-better-late-than-never/.

3. Andrew C. Hinderliter, "Methodological Issues for Studying Asexuality," *Archives of Sexual Behavior* 38, no. 5 (2009): 620, https://doi.org/10.1007/s10508-009-9502-x.

CHAPTER 2: EXPLANATION *VIA NEGATIVA*

1. Donna J. Drucker, "Marking Sexuality from 0–6: The Kinsey Scale in Online Culture," *Sexuality & Culture* 16, no. 3 (September 2012): 243–46, https://doi.org /10.1007/s12119-011-9122-1.

2. Alfred C. Kinsey, Wardell B. Pomeroy, and Clyde E. Martin, *Sexual Behavior in the Human Male* (Philadelphia and London: W. B. Saunders, 1948), 656.

3. Julie Kliegman, "How Zines Paved the Way for Asexual Recognition," *them.*, November 6, 2019, https://www.them.us/story/asexual-zines.

4. Andrew C. Hinderliter, "The Evolution of Online Asexual Discourse," PhD diss., University of Illinois at Urbana–Champaign, 2016.

5. Hinderliter, "The Evolution of Online Asexual Discourse."

6. Andrew C. Hinderliter, "How Is Asexuality Different from Hypoactive Sexual Desire Disorder?," *Psychology and Sexuality* 4, no. 2 (2013): 171–73, https://doi.org/10 .1080/19419899.2013.774165.

7. Hinderliter, "How Is Asexuality Different?" 172.

8. Lori A. Brotto and Morag A. Yule, "Physiological and Subjective Sexual Arousal in Self-Identified Asexual Women," *Archives of Sexual Behavior* 40, no. 4 (August 2011): 699–712, https://doi.org/10.1007/s10508-010-9671-7.

9. David Jay, "#10—The Masturbation Paradox," *Love from the Asexual Underground*, September 26, 2006, http://asexualunderground.blogspot.com/2006/09/10 -masturbation-paradox.html.

10. C. J. Chasin, "Asexuality and Re/Constructing Sexual Orientation," in *Expanding the Rainbow: Exploring the Relationships of Bi+, Polyamorous, Kinky, Ace, Intersex, and Trans People*, ed. Brandy L. Simula et al. (Boston: Brill, 2019).

CHAPTER 3: COMPULSORY SEXUALITY AND (MALE) ASEXUAL EXISTENCE

1. Adrienne Rich, "Compulsory Heterosexuality and Lesbian Existence," *Signs* 5, no. 4 (Summer 1980): 631–60, https://doi.org/10.1080/09574049008578015.

2. Rich, "Compulsory Heterosexuality and Lesbian Existence."

3. L. Kann, "Youth Risk Behavior Surveillance—United States, 2015," *MMWR Surveillance Summaries* 63, no. 4 (June 10, 2016), https://www.cdc.gov/healthyyouth /data/yrbs/pdf/2015/ss6506_updated.pdf.

4. J. M. Twenge, R. A. Sherman, et al. "Declines in Sexual Frequency among American Adults, 1989–2014," *Archives of Sexual Behavior* 46, no. 8 (November 2017): 2389, https://doi.org/10.1007/s10508-017-0953-1.

5. Kate Julian, "Why Are Young People Having So Little Sex?," *Atlantic*, December 2018, https://www.theatlantic.com/magazine/archive/2018/12/the-sex-recession/573949.

6. Jake Novak, "America's Sex Recession Could Lead to an Economic Depression," *CNBC*, October 25, 2019, https://www.cnbc.com/2019/10/25/americas-sex-recession -could-lead-to-an-economic-depression.html.

7. Novak, "America's Sex Recession Could Lead to an Economic Depression."

8. Alessandra Potenza, "People Are Having Less Sex—Maybe Because of all Our Screen Time," *Verge*, March 11, 2017, https://www.theverge.com/2017/3/11/14881062 /americans-sexual-activity-decline-study-happiness-internet-tv.

9. Tara Bahrampour, "'There Really Isn't Anything Magical about It': Why More Millennials Are Avoiding Sex," *Washington Post*, August 2, 2016, https://www.washington post.com/local/social-issues/there-isnt-really-anything-magical-about-it-why-more -millennials-are-putting-off-sex/2016/08/02/e7b73d6e-37f4-11e6-8f7c-d4c723a2becb _story.html.

10. Rachel Hills, *The Sex Myth: The Gap between Our Fantasies and Reality* (New York: Simon & Schuster, 2015), 15–16.

11. Sophie Gilbert, "How Hugh Hefner Commercialized Sex," *Atlantic*, September 28, 2017, https://www.theatlantic.com/entertainment/archive/2017/09/how-hugh -hefner-commercialized-sex/541368.

12. Caroline Bauer, Tristan Miller, et al., "The 2016 Asexual Community Survey Summary Report," Ace Community Survey, November 15, 2018, https://asexualcensus .files.wordpress.com/2018/11/2016_ace_community_survey_report.pdf.

13. Alan D. DeSantis, *Inside Greek U: Fraternities, Sororities, and the Pursuit of Power, Pleasure, and Prestige* (Lexington: University Press of Kentucky, 2007), 43–44.

14. Kim Parker, Juliana Menasce Horowitz, and Renee Stepler, "On Gender Differences, No Consensus on Nature vs. Nurture," Pew Research Center, December 5, 2017, https://www.pewsocialtrends.org/2017/12/05/on-gender-differences-no -consensus-on-nature-vs-nurture/#millennial-men-are-far-more-likely-than-those -in-older-generations-to-say-men-face-pressure-to-throw-a-punch-if-provoked-join -in-when-others-talk-about-women-in-a-sexual-way-and-have-many-sexual-par.

15. C. Brian Smith, "When Having Sex Is a Requirement for Being Considered 'A Real Man,'" *MEL Magazine*, 2018, https://melmagazine.com/en-us/story/when-having -sex-is-a-requirement-for-being-considered-a-real-man.

16. Ela Przybylo, "Masculine Doubt and Sexual Wonder: Asexually-Identified Men Talk About Their (A)sexualites," in *Asexualities: Feminist and Queer Perspectives*, ed. Megan Milks and KJ Cerankowski (New York: Routledge, 2014), 225–46.

17. Pryzyblo, "Masculine Doubt and Sexual Wonder."

18. Alim Kheraj, "Not Every Gay Man Is DTF," *GQ*, April 5, 2018, https://www .gq.com/story/not-every-gay-man-is-dtf.

19. Pryzyblo, "Masculine Doubt and Sexual Wonder."

20. Peter Baker, "The Woman Who Accidentally Started the Incel Movement," *Elle*, March 1, 2016, https://www.elle.com/culture/news/a34512/woman-who-started-incel-movement.

21. Marc Lamoureux, "This Group of Straight Men Is Swearing Off Women," *Vice*, September 24, 2015, https://www.vice.com/en_us/article/7bdwyx/inside-the-global-collective-of-straight-male-separatists.

22. Olivia Solon, "'Incel': Reddit Bans Misogynist Men's Group Blaming Women For Their Celibacy," *Guardian*, November 8, 2017, https://www.theguardian.com/technology/2017/nov/08/reddit-incel-involuntary-celibate-men-ban.

23. Ian Lovett and Adam Nagourney, "Video Rant, Then Deadly Rampage in California Town," *New York Times*, May 24, 2014, https://www.nytimes.com/2014/05/25/us/california-drive-by-shooting.html.

24. Gianluca Mezzofiore, "The Toronto Suspect Apparently Posted about an 'Incel Rebellion.' Here's What That Means," CNN, April 25, 2018, https://edition.cnn.com/2018/04/25/us/incel-rebellion-alek-minassian-toronto-attack-trnd/index.html.

25. Fox News, "Asexuality a Sexual Orientation?," August 21, 2012, https://video.foxnews.com/v/1797282177001.

26. Fox News, "Asexuality a Sexual Orientation?"

27. Fox News, "Asexuality a Sexual Orientation?"

28. Michel Foucault, *The History of Sexuality, Vol. 1* (New York: Random House, 1978), 19–23.

CHAPTER 4: JUST LET ME LIBERATE YOU

1. Rebecca Traister, "Why Consensual Sex Can Still Be Bad," *The Cut*, October 20, 2015, https://www.thecut.com/2015/10/why-consensual-sex-can-still-be-bad.html.

2. Nan D. Hunter, "Contextualizing the Sexuality Debates: A Chronology 1966–2005," in *Sex Wars: Sexual Dissent and Political Culture (10th Anniversary Edition)*, ed. Lisa Duggan and Nan D. Hunter (New York: Routledge, 2006), 22, 23.

3. Lisa Duggan, "Censorship in the Name of Feminism," *Sex Wars: Sexual Dissent and Political Culture (10th Anniversary Edition)*, ed. Lisa Duggan and Nan D. Hunter (New York: Routledge, 2006), 32.

4. Hunter, "Contextualizing the Sexuality Debates," 23–24.

5. Ellen Willis, "Lust Horizons: Is the Women's Movement Pro-Sex?" *No More Nice Girls: Countercultural Essays* (Minneapolis: University of Minnesota Press, 2012), 6–8.

6. Chloe Hall, "It's 2019 And Women Are Horny As Heck," *Elle*, January 24, 2019, https://www.elle.com/culture/a26006074/women-horny-2019.

7. Tracy Egan Morrissey, "The Year Women Got 'Horny,'" *New York Times*, December 13, 2019, https://www.nytimes.com/2019/12/13/style/horny-women.html.

8. "Totally Soaked," *The Cut*, 2019. https://www.thecut.com/tags/totally-soaked.

9. Framboise, "No True Sex Positive Feminist," *The Radical Prude*, March 25, 2012, https://radicalprude.blogspot.com/2012/03/no-true-sex-positive-feminist.html.

10. Framboise, "No True Sex Positive Feminist."

11. Gayle Rubin, "Thinking Sex: Notes for a Radical Theory of the Politics of Sexuality," in *Pleasure and Danger: Exploring Female Sexuality*, ed. Carole S. Vance (Boston: Routledge & Kegan Paul, 1984), 267–311.

12. Elisa Glick, "Sex Positive: Feminism, Queer Theory, and the Politics of Transgression," *Feminist Review*, no. 64 (Spring 2000): 19–45, www.jstor.org/stable /1395699.

13. Yasmin Nair, "Your Sex Is Not Radical," *Yasmin Nair*, June 27, 2015. http://yasminnair.net/content/your-sex-not-radical.

14. Rubin, "Thinking Sex."

15. Glick, "Sex Positive."

16. Rafia Zakaria, "Sex and the Muslim Feminist," *New Republic*, November 13, 2015, https://newrepublic.com/article/123590/sex-and-the-muslim-feminist.

17. Zakaria, "Sex and the Muslim Feminist."

18. Nair, "Your Sex Is Not Radical."

19. Breanne Fahs, "'Freedom To' and 'Freedom From': A New Vision for Sex-Positive Politics," *Sexualities* 17, no. 3 (2014): 267–90, https://doi.org/10.1177 /1363460713516334.

20. Julian, "Why Are Young People Having So Little Sex?"

21. Emily Bazelon, "The Return of the Sex Wars," *New York Times Magazine*, September 10, 2015, https://www.nytimes.com/2015/09/13/magazine/the-return-of-the -sex-wars.html.

22. Fahs, "'Freedom To' and 'Freedom From.'"

23. Lisa Downing, "What Is 'Sex-Critical' and Why Should We Care about It?," *Sex Critical*, July 27, 2012, http://sexcritical.co.uk/2012/07/27/what-is-sex-critical-and -why-should-we-care-about-it.

CHAPTER 5: WHITEWASHED

1. Asexual Census, "A History of Previous Ace Community Surveys," https:// asexualcensus.wordpress.com/faq/a-history-of-previous-ace-community-surveys.

2. Caroline Bauer et al., *The 2016 Asexual Community Survey Summary Report* (November 15, 2018), https://asexualcensus.files.wordpress.com/2018/11/2016_ace _community_survey_report.pdf.

3. Bauer et al., *The 2016 Asexual Community Survey Summary Report*.

4. Combahee River Collective, "The Combahee River Collective Statement," 1977, https://americanstudies.yale.edu/sites/default/files/files/Keyword%20Coalition _Readings.pdf.

5. Kimberlé Crenshaw, "Demarginalizing the Intersection of Race and Sex: A Black Feminist Critique of Antidiscrimination Doctrine, Feminist Theory, and Anti-racist Politics," *University of Chicago Legal Forum* 1989, no. 1, article 8 (1989), http:// chicagounbound.uchicago.edu/uclf/vol1989/iss1/8.

6. Pauline E. Schloesser, *The Fair Sex: White Women and Racial Patriarchy in the Early American Republic* (New York: New York University Press, 2002), 54.

7. Andrea Lim, "The Alt-Right's Asian Fetish," *New York Times*, January 6, 2018, https://www.nytimes.com/2018/01/06/opinion/sunday/alt-right-asian-fetish.html.

8. Craig Kilborn, "Sebastian, the Asexual Icon," *The Late Late Show with Craig Kilborn*, CBS, https://www.youtube.com/watch?v=YdlVAvjvKec and: https://www .youtube.com/watch?time_continue=34&v=8-tUM1FZH7U&feature=emb_logo.

9. Sara Ghaleb, "Asexuality Is Still Hugely Misunderstood. TV Is Slowly Changing That," *Vox*, March 26, 2018, https://www.vox.com/culture/2018/3/26/16291562 /asexuality-tv-history-bojack-shadowhunters-game-of-thrones.

10. *Game of Thrones*, "The Laws of Gods and Men," season 4, episode 6, May 11, 2014, https://www.youtube.com/watch?v=YK8zhFnsBGA.

11. *BoJack Horseman*, "Stupid Piece of Sh*t," season 4, episode 6, September 8, 2017.

12. Anthony F. Bogaert, "Asexuality: Prevalence and Associated Factors in a National Probability Sample," *Journal of Sex Research* 41, no. 3 (August 2004): 279–87, www.jstor.org/stable/4423785.

13. GLAAD Media Institute, "Where We Are On TV: 2019–2020," https://www.glaad.org/sites/default/files/GLAAD%20WHERE%20WE%20ARE%20ON%20TV%202019%202020.pdf.

14. Carlos Aguilar, "*BoJack Horseman*'s Biggest Mystery: Is Todd Supposed to Be Latino?" *Vulture*, September 19, 2018, https://www.vulture.com/2018/09/bojack-horseman-todd-chavez-latino.html.

15. Adrienne Green, "How Black Girls Aren't Presumed to Be Innocent," *Atlantic*, June 29, 2017, https://www.theatlantic.com/politics/archive/2017/06/black-girls-innocence-georgetown/532050.

16. Ianna Hawkins Owen, "On the Racialization of Asexuality," in *Asexualities: Feminist and Queer Perspectives*, ed. KJ Cerankowski and Megan Milks (New York: Routledge, 2014).

17. Sherronda J. Brown, "Black Asexuals Are Not Unicorns, There Are More of Us Than We Know," *Black Youth Project*, October 25, 2019, http://blackyouthproject.com/black-asexuals-are-not-unicorns-there-are-more-of-us-than-we-know.

18. Akwaeke Emezi, "This Letter Isn't For You: On the Toni Morrison Quote That Changed My Life," *them.*, August 7, 2019, https://www.them.us/story/toni-morrison.

CHAPTER 6: IN SICKNESS AND IN HEALTH

1. Katherine Angel, "The History of 'Female Sexual Dysfunction' as a Mental Disorder in the 20th Century," *Current Opinion in Psychiatry* 23, no. 6 (November 2010): 536–41, https://doi.org/10.1097/YCO.0b013e32833db7a1.

2. American Psychiatric Association, *Diagnostic and Statistical Manual of Mental Disorders: Fifth Edition* (Arlington, VA: American Psychiatric Association, 2013), 433, 440.

3. Lori A. Brotto, "The *DSM* Criteria for Hypoactive Sexual Desire Disorder in Women," *Archives of Sexual Behavior* 39, no. 2 (April 2010): 221–39, https://doi.org/10.1007/s10508-009-9543-1.

4. Peter M. Cryle and Alison M. Moore, *Frigidity: An Intellectual History* (New York: Palgrave Macmillan, 2011), 47.

5. Rossella E. Nappi et al., "Management of Hypoactive Sexual Desire Disorder in Women: Current and Emerging Therapies," *International Journal of Women's Health* 2010, no. 2 (August 2010): 167–75, https://doi.org/10.2147/ijwh.s7578.

6. Kristina Gupta and Thea Cacchioni, "Sexual Improvement as If Your Health Depends on It: An Analysis of Contemporary Sex Manuals," *Feminism & Psychology* 23, no. 4 (2013): 442–458, https://doi.org/10.1177/0959353513498070.

7. Jonathan M. Metzl, "Why 'Against Health'?" in *Against Health: How Health Became the New Morality*, ed. Jonathan M. Metzl and Anna Kirkland (New York: New York University Press, 2010), 2.

8. Laura Gilbert, "FDA Panel Rejects P&G Female Sex-Drive Patch," *Market-Watch*, December 2, 2014, https://www.marketwatch.com/story/fda-panel-rejects-pgs-female-sex-drive-patch.

9. Brigid Schulte, "From 1952–2015: The Path to 'Female Viagra' Has Been a Rocky One," *Washington Post*, August 18, 2015, https://www.washingtonpost.com/news/to-your-health/wp/2015/08/17/female-viagra-could-get-fda-approval-this-week.

10. Gardiner Harris, "Pfizer Gives Up Testing Viagra on Women," *New York Times*, February 28, 2004, https://www.nytimes.com/2004/02/28/business/pfizer-gives-up-testing-viagra-on-women.html.

11. T. S. Sathyanarayana Rao and Chittaranjan Andrade, "Flibanserin: Approval of a Controversial Drug For A Controversial Disorder," *Indian Journal of Psychiatry*, 57, no. 3 (2015): 221–23, https://doi.org/10.4103/0019-5545.166630.

12. Andrew Pollack, "F.D.A. Approves Addyi, a Libido Pill for Women," *New York Times*, August 18, 2015, https://www.nytimes.com/2015/08/19/business/fda-approval-addyi-female-viagra.html.

13. Jennifer Block and Liz Canner, "The 'Grassroots Campaign' for 'Female Viagra' Was Actually Funded by Its Manufacturer," *The Cut*, September 8, 2016, https://www.thecut.com/2016/09/how-addyi-the-female-viagra-won-fda-approval.html.

14. Katie Thomas and Gretchen Morgenson, "The Female Viagra, Undone by a Drug Maker's Dysfunction," *New York Times*, April 9, 2016, https://www.nytimes.com/2016/04/10/business/female-viagra-addyi-valeant-dysfunction.html.

15. Katie Thomas, "New Sex Drug for Women to Improve Low Libido Is Approved by the F.D.A.," *New York Times*, June 21, 2019, https://www.nytimes.com/2019/06/21/health/vyleesi-libido-women.html.

16. Thomas, "New Sex Drug for Women to Improve Low Libido Is Approved by the F.D.A."

17. Richard Balon, "The *DSM* Criteria of Sexual Dysfunction: Need for a Change," *Journal of Sex & Marital Therapy* 34, no. 3 (2008): 186–97, doi:10.1080/00926230701866067.

18. Andrew C. Hinderliter, "How Is Asexuality Different from Hypoactive Sexual Desire Disorder?," *Psychology and Sexuality* 4, no. 2 (2013): 171–73, doi.org/10.1080/19419899.2013.774165.

19. American Psychiatric Association, *Diagnostic and Statistical Manual of Mental Disorders: Fifth Edition* (Arlington, VA: American Psychiatric Association, 2013), 434, 443.

20. Grace Medley et al., "Sexual Orientation and Estimates of Adult Substance Use and Mental Health: Results from the 2015 National Survey on Drug Use and Health," SAMHSA, https://www.samhsa.gov/data/sites/default/files/NSDUH-SexualOrientation-2015/NSDUH-SexualOrientation-2015/NSDUH-SexualOrientation-2015.htm.

21. Hinderliter, "How Is Asexuality Different from Hypoactive Sexual Desire Disorder?"

22. Mikala Jamison, "Horny Pens for All," *Outline*, December 30, 2019, https://theoutline.com/post/8481/every-woman-deserves-to-try-vyleesi-aka-the-horny-pen-if-she-wants.

23. Lori Brotto et al., "Asexuality: An Extreme Variant of Sexual Desire Disorder?" *Journal of Sexual Medicine* 12, no. 3 (March 2015): 646–60, https://doi.org/10.1111/jsm.12806.

24. Neel Burton, "When Homosexuality Stopped Being a Mental Disorder," *Psychology Today*, September 18, 2015, https://www.psychologytoday.com/us/blog/hide-and-seek/201509/when-homosexuality-stopped-being-mental-disorder.

25. Oliver Wendell Holmes and Supreme Court of the United States, U.S. Reports: Buck v. Bell, 274 U.S. 200 (1927), Library of Congress, https://www.loc.gov /item/usrep274200.

26. Adam Cohen, *Imbeciles: The Supreme Court, American Eugenics, and the Sterilization of Carrie Buck* (New York: Penguin Books, 2016), 6–10, 26–39.

27. Paul Lombardo, *Three Generations, No Imbeciles: Eugenics, the Supreme Court, and Buck v. Bell* (Baltimore: Johns Hopkins Press, 2010), 49.

28. Jules Hathaway, "The Spirit of Buck V. Bell Survives in Our Demonizing of Marginalized Groups," *Bangor Daily News*, April 30, 2017, https://bangordailynews .com/2017/04/30/opinion/contributors/the-spirit-of-buck-v-bell-survives-in-our -demonizing-of-marginalized-groups.

29. Eunjung Kim, "Asexuality in Disability Narratives," *Sexualities* 14, no. 4 (2011): 479–93, https://doi.org/10.1177/1363460711406463.

30. Katharine Quarmby, "Disabled and Fighting for a Sex Life," *Atlantic*, March 11, 2015, https://www.theatlantic.com/health/archive/2015/03/sex-and-disability /386866.

31. Margaret A. Nosek et al., "Sexual Functioning among Women with Physical Disabilities," *Archives of Physical Medicine and Rehabilitation* 77 (1996): 107–15, https:// doi.org/10.1016/S0003-9993(96)90154-9.

32. Ariel Henley, "Why Sex Education for Disabled People Is So Important," *Teen Vogue*, October 5, 2017, https://www.teenvogue.com/story/disabled-sex-ed.

33. Wendy Lu, "Dating With a Disability," *New York Times*, December 8, 2016, https://www.nytimes.com/2016/12/08/well/family/dating-with-a-disability.html.

34. Karen Cuthbert, "You Have to Be Normal to Be Abnormal: An Empirically Grounded Exploration of the Intersection of Asexuality and Disability," *Sociology* 51, no. 2 (2017): 241–57, doi.org/10.1177/0038038515587639.

35. Cuthbert, "You Have to Be Normal to Be Abnormal."

36. Antonio Centeno and Raúl de la Morena, dirs., *Yes, We Fuck!* 2015.

37. Andrew Gurza, *Disability after Dark*, https://www.stitcher.com/podcast/andrew -gurza/disabilityafterdark.

38. Maïa de la Baume, "Disabled People Say They, Too, Want a Sex Life, and Seek Help in Attaining It," *New York Times*, July 4, 2013, https://www.nytimes.com/2013 /07/05/world/europe/disabled-people-say-they-too-want-a-sex-life-and-seek-help-in -attaining-it.html.

39. Maureen S. Milligan and Alfred H. Neufeldt, "The Myth of Asexuality: A Survey of Social and Empirical Evidence," *Sexuality and Disability* 19, no. 2 (2001): 91–109, https://doi.org/10.1023/A:1010621705591.

40. Kristina Gupta, "Happy Asexual Meets *DSM*," *Social Text Journal*, October 24, 2013, https://socialtextjournal.org/periscope_article/happy-asexual-meets-dsm/.

41. Sciatrix, "The Construct of the 'Unassailable Asexual,'" Knights of the Shaded Triangle (forum), October 23, 2010, http://shadedtriangle.proboards.com/thread/18.

42. Sciatrix, "The Construct of the 'Unassailable Asexual'"; Cuthbert, "You Have to Be Normal to Be Abnormal."

43. Nicola Davis, "Scientists Quash Idea of Single 'Gay Gene,'" *Guardian*, August 29, 2019, https://www.theguardian.com/science/2019/aug/29/scientists-quash-idea-of -single-gay-gene.

44. Arthur Krystal, "Why We Can't Tell the Truth About Aging," *New Yorker*, October 28, 2019, https://www.newyorker.com/magazine/2019/11/04/why-we-cant-tell
-the-truth-about-aging.

45. Heather Havrilesky, "Ask Polly: 'I'm Trying to Go Gray and I Hate It!,'" *Cut*,
December 18, 2019, https://www.thecut.com/2019/12/ask-polly-im-trying-to-go-gray
-and-i-hate-it.html.

CHAPTER 7: ROMANCE, RECONSIDERED

1. Yumi Sukugawa, "I Think I Am in Friend-Love With You," *Sadie Magazine*,
2012, retrieved from: https://therumpus.tumblr.com/post/36880088831/i-think-i-am
-in-friend-love-with-you-written-by.

2. Kim Brooks, "I'm Having a Friendship Affair," *The Cut*, December 22, 2015,
https://www.thecut.com/2015/12/friendship-affair-c-v-r.html.

3. Alex Mar, "Into the Woods: How Online Urban Legend Slender Man Inspired
Children to Kill," *Guardian*, December 7, 2017, https://www.theguardian.com/news
/2017/dec/07/slender-man-into-the-woods-how-an-online-bogeyman-inspired
-children-to-kill.

4. Mary Embree, "The Murder of the Century," *HuffPost*, May 21, 2013, https://
www.huffpost.com/entry/the-murder-of-the-century_b_3312652.

5. Embree, "The Murder of the Century."

6. "We Were Not Lesbians, Says Former Juliet Hulme," *New Zealand Herald*,
March 5, 2006, https://www.nzherald.co.nz/nz/news/article.cfm?c_id=1&objectid
=10371147.

7. Lisa M. Diamond, "What Does Sexual Orientation Orient? A Biobehavioral
Model Distinguishing Romantic Love and Sexual Desire," *Psychological Review* 110,
no. 1 (2003): 173–92, https://doi.org/10.1037//0033-295X.110.1.173.

8. Dorothy Tennov, *Love and Limerence: The Experience of Being in Love* (New York:
Scarborough House, 1979), 74.

9. Marta Figlerowicz and Ayesha Ramachandran, "The Erotics of Mentorship,"
Boston Review, April 23, 2018, http://bostonreview.net/education-opportunity-gender
-sexuality-class-inequality/marta-figlerowicz-ayesha-ramachandran.

10. Joe Fassler, "How My High School Teacher Became My Abuser," *Catapult*,
July 30, 2018, https://catapult.co/stories/how-my-high-school-teacher-became-my
-abuser.

11. Fassler, "How My High School Teacher Became My Abuser."

12. Brooks, "I'm Having a Friendship Affair."

13. Fassler, "How My High School Teacher Became My Abuser."

14. Helen Fisher, *Why We Love: The Nature and Chemistry of Romantic Love* (New
York: Henry Holt, 2004), 101–2.

15. Victor Karandashev, *Romantic Love in Cultural Contexts* (Switzerland: Springer,
2017), 30–32.

16. *Grey's Anatomy*, "Raindrops Keep Falling On My Head," season 2, episode 1,
September 25, 2005, https://www.youtube.com/watch?v=9DN4Dw3tyLY.

17. Kayte Huszar, "10 'Grey's Anatomy' Quotes That Remind You of Your Person," *Odyssey Online*, March 21, 2016, https://www.theodysseyonline.com/10-greys
-anatomy-quotes-you-either-tell-or-relate-to-your-person.

18. Alexander Blok, "When You Stand in My Path," from *The Penguin Book of Russian Poetry*, ed. Robert Chandler et al. (New York: Penguin, 2015), 189.

19. Demi Lovato, vocalist, "Tell Me You Love Me," by Kirby Lauryen et al., track 2 on *Tell Me You Love Me*, Hollywood, Island, Safehouse Records, 2017.

20. Danny M. Lavery, "Dear Prudence: The 'Tepidly Panromantic' Edition," *Slate*, January 24, 2018, https://slate.com/human-interest/2018/01/dear-prudence-podcast -the-tepidly-panromantic-edition.html.

21. Danny M. Lavery, "Dear Prudence: The 'Relentlessly Friendly Neighbor' Edition," *Slate*, February 21, 2018, https://slate.com/human-interest/2018/02/dear -prudence-podcast-the-relentlessly-friendly-neighbor-edition.html.

22. Elizabeth Brake, *Minimizing Marriage: Marriage, Morality, and the Law* (Oxford, UK: Oxford University Press, 2011), 88–90.

23. Drake Baer, "There's a Word for the Assumption that Everybody Should Be in a Relationship," *Cut*, March 8, 2017, https://www.thecut.com/2017/03/amatonormativity -everybody-should-be-coupled-up.html.

24. Anthony Kennedy and Supreme Court of the United States, Obergefell v. Hodges, 576 (2015).

25. Drake Baer, "There's a Word for the Assumption that Everybody Should Be in a Relationship."

26. Manu Raju, "Graham on Bachelorhood: I'm Not 'Defective,'" *Politico*, June 11, 2015, https://www.politico.com/story/2015/06/graham-on-bachelorhood-im-not -defective-118896.

27. Lisa Wade, *American Hookup: The New Culture of Sex on Campus* (New York: W. W. Norton, 2017), 145.

28. Vicki Larson, "Marriage Benefits Are an Antiquated Custom That Hold Back Society," *Quartz*, December 11, 2017, https://qz.com/quartzy/1148773/marriage -should-not-come-with-any-social-benefits-or-privileges.

29. Julian Baggini, "Why You Should Be Allowed to 'Marry' Your Sister," *Prospect Magazine*, July 2, 2018, https://www.prospectmagazine.co.uk/philosophy/why-you -should-be-allowed-to-marry-your-sister.

30. Jane Taber, "Elderly American Caregiver Being Deported Has Been Granted Temporary Visa," *Globe and Mail*, November 15, 2012, https://www.theglobeandmail .com/news/national/elderly-american-caregiver-being-deported-has-been-granted -temporary-visa/article5328771.

31. Elizabeth Brake, "Why Can't We Be (Legally-Recognized) Friends?," *Forum for Philosophy*, September 14, 2015, https://blogs.lse.ac.uk/theforum/why-cant-we-be -legally-recognized-friends.

32. Jack Julian, "79-Year-Old Finally a Permanent Resident 7 Years after Deportation Saga," *CBC News*, February 13, 2019, https://www.cbc.ca/news/canada/nova -scotia/nancy-inferrera-permanent-residency-mildred-sanford-guysborough -1.5017153.

33. Baggini, "Why You Should Be Allowed to Marry Your Sister."

34. Tamara Metz, *Untying the Knot: Marriage, the State, and the Case for Their Divorce* (Princeton, NJ: Princeton University Press, 2010), 119–51.

35. Lillian Faderman, "Nineteenth-Century Boston Marriages as a Lesson for Today," in *Boston Marriages: Romantic But Asexual Relationships Among Contemporary*

Lesbians, ed. Esther Rothblum and Kathleen A. Brehony (Amherst: University of Massachusetts Press, 1993), 59–62.

36. Kim Parker and Eileen Patten, "The Sandwich Generation: Rising Financial Burdens for Middle-Aged Americans," Pew Research Center, January 30, 2013, https://www.pewsocialtrends.org/2013/01/30/the-sandwich-generation/.

CHAPTER 8: THE GOOD-ENOUGH REASON

1. Miranda Fricker, *Epistemic Injustice: Power and the Ethics of Knowing* (Oxford, UK: Oxford University Press, 2007), 147–54.

2. Queenie of Aces, "Mapping the Grey Area of Sexual Experience: Consent, Compulsory Sexuality, and Sex Normativity," *Concept Awesome*, January 11, 2015, https://queenieofaces.wordpress.com/2015/01/11/mapping-the-grey-area-of-sexual -experience.

3. StarchyThoughts, "Hermeneutical Injustice in Consent and Asexuality," Tumblr, March 18, 2016, https://starchythoughts.tumblr.com/post/141266238674.

4. Kersti Yllö, "Marital Rape in a Global Context: From 17th Century to Today," Oxford University Press blog, November 13, 2017, https://blog.oup.com/2017/11 /marital-rape-global-context.

5. Victoria Barshis, "The Question of Marital Rape," *Women's Studies International Forum* 6, no. 4 (1983): 383–93, https://doi.org/10.1016/0277-5395(83)90031-6.

6. Anna Brand, "Trump Lawyer: You Can't Rape Your Spouse," MSNBC, July 28, 2015, http://www.msnbc.com/msnbc/trump-lawyer-you-cant-rape-your-spouse.

7. Eric Berkowitz, "'The Rape-Your-Wife Privilege': The Horrifying Modern Legal History Of Marital Rape," *Salon*, August 8, 2015, https://www.salon.com /2015/08/08/the_rape_your_wife_privilege_the_horrifying_modern_legal_history _of_marital_rape.

8. Molly Redden, "GOP Congressional Candidate: Spousal Rape Shouldn't Be a Crime," *Mother Jones*, January 15, 2014, https://www.motherjones.com/politics /2014/01/gop-congressional-candidate-richard-dick-black-spousal-rape-not-a -crime/.

9. Julie Carr Smyth and Steve Karnowski, "Some States Seek to Close Loopholes in Marital Rape Laws," *AP News*, May 4, 2019, https://apnews.com/3a11fee6d0e 449ce81f6c8a50601c687.

10. Kyle Mantyla, "Schlafly Reiterates View That Married Women Cannot Be Raped By Husbands," *RightWing Watch*, May 7, 2008, https://www.rightwingwatch .org/post/schlafly-reiterates-view-that-married-women-cannot-be-raped-by-husbands.

11. Abiola Abrams, "Intimacy Intervention: 'Do My Wife Duties Include Sex?'" *Essence*, August 19, 2014, https://www.essence.com/love/intimacy-intervention-do -my-wife-duties-include-sex.

12. D. A. Wolf, "Do We Owe Our Spouses Sex?" *HuffPost*, October 15, 2011, https://www.huffpost.com/entry/do-we-owe-our-spouses-sex_b_927484.

13. Quora, "Is Having Sex with Your Spouse Your Obligation, Duty or Right?" https://www.quora.com/Is-having-sex-with-your-spouse-your-obligation-duty-or -right.

14. MetaFilter, "What Are the Sexual Obligations of a Husband or Wife?" March 8, 2006, https://ask.metafilter.com/33981/What-are-the-sexual-obligations-of-a -husband-or-wife.

15. Cari Romm, "A Sex Therapist on How She'd Approach the Sexual Problems in 'On Chesil Beach,'" *The Cut*, May 21, 2018, https://www.thecut.com/2018/05/a-sex-therapist-on-the-sexual-problems-in-on-chesil-beach.html.

16. Melissa Dahl, "A New Book Claims We've Entered the Sexual Pharmaceutical Era," *The Cut*, October 26, 2015, https://www.thecut.com/2015/10/weve-entered-the-sexual-pharmaceutical-era.html.

17. Susan Brownmiller, *Against Our Will: Men, Women, and Rape* (New York: Fawcett Columbine, 1975), 15.

18. Lauren Wolfe, "Gloria Steinem on Rape in War, Its Causes, and How to Stop It," *Atlantic*, February 8, 2012, https://www.theatlantic.com/international/archive/2012/02/gloria-steinem-on-rape-in-war-its-causes-and-how-to-stop-it/252470.

19. Jane C. Hood, "Why Our Society Is Rape-Prone," *New York Times*, May 16, 1989, https://www.nytimes.com/1989/05/16/opinion/why-our-society-is-rapeprone.html.

20. Charles M. Blow, "This Is a Man Problem," *New York Times*, November 19, 2017, https://www.nytimes.com/2017/11/19/opinion/sexual-harassment-men.html.

21. Elizabeth Weingarten, "A Fresh Approach to Understanding Sexual Assault: A Conversation with Betsy Levy Paluck," *Behavioral Scientist*, November 20, 2018, https://behavioralscientist.org/a-fresh-approach-to-understanding-sexual-assault-a-conversation-with-betsy-levy-paluck.

22. Cameron Kimble and Inimal M. Chettiar, "Sexual Assault Remains Dramatically Underreported," Brennan Center for Justice, October 4, 2018, https://www.brennancenter.org/our-work/analysis-opinion/sexual-assault-remains-dramatically-underreported.

23. Catharine A. MacKinnon, "Sexuality, Pornography, and Method: 'Pleasure under Patriarchy,'" *Ethics* 99, no. 2 (January1989): 323, www.jstor.org/stable/2381437.

24. Catharine A. MacKinnon, "Sex and Violence: A Perspective," in *Feminism Unmodified: Discourses on Life and Law* (Cambridge, MA: Harvard University Press, 1987), 86–87.

25. Leslie Houts, "But Was It Wanted?: Young Women's First Voluntary Sexual Intercourse," *Journal of Family Issues* 26, no. 8 (2005): 1082–1102, https://doi.org/10.1177/0192513X04273582.

26. Lucia F. O'Sullivan and Elizabeth Rice Allgeier, "Feigning Sexual Desire: Consenting to Unwanted Sexual Activity in Heterosexual Dating Relationships," *Journal of Sex Research* 35, no. 3 (1998): 234–43, https://doi.org/10.1080/00224499809551938.

27. Emily Nagoski, "Enthusiastic, Willing, Unwilling, Coerced," *The Dirty Normal*, April 30, 2011, https://www.thedirtynormal.com/post/2011/04/30/enthusiastic-willing-unwilling-coerced/; Elizabeth Leuw, "Willing Consent," *Prismatic Entanglements*, May 17, 2011, https://prismaticentanglements.com/2011/05/17/willing-consent.

28. Meg-John Barker and Justin Hancock, *Enjoy Sex (How, When, and If You Want To)* (London: Icon Books, 2017), 156.

CHAPTER 9: PLAYING WITH OTHERS

1. Bogaert, "Asexuality,"279–87.

2. Leonore Tiefer, *Sex Is Not a Natural Act and Other Essays* (Boulder, CO: Westview Press, 1995), 39.

3. Donald G. Dutton and Arthur P. Aron, "Some Evidence for Heightened Sexual Attraction Under Conditions of High Anxiety," *Journal of Personality and Social Psychology* 30, no. 4 (1974): 510–17, https://doi.org/10.1037/h0037031.

4. William Jankowiak et al., "The Half of the World That Doesn't Make Out," *Sapiens*, February 10, 2016, https://www.sapiens.org/culture/is-romantic-kissing-a-human -universal.

5. William Jankowiak et al., "Is the Romantic-Sexual Kiss a Near Human Universal?" *American Anthropologist* 117, no. 3 (September 2015): 535–39, https://doi.org /10.1111/aman.12286.

6. Meg-John Barker, Rosalind Gill, and Laura Harvey, "The Sexual Imperative," in *Mediated Intimacy: Sex Advice in Media Culture* (Cambridge: Polity Press, 2018).

7. Mary Fissell, "When the Birds and the Bees Were Not Enough: Aristotle's Masterpiece," *Public Domain Review*, August 19, 2015, https://publicdomainreview.org /essay/when-the-birds-and-the-bees-were-not-enough-aristotle-s-masterpiece.

8. Barker et al., "The Sexual Imperative."

9. Meg-John Barker et al., "Sex as Necessary for Relationships," in *Mediated Intimacy: Sex Advice in Media Culture* (Cambridge: Polity Press, 2018).

10. Anagnori, "Sex Therapy's Blind Spot," Tumblr, October 6, year unknown, https://anagnori.tumblr.com/post/178801800354/sex-therapys-blind-spot.

11. Joan McFadden, "'I Don't Think We'll Ever Have Sex Again': Our Happy, Cuddly, Celibate Marriage," *Guardian*, April 15, 2017, https://www.theguardian.com /lifeandstyle/2017/apr/15/celibate-marriage-sex-sexless-relationship.

12. McFadden, "'I Don't Think We'll Ever Have Sex Again': Our Happy, Cuddly, Celibate Marriage."

13. K. R. Mitchell et al., "Sexual Function in Britain: Findings from the Third National Survey of Sexual Attitudes and Lifestyles (Natsal-3)," *Lancet* 382, no. 9907 (November 2013): 1817–29, https://doi.org/10.1016/S0140-6736(13)62366-1.

14. Anagnori, "Sex Therapy's Blind Spot."

15. Sarah Barmak, "The Misunderstood Science of Sexual Desire," *The Cut*, April 26, 2018, https://www.thecut.com/2018/04/the-misunderstood-science-of-sexual -desire.html.

16. Karin Jones, "What Sleeping with Married Men Taught Me About Infidelity," *New York Times*, April 6, 2018, https://www.nytimes.com/2018/04/06/style/modern -love-sleeping-with-married-men-infidelity.html.

CHAPTER 11: WHERE ARE WE GOING, WHERE HAVE WE BEEN?

1. Cam Awkward-Rich, "Prude Manifesto," *Watch-Listen-Read*, https://www.watch -listen-read.com/english/Cam-Awkward-Rich-A-Prudes-Manifesto-id-395533.

2. Ela Przybylo, *Asexual Erotics: Intimate Readings of Compulsory Sexuality* (Columbus: Ohio State University Press, 2019), 20.

3. Audre Lorde, *The Uses of the Erotic: The Erotic as Power* (New York: Out & Out Books, 1978), 89.

4. Lorde, *The Uses of the Erotic*, 89.

5. Kristina Gupta, "Compulsory Sexuality: Evaluating an Emerging Concept," *Signs* 41, no. 1 (Autumn 2015): 131–54, https://doi.org/10.1086/681774.

6. Adrienne Rich, "Compulsory Heterosexuality and Lesbian Existence," *Signs* 5, no. 4 (Summer 1980): 631–60, https://doi.org/10.1080/09574049008578015.

INDEX

abuse, 97–99, 143. *See also* sexual violence

acceptance, 43, 99–103. *See also* sexual liberation

ace. *See* asexuality

Ace Community Survey, 38, 68

Ace Inclusion Guide for High Schools, 184

ace men, 21, 39–40, 41. *See also* asexuality; *names of specific men*

ace movement, 18, 183–84. *See also* AVEN (Asexuality Visibility and Education Network)

ace women, 21, 52, 54–56. *See also* asexuality; *names of specific women*

Addyi, 87

aesthetic attraction, 14, 27–28, 115, 117. *See also* emotional attraction; romantic attraction; sexual attraction

agency, 45–46, 52, 65, 82–83. *See also* sex-positive feminism

aging, 94, 102, 132, 133–34, 184, 185

Alicia, 26, 115, 141, 166

Alison, 156–57

allosexual (allo), as term, 8

Alptraum, Lux, 157

amatonormativity, 127–29, 131–33, 134, 183, 185. *See also* compulsory sexuality; dating norms; marriage; relationship scripts; romantic love; social conditioning

Amish community, 151

Anagnori, 155, 162

Anna, 171–79

Antony, 40

Archives of Sexual Behavior (publication), 13

aromanticism, 28, 30, 81, 118–19, 123–31. *See also* asexuality; romantic love

The Asexual Agenda (blog), 30

Asexual Artists (website), 57

Asexual Awareness Week, 183

asexuality: overview, 5–7, 15–16, 180–84, 187–89; acceptance of, 43, 99–103; author's personal experiences with, 5, 9–15, 49, 72 74, 83 84; as compared to *Naked Attraction* show, 23–24, 27–28; definition of, 5, 13, 19–20; flags and symbols of, 30, 69; fluidity of, 100–101; as illness, 86–92; internet community on, 17–18; negative stereotypes of, 37, 43–44; oppression and, 69–72; people with disabilities and, 85–86, 94–97, 101–3, 184; power of language and, 17–19, 25–27, 111–19, 121–23; race and community of, 68–69, 77–79, 184; representation and, 32, 74–82, 126; sexual drive and, 20–22; transgender identity and, 39–40, 69–70, 80, 171–79; variations of, 25–27, 64–65, 68, 101–2. *See also* aromanticism; *names of types of*; romantic love; sexual attraction; sexual behavior; sexual drive; sexual repression

asexuality.org, 19. *See also* AVEN (Asexuality Visibility and Education Network)

Asexuality Visibility and Education Network. *See* AVEN (Asexuality Visibility and Education Network)

Miller, Zii, 36, 40, 182
Milligan, Maureen, 96
mimetic desire, 171–72
Minaj, Nicki, 53
Minassian, Alek, 41
Moore, Alison Downham, 86
Mormon communities, 173, 175
Morrison, Toni, 84
music, 53, 58, 65, 93
Muslim feminism, 60–61

Nagoski, Emily, 145–47
Nair, Yasmin, 56, 61
National Survey of Sexual Attitudes
    and Lifestyles (NATSAL), 157
negotiation, 147–49
Neufeldt, Aldred, 96
Noah, 115–17, 166–67, 168
nonsexual, as term, 18
nonsexual romantic love, 107–9
nonverbal cues, 148–49. See also
    consent

Official Asexual Society, 19
OKCupid, 62
On Our Backs (publication), 65
open relationships, 10–11, 159, 165–66,
    167, 170, 178
oppression, racial–sexual, 69–72
Orthodox Jewish community, 151
Owen, Ianna Hawkins, 77

pansexuality, 5, 27, 124
parenting, 110, 185–87
Parker, Pauline, 109–10, 114
patriarchy, 50–52, 56
pharmaceutical drugs, 31, 87–88, 141
phenomenology, 116–17
Phoenix, Lola, 25–26, 149
Plato, 181
platonic love, 113–17. See also romantic
    love
Playboy, 37, 38
political radicalism and sexuality, 50–52,
    54–56, 58–61
population statistics, 75

pornography, 51, 52
Przybylo, Ela, 35, 39, 40, 180–81
psychiatric sickness, 86–92
puberty, 7, 13–14, 111

Queenie of Aces, 138
queerplatonic partners (QPP), 118–21,
    122, 123

race: asexual community and, 32, 68–69,
    77–79, 184; oppression and asex-
    uality, 69–72; representation and,
    74–82, 126; stereotypes of, 72–74,
    77, 84. See also class and sexuality;
    feminist politics; identity politics
rape, 66, 139, 142–45. See also sexual
    violence
Rape, Abuse & Incest National Net-
    work, 145
relationship scripts, 150–55, 173–74.
    See also amatonormativity, dating
    norms; marriage
religion, 33–34, 38, 42, 98
representation, 32, 74–82, 126. See also
    erasure
Resources for Ace Survivors, 145
responsive desire, 163–64
Rich, Adrienne, 34–35, 98, 187
Rodger, Elliot, 41
romance in literature, 125–27
romantic attraction, 28, 110, 112–13. See
    also aesthetic attraction; emotional
    attraction; lust; sexual attraction
romantic love: amatonormativity of,
    127–29, 131–33; author's personal
    experiences with, 115–17; case
    studies of, 109–10; Diamond on,
    110–11, 113; friend-love, 107–8,
    113; language and categoriza-
    tion of, 111–19, 121–23. See also
    aromanticism
Rubin, Gayle, 55, 59
Ruth, 176

sadomasochism, 51
Sakugawa, Yumi, 107, 122

ABOUT THE AUTHOR

ANGELA CHEN is a journalist and writer. Her reporting and criticism have appeared in the *Wall Street Journal, Atlantic, Guardian, Paris Review, Lapham's Quarterly*, and elsewhere. Chen is a member of the ace community and has spoken about asexuality at academic conferences and events including World Pride. Connect with her on Twitter @chengela.